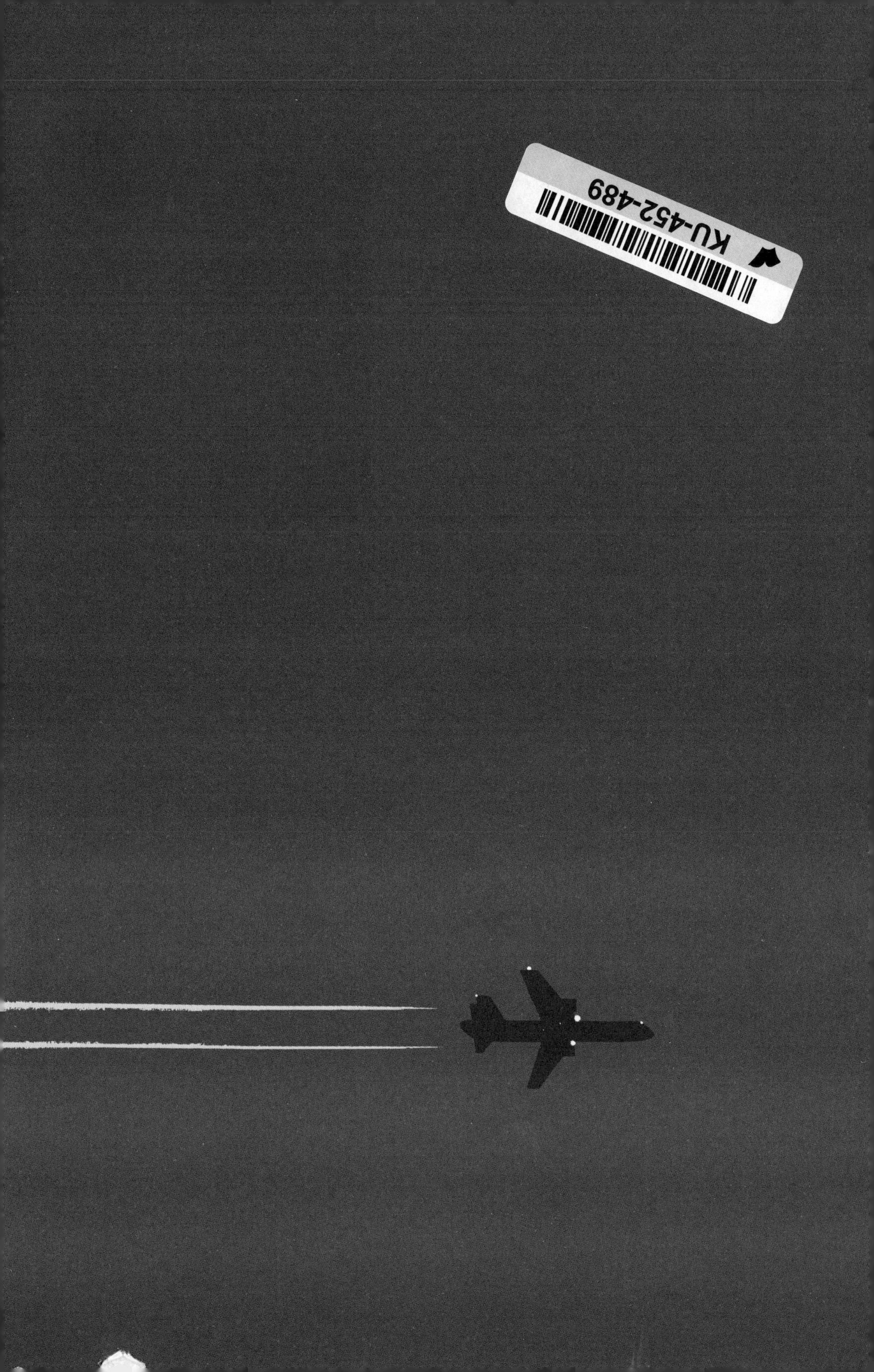

Killing and Dying

killi

and

Dyir

SIX STORIES BY ADRIAN TOMINE

Faber and Faber

ALSO BY ADRIAN TOMINE

Sleepwalk and Other Stories

32 Stories: The Complete Optic Nerve Mini-Comics

Summer Blonde

Scrapbook (Uncollected Work: 1990–2004)

Shortcomings

Scenes from an Impending Marriage

New York Drawings

FOR CHRIS AND SATSUKI

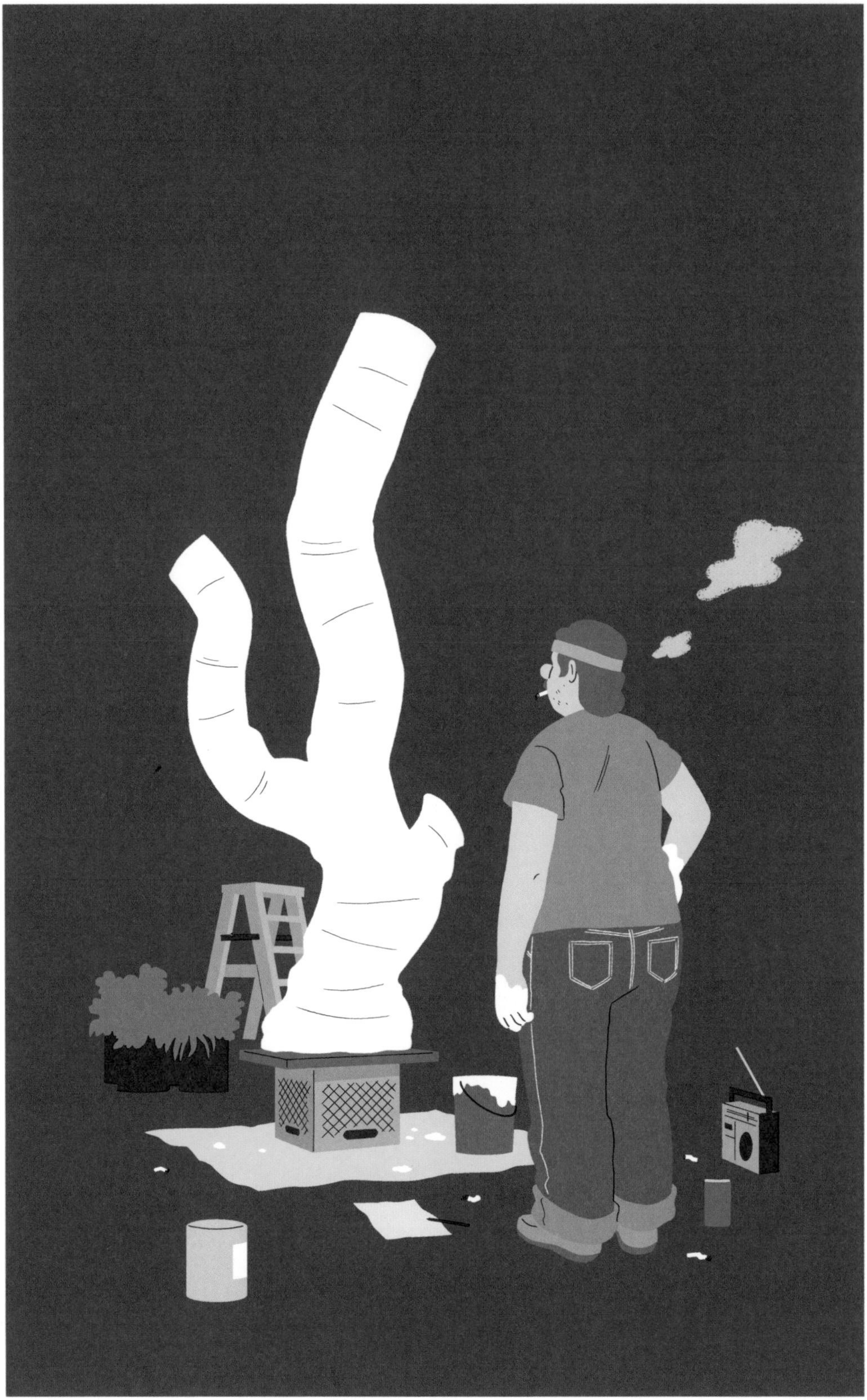

CONTENTS

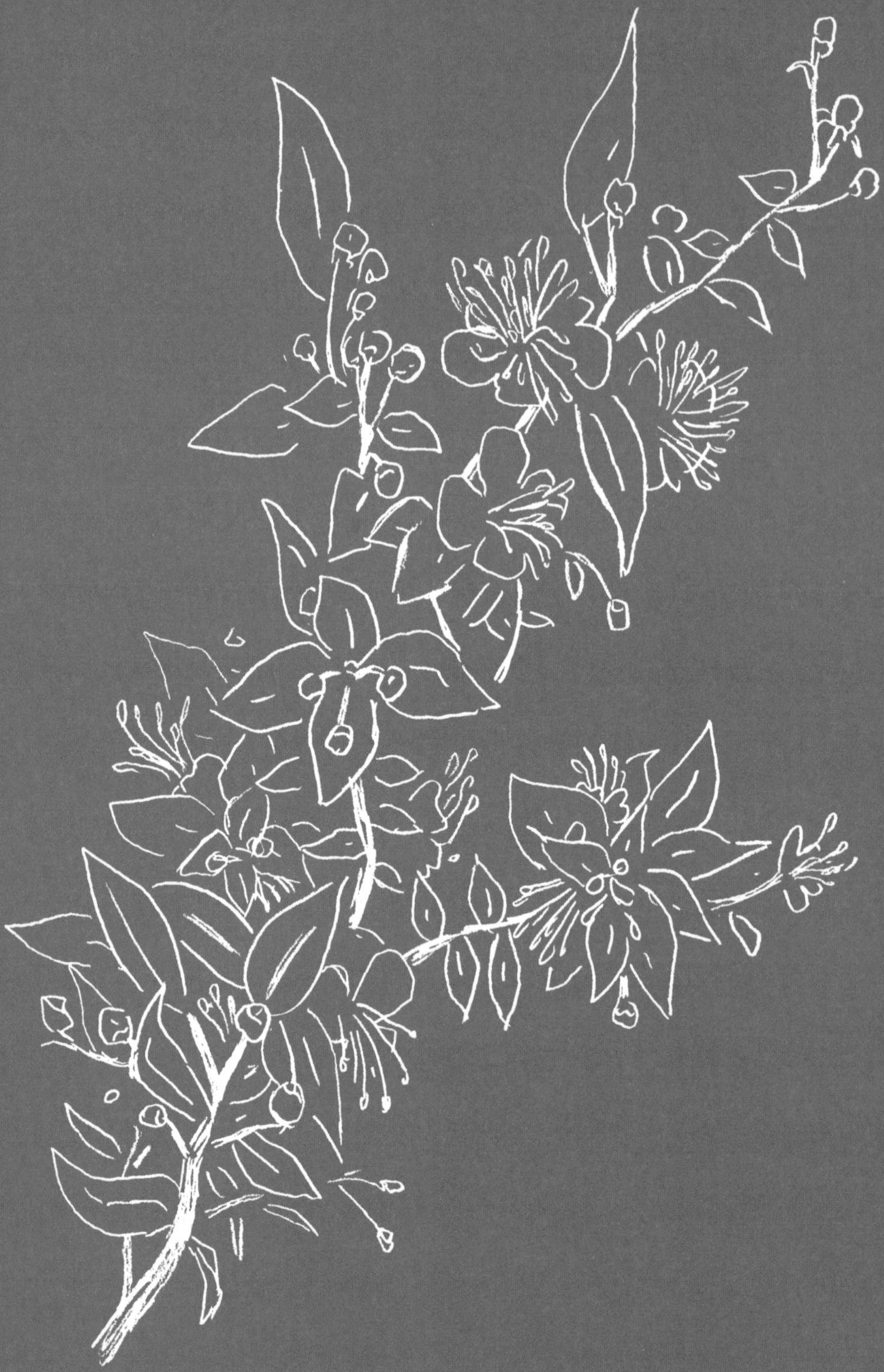

A BRIEF HISTORY of
the ART FORM KNOWN as
"HORTISCULPTURE"

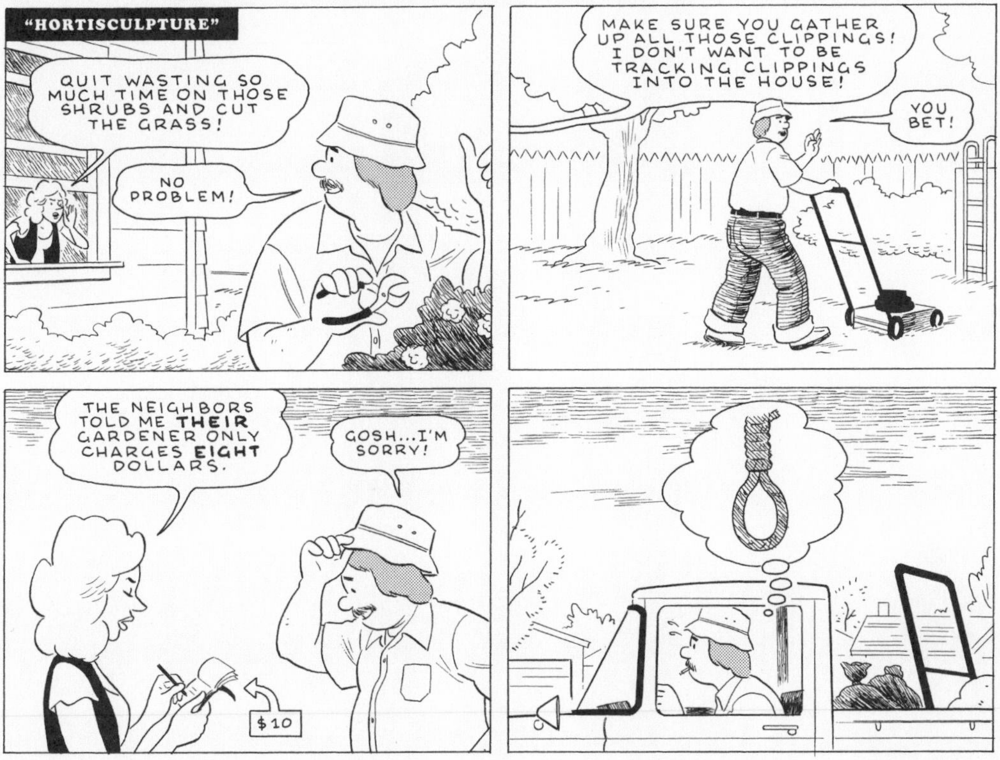
"HORTISCULPTURE"
QUIT WASTING SO MUCH TIME ON THOSE SHRUBS AND CUT THE GRASS!
NO PROBLEM!
MAKE SURE YOU GATHER UP ALL THOSE CLIPPINGS! I DON'T WANT TO BE TRACKING CLIPPINGS INTO THE HOUSE!
YOU BET!
THE NEIGHBORS TOLD ME **THEIR** GARDENER ONLY CHARGES **EIGHT** DOLLARS.
GOSH...I'M SORRY!
$10

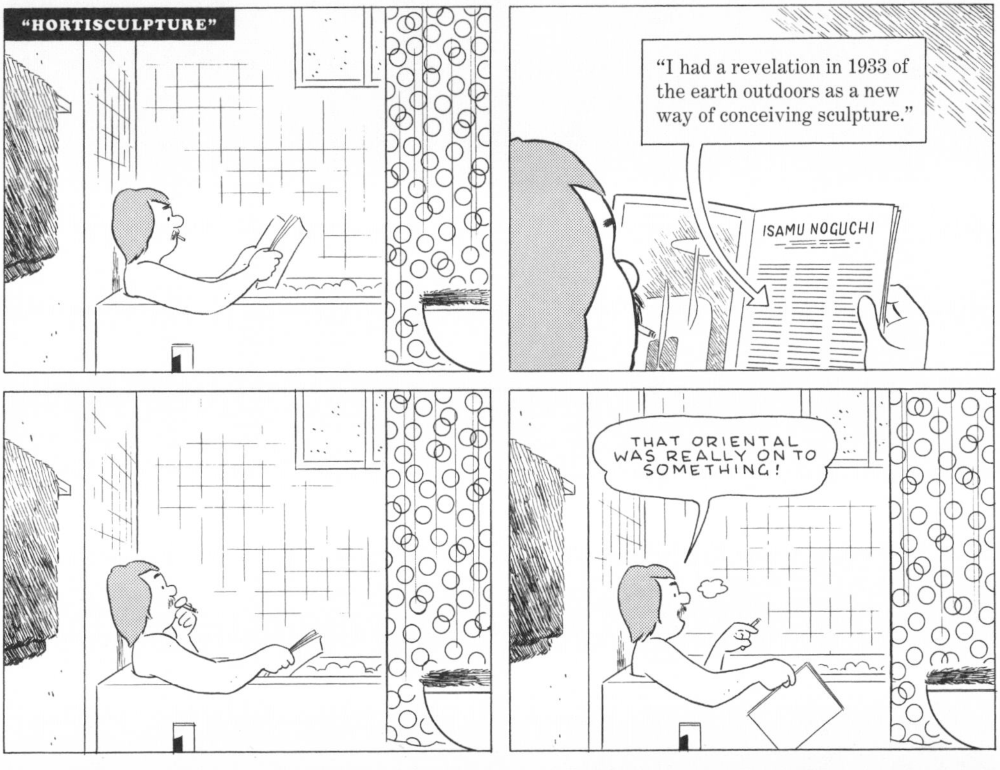
"HORTISCULPTURE"
"I had a revelation in 1933 of the earth outdoors as a new way of conceiving sculpture."
ISAMU NOGUCHI
THAT ORIENTAL WAS REALLY ON TO SOMETHING!

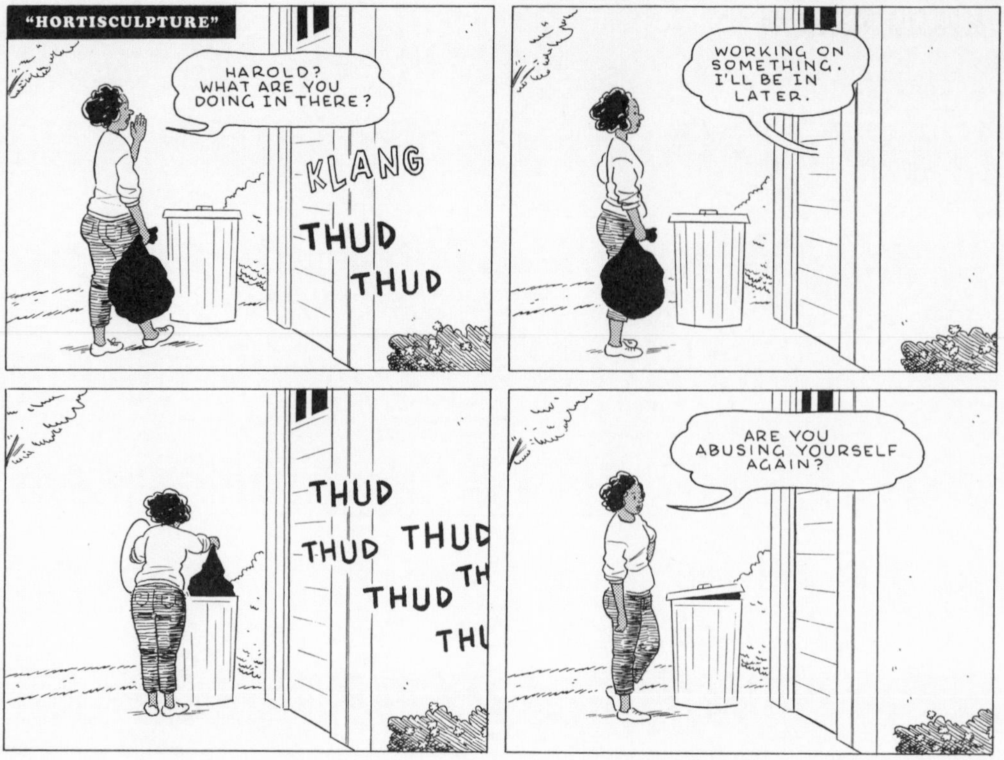
"HORTISCULPTURE"
HAROLD? WHAT ARE YOU DOING IN THERE?
KLANG
THUD
THUD
WORKING ON SOMETHING. I'LL BE IN LATER.
THUD
THUD THUD
THUD TH
THU
ARE YOU ABUSING YOURSELF AGAIN?

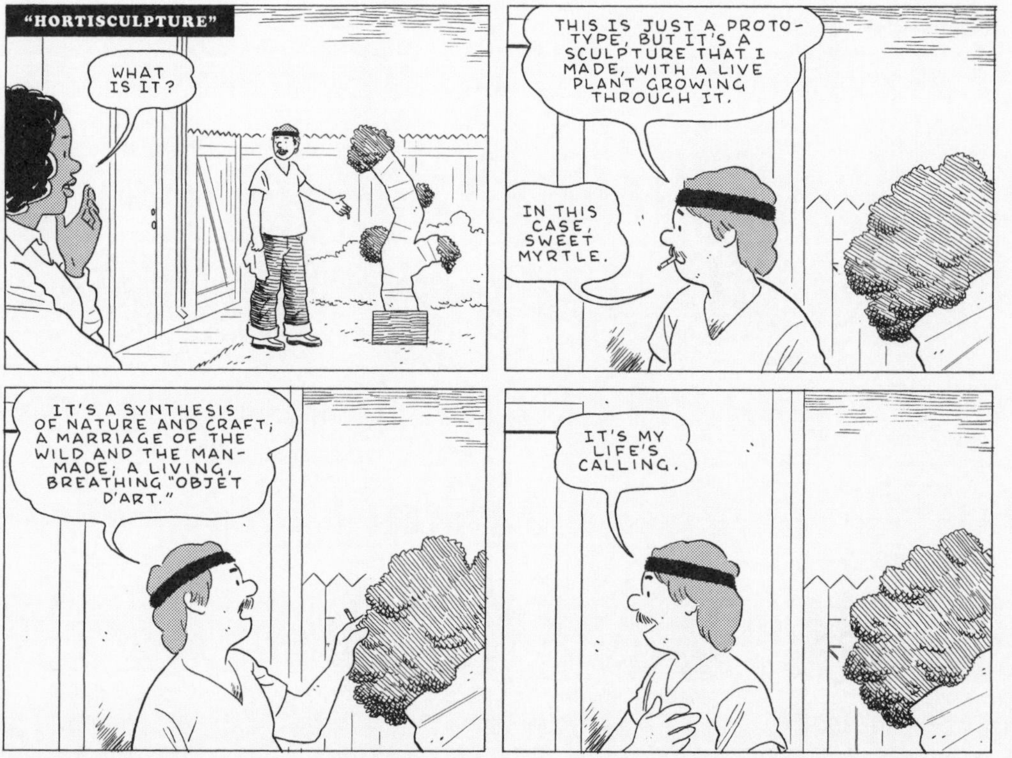
"HORTISCULPTURE"
WHAT IS IT?
THIS IS JUST A PROTOTYPE, BUT IT'S A SCULPTURE THAT I MADE, WITH A LIVE PLANT GROWING THROUGH IT.
IN THIS CASE, SWEET MYRTLE.
IT'S A SYNTHESIS OF NATURE AND CRAFT; A MARRIAGE OF THE WILD AND THE MAN-MADE; A LIVING, BREATHING "OBJET D'ART."
IT'S MY LIFE'S CALLING.

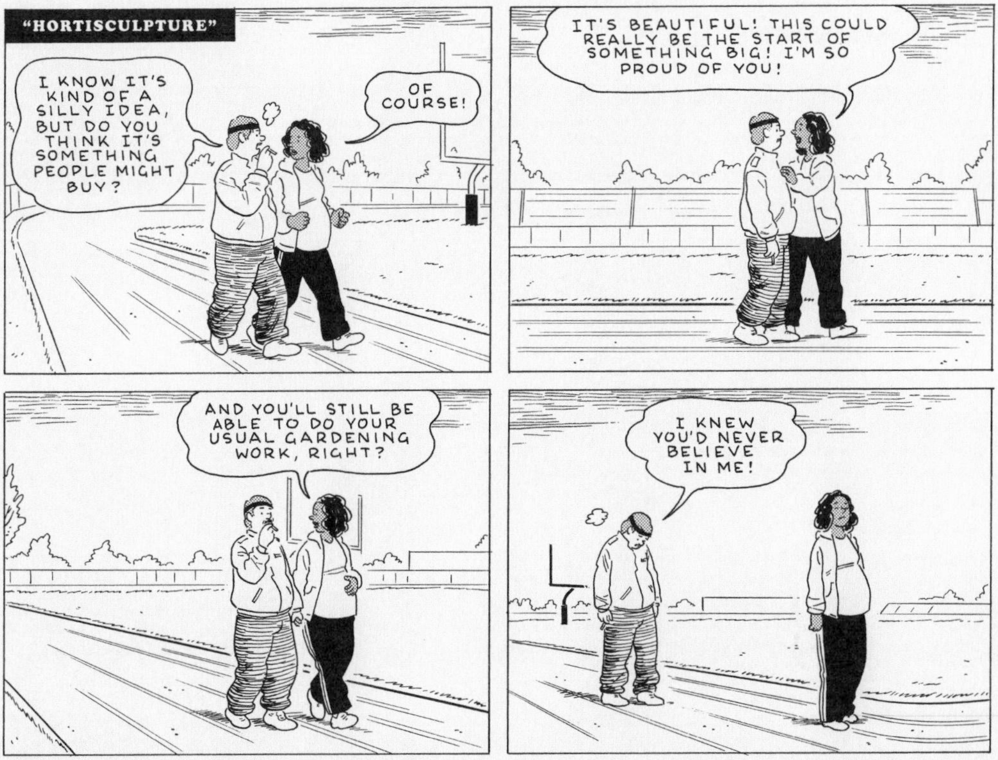
"HORTISCULPTURE"
I KNOW IT'S KIND OF A SILLY IDEA, BUT DO YOU THINK IT'S SOMETHING PEOPLE MIGHT BUY?
OF COURSE!
IT'S BEAUTIFUL! THIS COULD REALLY BE THE START OF SOMETHING BIG! I'M SO PROUD OF YOU!
AND YOU'LL STILL BE ABLE TO DO YOUR USUAL GARDENING WORK, RIGHT?
I KNEW YOU'D NEVER BELIEVE IN ME!

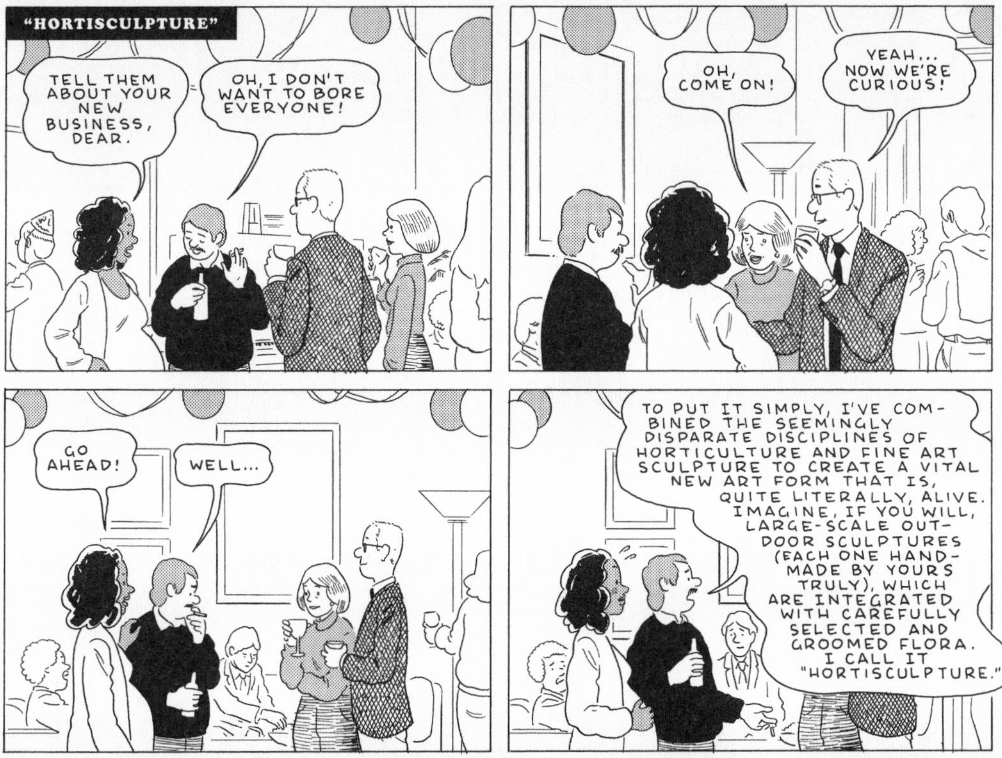
"HORTISCULPTURE"
TELL THEM ABOUT YOUR NEW BUSINESS, DEAR.
OH, I DON'T WANT TO BORE EVERYONE!
OH, COME ON!
YEAH... NOW WE'RE CURIOUS!
GO AHEAD!
WELL...
TO PUT IT SIMPLY, I'VE COMBINED THE SEEMINGLY DISPARATE DISCIPLINES OF HORTICULTURE AND FINE ART SCULPTURE TO CREATE A VITAL NEW ART FORM THAT IS, QUITE LITERALLY, ALIVE. IMAGINE, IF YOU WILL, LARGE-SCALE OUTDOOR SCULPTURES (EACH ONE HANDMADE BY YOURS TRULY), WHICH ARE INTEGRATED WITH CAREFULLY SELECTED AND GROOMED FLORA. I CALL IT "HORTISCULPTURE."

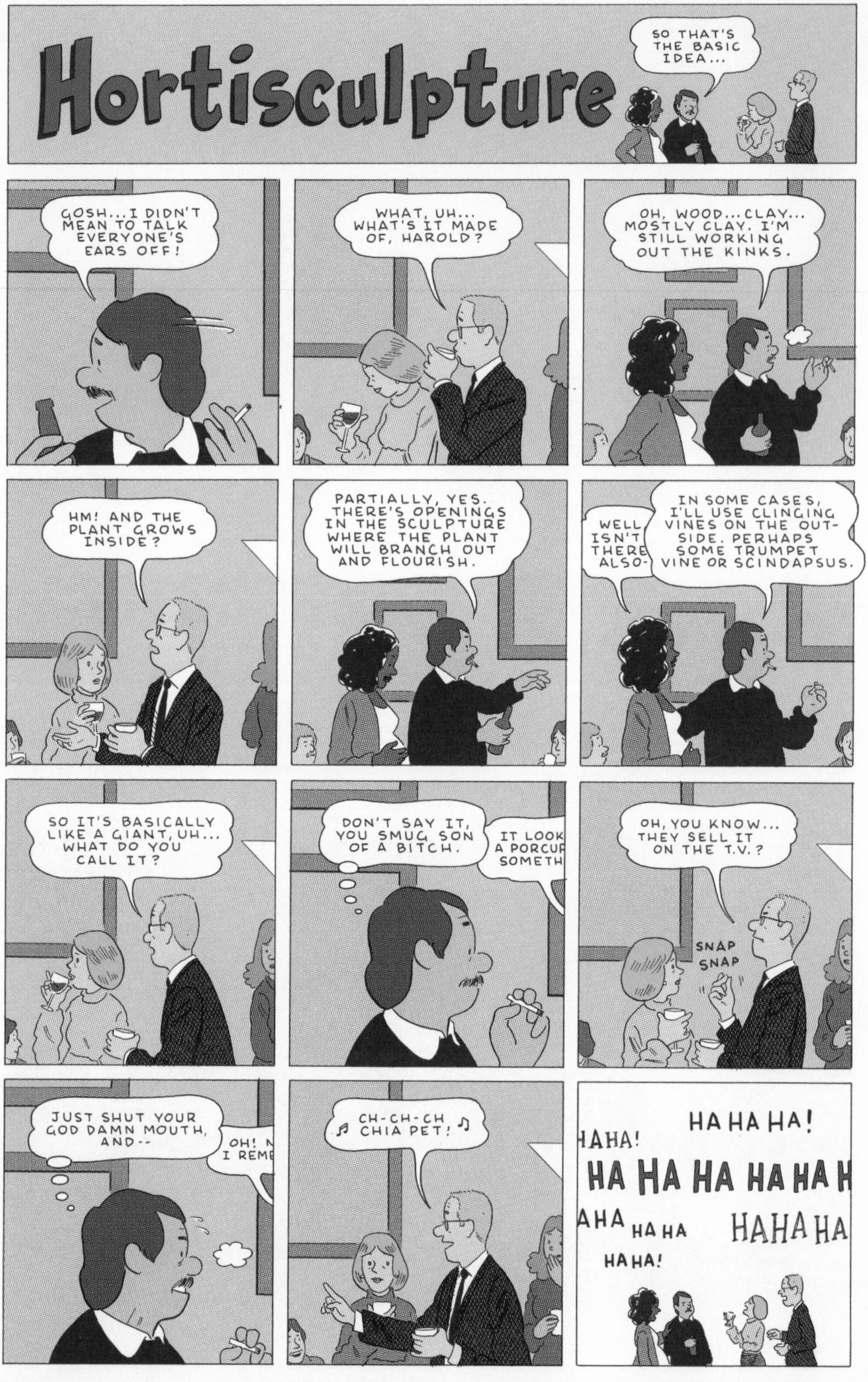
Hortisculpture
SO THAT'S THE BASIC IDEA...
GOSH...I DIDN'T MEAN TO TALK EVERYONE'S EARS OFF!
WHAT, UH... WHAT'S IT MADE OF, HAROLD?
OH, WOOD...CLAY... MOSTLY CLAY. I'M STILL WORKING OUT THE KINKS.
HM! AND THE PLANT GROWS INSIDE?
PARTIALLY, YES. THERE'S OPENINGS IN THE SCULPTURE WHERE THE PLANT WILL BRANCH OUT AND FLOURISH.
WELL, ISN'T THERE ALSO-
IN SOME CASES, I'LL USE CLINGING VINES ON THE OUT-SIDE. PERHAPS SOME TRUMPET VINE OR SCINDAPSUS.
SO IT'S BASICALLY LIKE A GIANT, UH... WHAT DO YOU CALL IT?
DON'T SAY IT, YOU SMUG SON OF A BITCH.
IT LOOK A PORCUP SOMETH
OH, YOU KNOW... THEY SELL IT ON THE T.V.?
SNAP SNAP
JUST SHUT YOUR GOD DAMN MOUTH, AND--
OH! N I REME
CH-CH-CH CHIA PET!
HA HA HA!
HAHA!
HA HA HA HA HA HA H
AHA HA HA HAHAHA HA
HA HA!

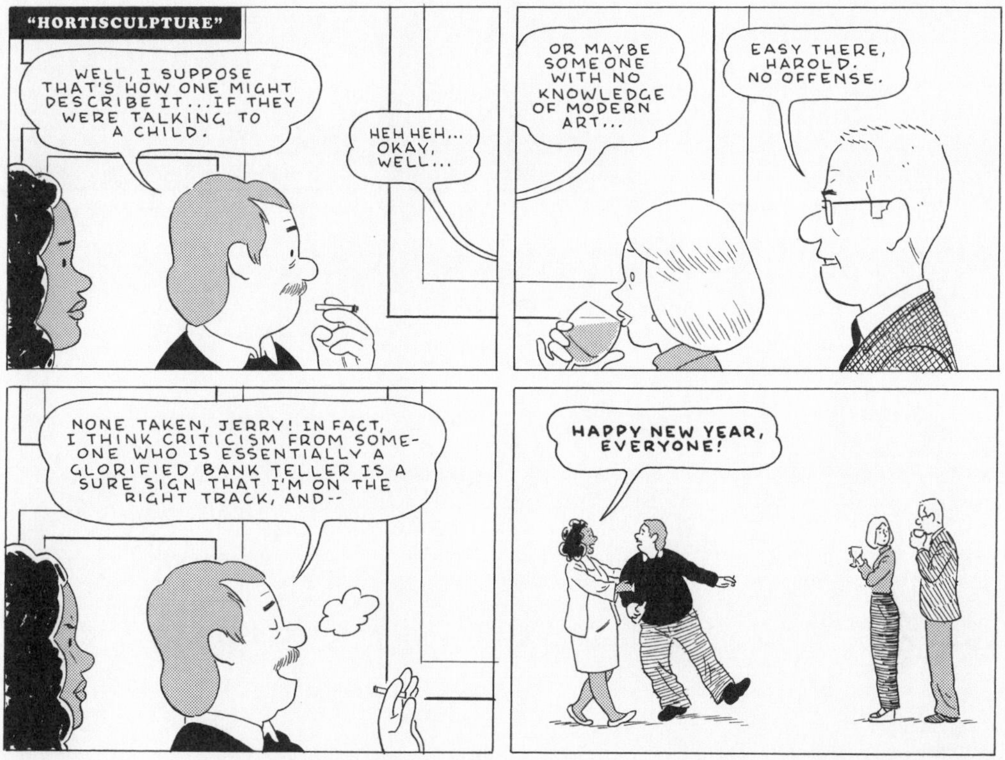
"HORTISCULPTURE"
WELL, I SUPPOSE THAT'S HOW ONE MIGHT DESCRIBE IT...IF THEY WERE TALKING TO A CHILD.
HEH HEH... OKAY, WELL...
OR MAYBE SOMEONE WITH NO KNOWLEDGE OF MODERN ART...
EASY THERE, HAROLD. NO OFFENSE.
NONE TAKEN, JERRY! IN FACT, I THINK CRITICISM FROM SOME-ONE WHO IS ESSENTIALLY A GLORIFIED BANK TELLER IS A SURE SIGN THAT I'M ON THE RIGHT TRACK, AND--
HAPPY NEW YEAR, EVERYONE!

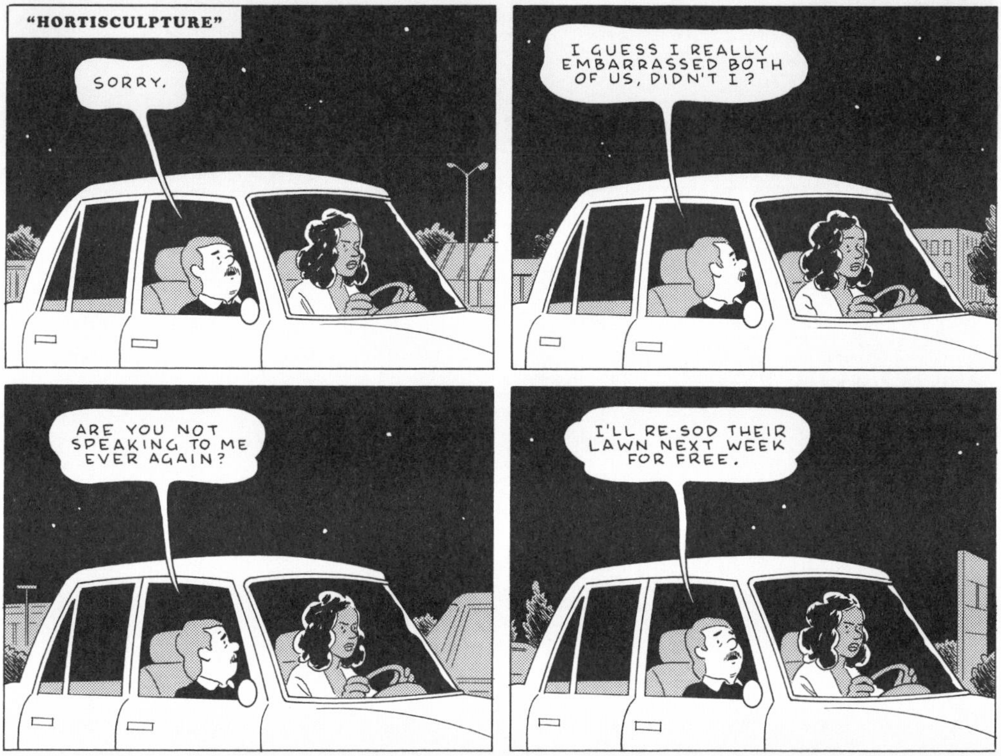
"HORTISCULPTURE"
SORRY.
I GUESS I REALLY EMBARRASSED BOTH OF US, DIDN'T I?
ARE YOU NOT SPEAKING TO ME EVER AGAIN?
I'LL RE-SOD THEIR LAWN NEXT WEEK FOR FREE.

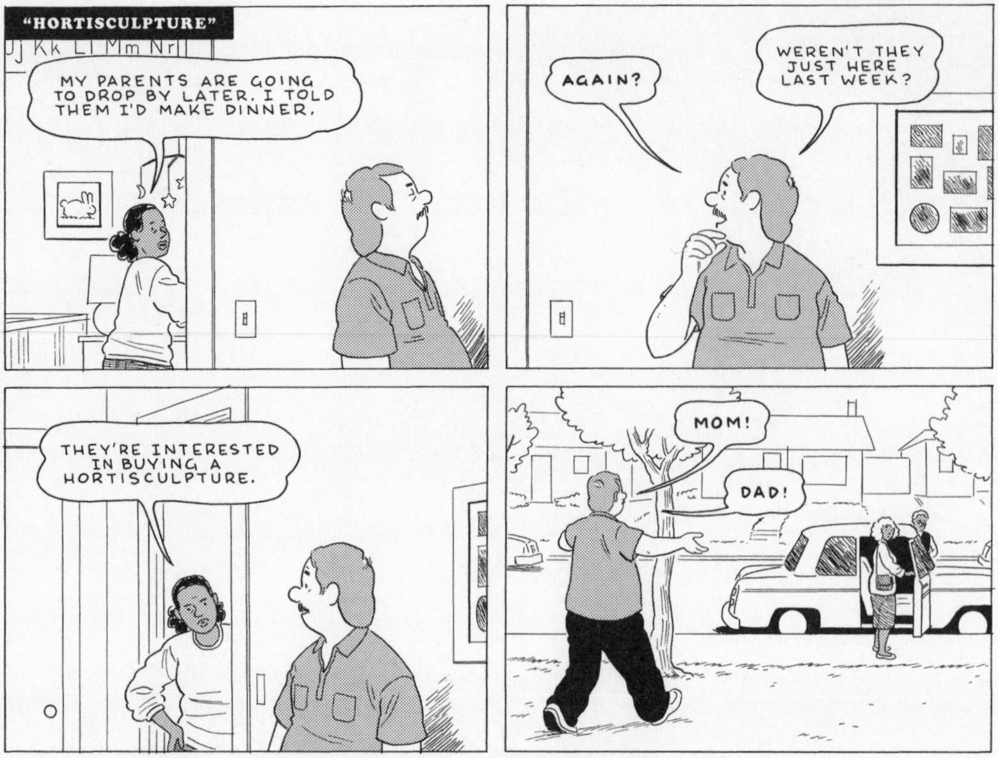
"HORTISCULPTURE"
MY PARENTS ARE GOING TO DROP BY LATER. I TOLD THEM I'D MAKE DINNER.
AGAIN?
WEREN'T THEY JUST HERE LAST WEEK?
THEY'RE INTERESTED IN BUYING A HORTISCULPTURE.
MOM!
DAD!

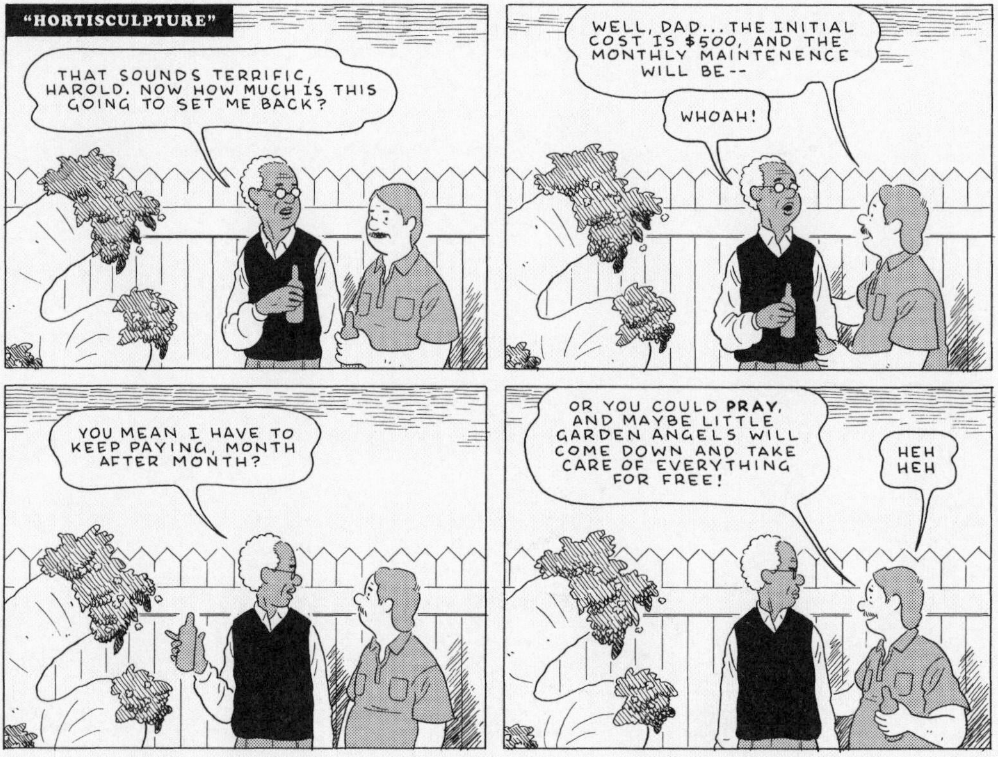
"HORTISCULPTURE"
THAT SOUNDS TERRIFIC, HAROLD. NOW HOW MUCH IS THIS GOING TO SET ME BACK?
WELL, DAD... THE INITIAL COST IS $500, AND THE MONTHLY MAINTENENCE WILL BE--
WHOAH!
YOU MEAN I HAVE TO KEEP PAYING, MONTH AFTER MONTH?
OR YOU COULD PRAY, AND MAYBE LITTLE GARDEN ANGELS WILL COME DOWN AND TAKE CARE OF EVERYTHING FOR FREE!
HEH HEH

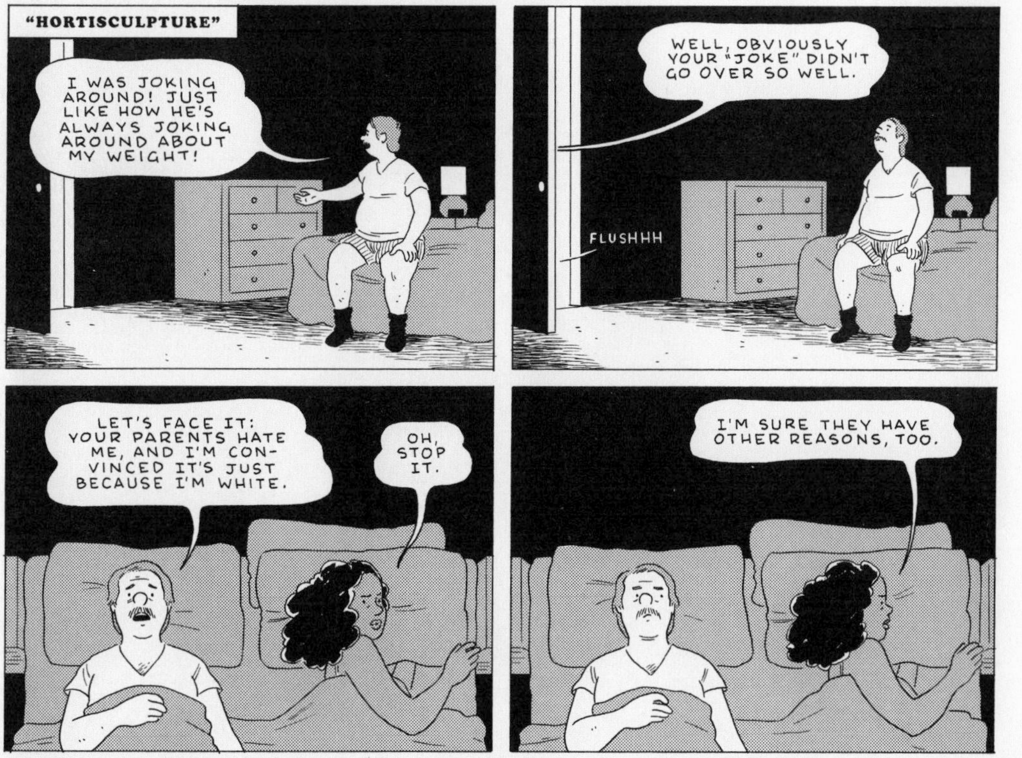
"HORTISCULPTURE"
I WAS JOKING AROUND! JUST LIKE HOW HE'S ALWAYS JOKING AROUND ABOUT MY WEIGHT!
WELL, OBVIOUSLY YOUR "JOKE" DIDN'T GO OVER SO WELL.
FLUSHHH
LET'S FACE IT: YOUR PARENTS HATE ME, AND I'M CONVINCED IT'S JUST BECAUSE I'M WHITE.
OH, STOP IT.
I'M SURE THEY HAVE OTHER REASONS, TOO.

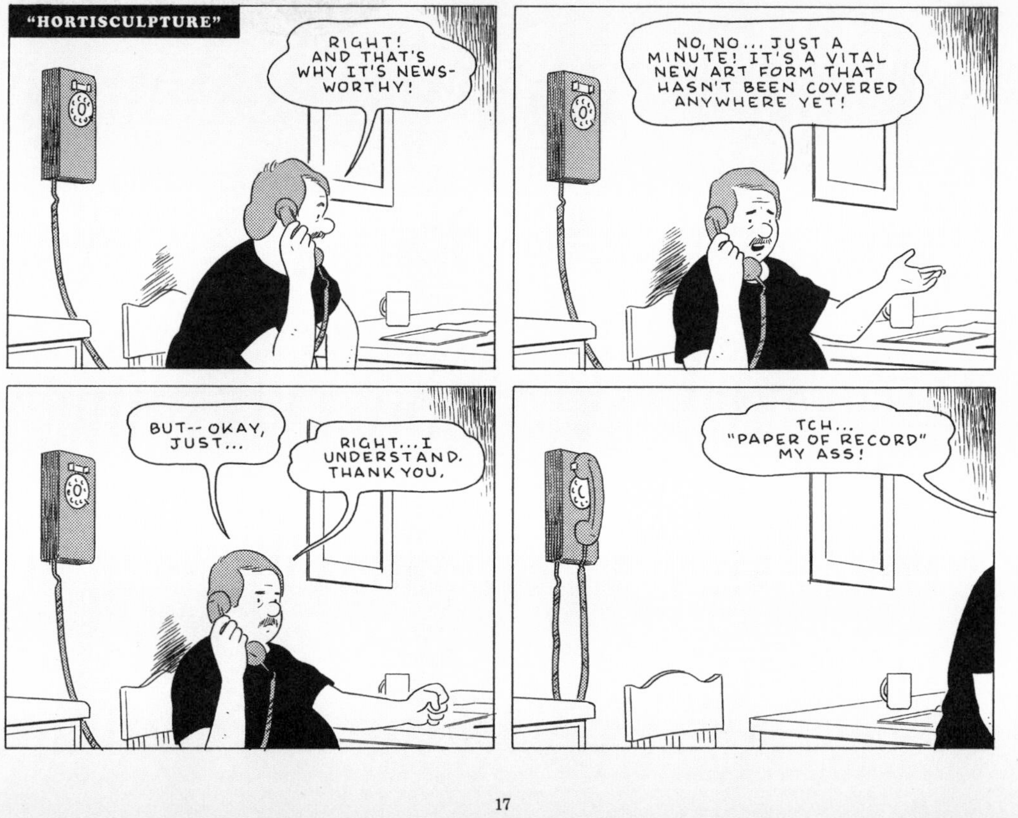
"HORTISCULPTURE"
RIGHT! AND THAT'S WHY IT'S NEWSWORTHY!
NO, NO... JUST A MINUTE! IT'S A VITAL NEW ART FORM THAT HASN'T BEEN COVERED ANYWHERE YET!
BUT-- OKAY, JUST...
RIGHT... I UNDERSTAND. THANK YOU.
TCH... "PAPER OF RECORD" MY ASS!

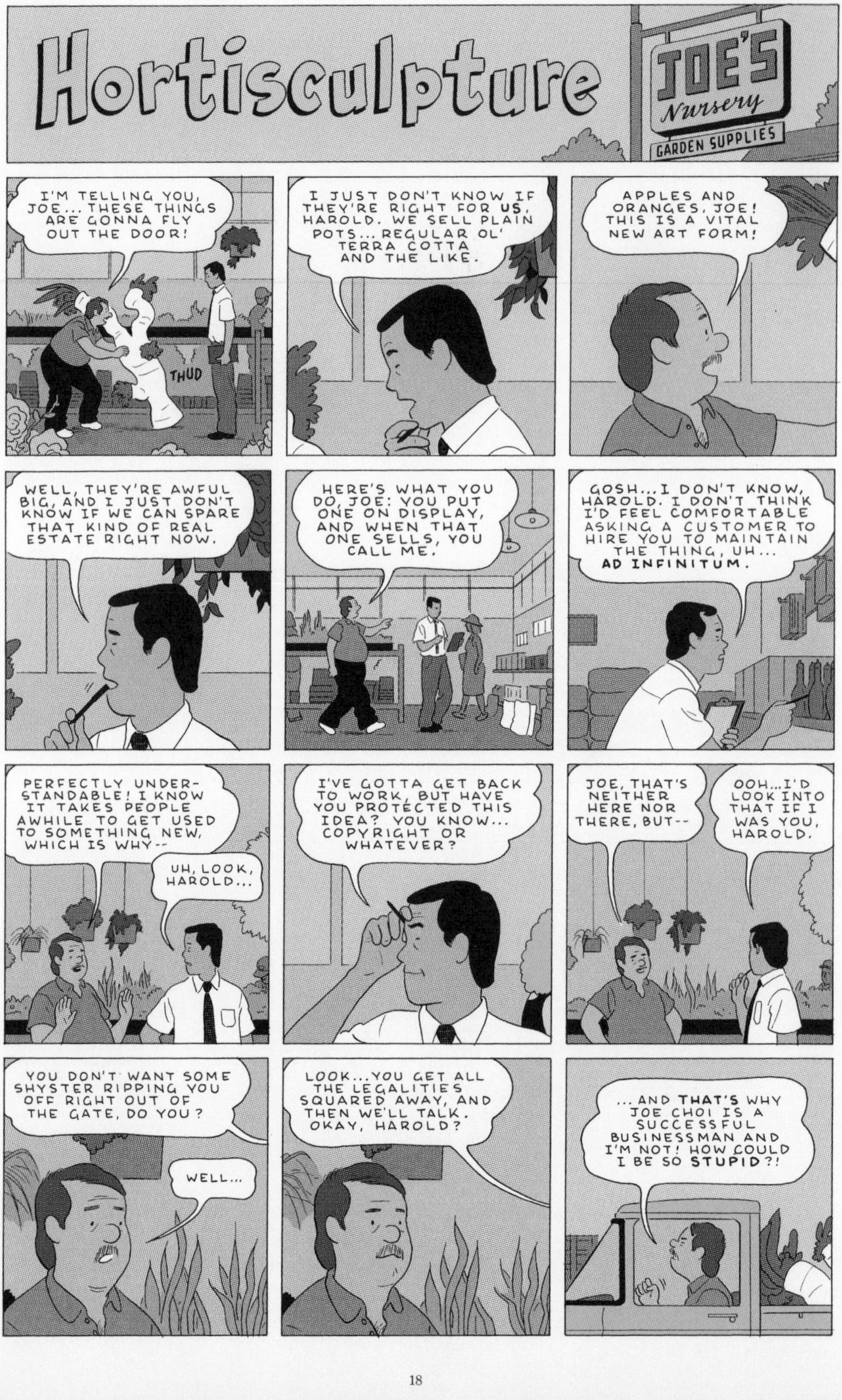
Hortisculpture
JOE'S Nursery
GARDEN SUPPLIES
I'M TELLING YOU, JOE... THESE THINGS ARE GONNA FLY OUT THE DOOR!
THUD
I JUST DON'T KNOW IF THEY'RE RIGHT FOR US, HAROLD. WE SELL PLAIN POTS... REGULAR OL' TERRA COTTA AND THE LIKE.
APPLES AND ORANGES, JOE! THIS IS A VITAL NEW ART FORM!
WELL, THEY'RE AWFUL BIG, AND I JUST DON'T KNOW IF WE CAN SPARE THAT KIND OF REAL ESTATE RIGHT NOW.
HERE'S WHAT YOU DO, JOE: YOU PUT ONE ON DISPLAY, AND WHEN THAT ONE SELLS, YOU CALL ME.
GOSH... I DON'T KNOW, HAROLD. I DON'T THINK I'D FEEL COMFORTABLE ASKING A CUSTOMER TO HIRE YOU TO MAINTAIN THE THING, UH... AD INFINITUM.
PERFECTLY UNDERSTANDABLE! I KNOW IT TAKES PEOPLE AWHILE TO GET USED TO SOMETHING NEW, WHICH IS WHY--
UH, LOOK, HAROLD...
I'VE GOTTA GET BACK TO WORK, BUT HAVE YOU PROTECTED THIS IDEA? YOU KNOW... COPYRIGHT OR WHATEVER?
JOE, THAT'S NEITHER HERE NOR THERE, BUT--
OOH... I'D LOOK INTO THAT IF I WAS YOU, HAROLD.
YOU DON'T WANT SOME SHYSTER RIPPING YOU OFF RIGHT OUT OF THE GATE, DO YOU?
WELL...
LOOK... YOU GET ALL THE LEGALITIES SQUARED AWAY, AND THEN WE'LL TALK. OKAY, HAROLD?
... AND THAT'S WHY JOE CHOI IS A SUCCESSFUL BUSINESSMAN AND I'M NOT! HOW COULD I BE SO STUPID?!

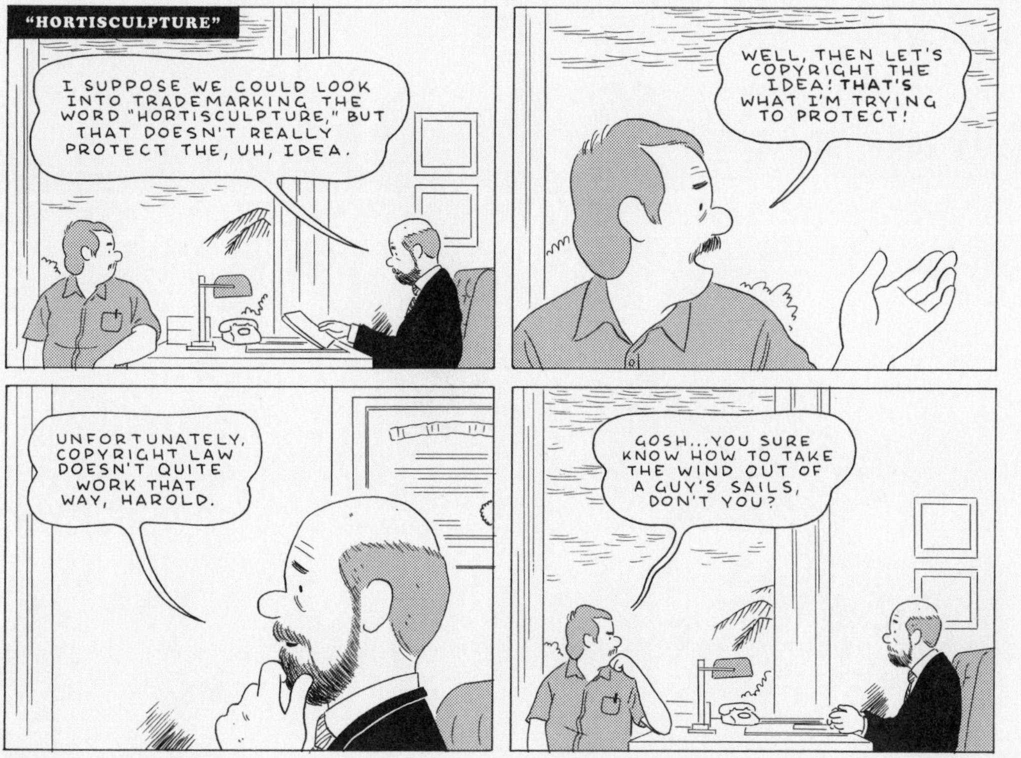
"HORTISCULPTURE"
I SUPPOSE WE COULD LOOK INTO TRADEMARKING THE WORD "HORTISCULPTURE," BUT THAT DOESN'T REALLY PROTECT THE, UH, IDEA.
WELL, THEN LET'S COPYRIGHT THE IDEA! THAT'S WHAT I'M TRYING TO PROTECT!
UNFORTUNATELY, COPYRIGHT LAW DOESN'T QUITE WORK THAT WAY, HAROLD.
GOSH... YOU SURE KNOW HOW TO TAKE THE WIND OUT OF A GUY'S SAILS, DON'T YOU?

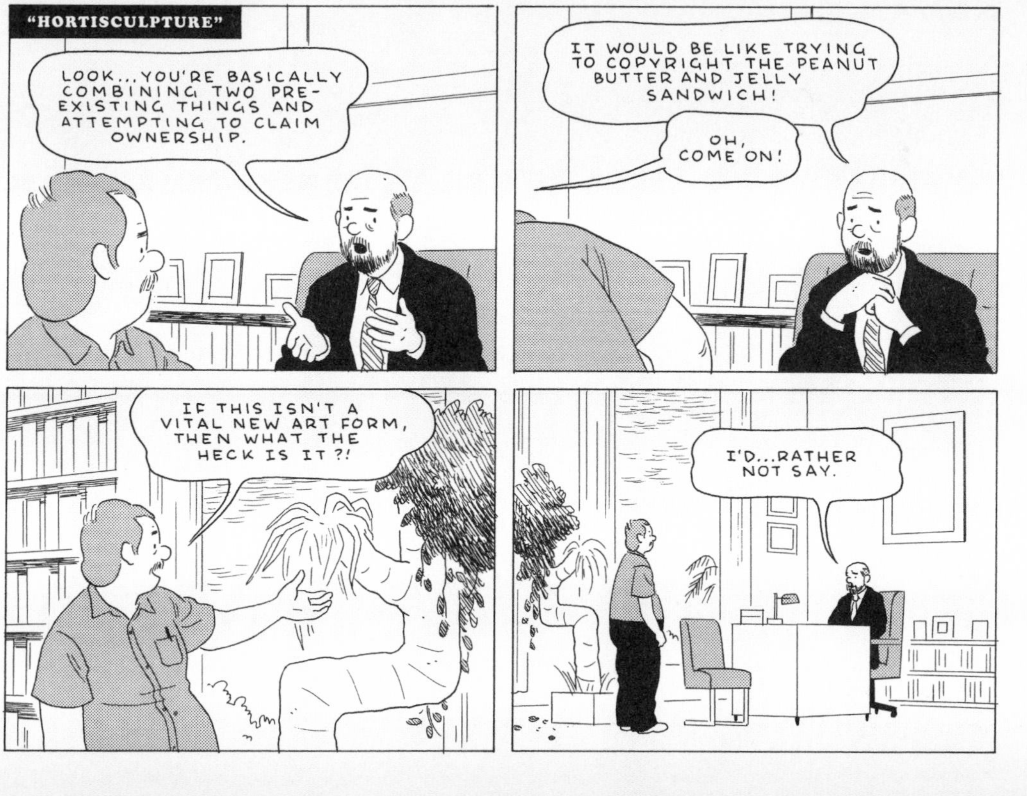
"HORTISCULPTURE"
LOOK... YOU'RE BASICALLY COMBINING TWO PRE-EXISTING THINGS AND ATTEMPTING TO CLAIM OWNERSHIP.
IT WOULD BE LIKE TRYING TO COPYRIGHT THE PEANUT BUTTER AND JELLY SANDWICH!
OH, COME ON!
IF THIS ISN'T A VITAL NEW ART FORM, THEN WHAT THE HECK IS IT?!
I'D... RATHER NOT SAY.

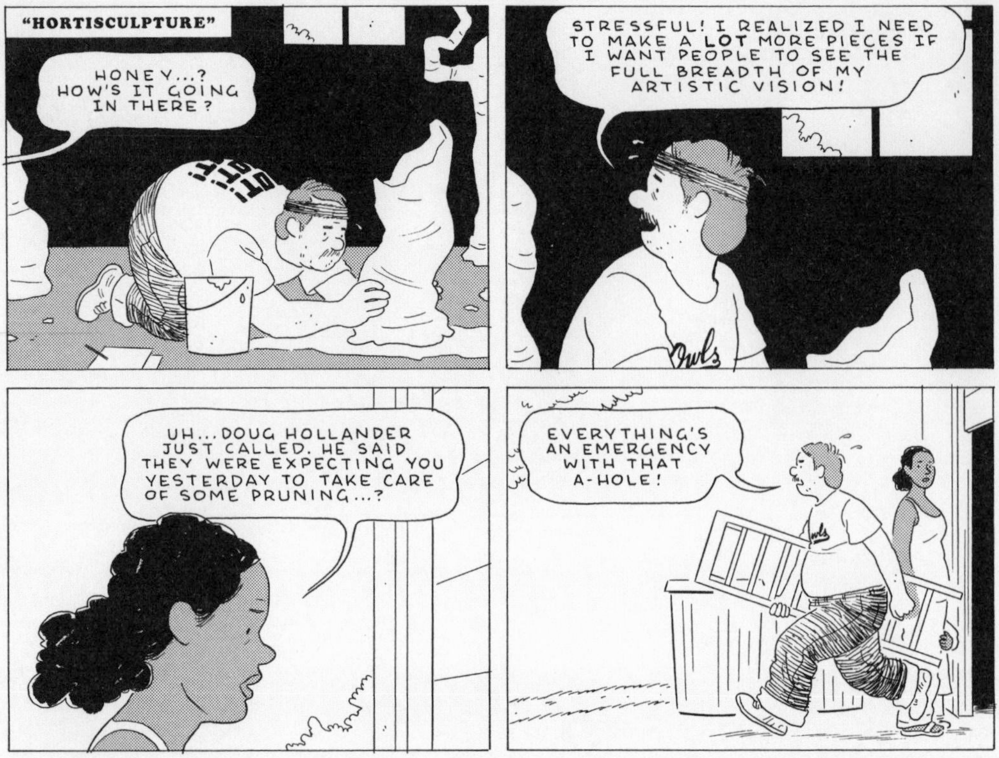
"HORTISCULPTURE"
HONEY...? HOW'S IT GOING IN THERE?
STRESSFUL! I REALIZED I NEED TO MAKE A LOT MORE PIECES IF I WANT PEOPLE TO SEE THE FULL BREADTH OF MY ARTISTIC VISION!
Owls
UH... DOUG HOLLANDER JUST CALLED. HE SAID THEY WERE EXPECTING YOU YESTERDAY TO TAKE CARE OF SOME PRUNING...?
EVERYTHING'S AN EMERGENCY WITH THAT A-HOLE!
Owls

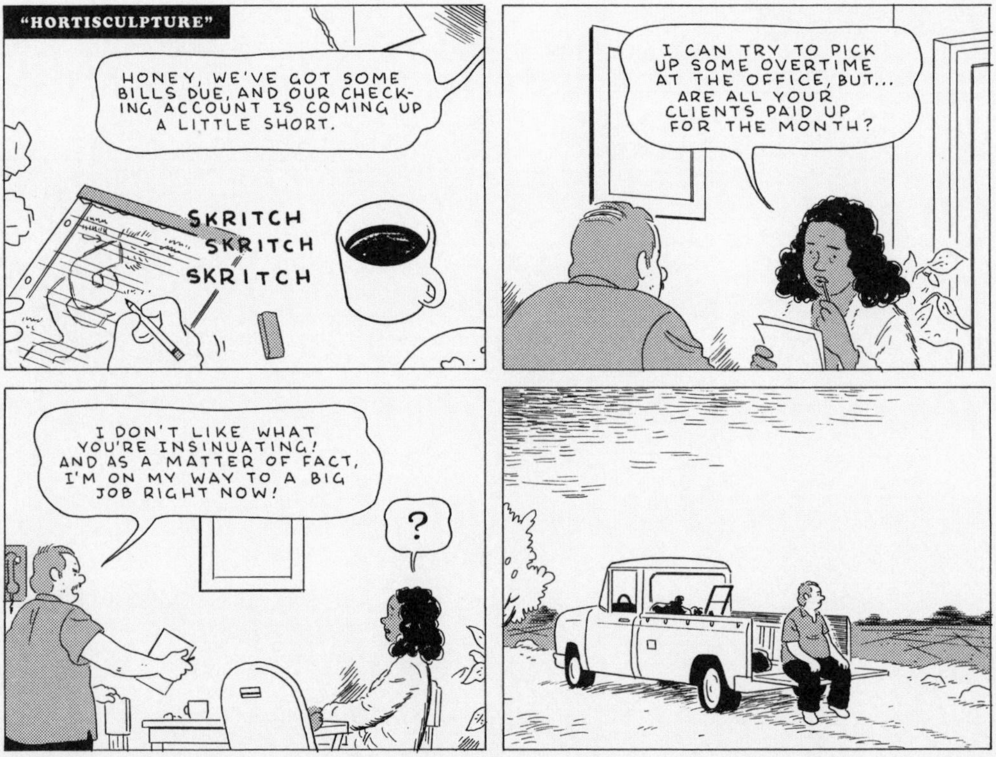
"HORTISCULPTURE"
HONEY, WE'VE GOT SOME BILLS DUE, AND OUR CHECKING ACCOUNT IS COMING UP A LITTLE SHORT.
SKRITCH SKRITCH SKRITCH
I CAN TRY TO PICK UP SOME OVERTIME AT THE OFFICE, BUT... ARE ALL YOUR CLIENTS PAID UP FOR THE MONTH?
I DON'T LIKE WHAT YOU'RE INSINUATING! AND AS A MATTER OF FACT, I'M ON MY WAY TO A BIG JOB RIGHT NOW!
?

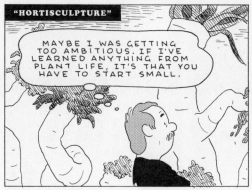

"HORTISCULPTURE"
MAYBE I WAS GETTING TOO AMBITIOUS. IF I'VE LEARNED ANYTHING FROM PLANT LIFE, IT'S THAT YOU HAVE TO START SMALL.
THE TRUTH IS, GOOD WORK WILL SELL ITSELF. AND WHAT BETTER GALLERY THAN MY OWN FRONT YARD?
AH... POTENTIAL CUSTOMERS AT NINE O' CLOCK!

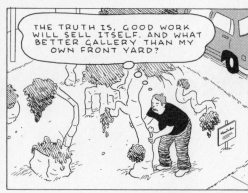

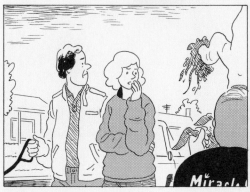

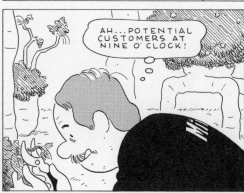

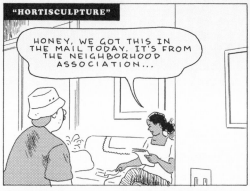

"HORTISCULPTURE"
HONEY, WE GOT THIS IN THE MAIL TODAY. IT'S FROM THE NEIGHBORHOOD ASSOCIATION...
I-I DON'T KNOW IF YOU'RE IN THE MOOD FOR THIS RIGHT NOW, BUT--
FWIP
..."UNSIGHTLY AND INCONGRUOUS"... "A BLIGHT ON THE NEIGHBORHOOD"... "PLEASE RECONSIDER"...
I WILL NOT BE BULLIED.
KRKL

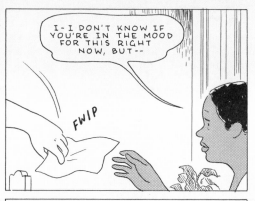

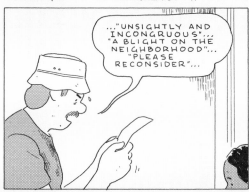

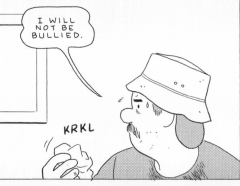

Hortisculpture

THANK YOU AND WELCOME TO THE GRAND RE-OPENING OF CITY HALL!

AND THANK YOU, HAROLD, FOR GRACING OUR HUMBLE GROUNDS WITH YOUR BEAUTIFUL AND INNOVATIVE CREATIONS.

CLAP CLAP CLAP CLAP CLAP WHO CLAP CLAP

THANK YOU, MR. MAYOR. THANK YOU.

WELL...IT WASN'T LONG AGO THAT I WAS JUST A SIMPLE GARDENER WITH A DREAM AND A VISION. SO I CAN ASSURE YOU: NONE OF THIS IS LOST ON ME.

AND NOW...I'D LIKE TO TAKE THIS OPPORTUNITY TO SETTLE SOME SCORES.

JERRY TUCKER: YOU CAN TAKE YOUR PATRON-IZING TONE AND YOUR STUPID "CHIA PET" JOKE AND SHOVE THEM UP YOUR ASS.

JOE CHOI: NOT ONLY WILL I NEVER ALLOW YOU TO SELL MY WORK, I HOPE YOUR ENTIRE BUSINESS GOES UP IN FLAMES.

AND TO MY BROTHER LEO: YOU... WELL, YOU WERE ACTUALLY RIGHT ABOUT THAT COPYRIGHT STUFF, BUT STILL-- YOU WEREN'T VERY ENCOURAGING, SO SCREW YOU.

AND TO ALL MY NEIGH-BORS: YOU CAN STOP WITH THE PETITIONS BECAUSE I JUST PUR-CHASED A HOME IN GREENLEAF ESTATES, SO YOUR NEIGHBORHOOD SHALL NO LONGER BE "BLIGHTED" BY MY ART.

THANK YOU ALL FOR COMING! I'LL BE SIGNING AUTOGRAPHS IN THE ROTUNDA!

CLAP WHOO LAP YEAH! AP LAP CLAP CLAP CLAP CLAP CLAP CLAP CLAP WHOO CLAP CLAP

WHO KNEW THERE WERE SCULPTURE GROUPIES?

WHAT ARE YOU THINKING ABOUT, HONEY?

HM? OH... NOTHING.

22

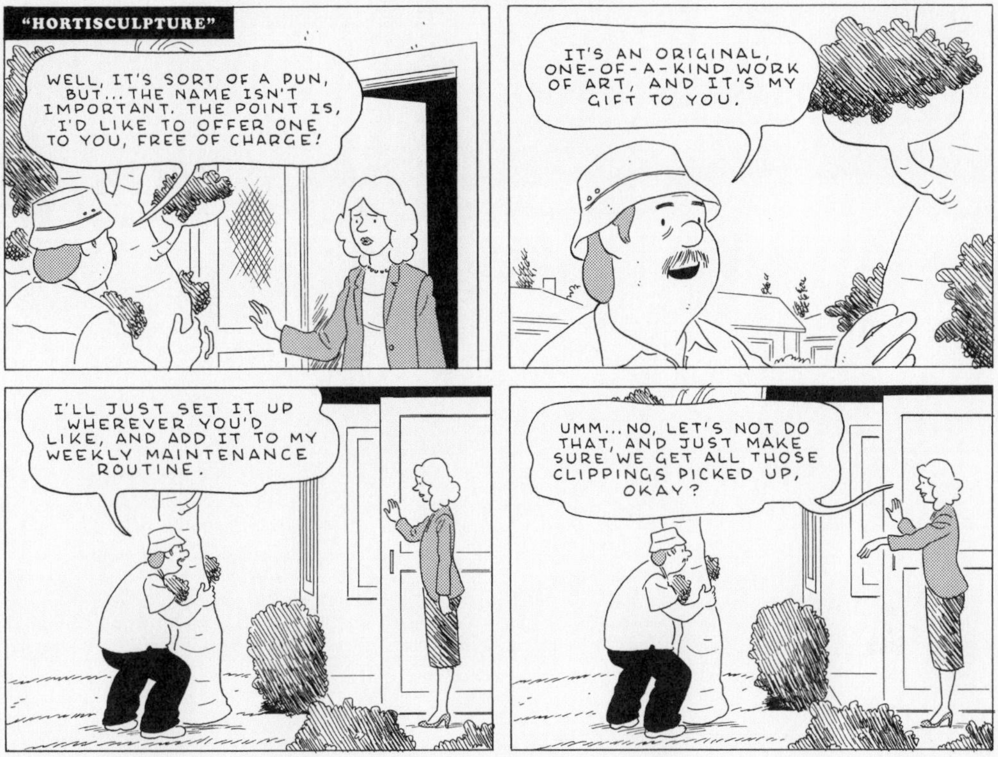
"HORTISCULPTURE"
WELL, IT'S SORT OF A PUN, BUT... THE NAME ISN'T IMPORTANT. THE POINT IS, I'D LIKE TO OFFER ONE TO YOU, FREE OF CHARGE!
IT'S AN ORIGINAL, ONE-OF-A-KIND WORK OF ART, AND IT'S MY GIFT TO YOU.
I'LL JUST SET IT UP WHEREVER YOU'D LIKE, AND ADD IT TO MY WEEKLY MAINTENANCE ROUTINE.
UMM... NO, LET'S NOT DO THAT, AND JUST MAKE SURE WE GET ALL THOSE CLIPPINGS PICKED UP, OKAY?

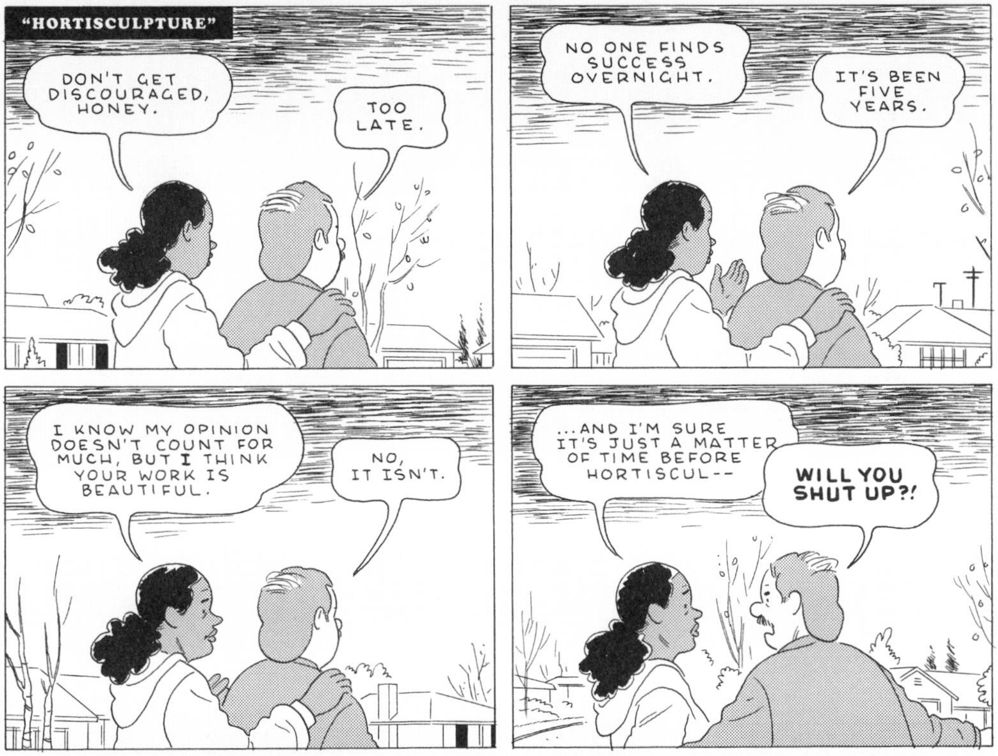
"HORTISCULPTURE"
DON'T GET DISCOURAGED, HONEY.
TOO LATE.
NO ONE FINDS SUCCESS OVERNIGHT.
IT'S BEEN FIVE YEARS.
I KNOW MY OPINION DOESN'T COUNT FOR MUCH, BUT I THINK YOUR WORK IS BEAUTIFUL.
NO, IT ISN'T.
...AND I'M SURE IT'S JUST A MATTER OF TIME BEFORE HORTISCUL--
WILL YOU SHUT UP?!

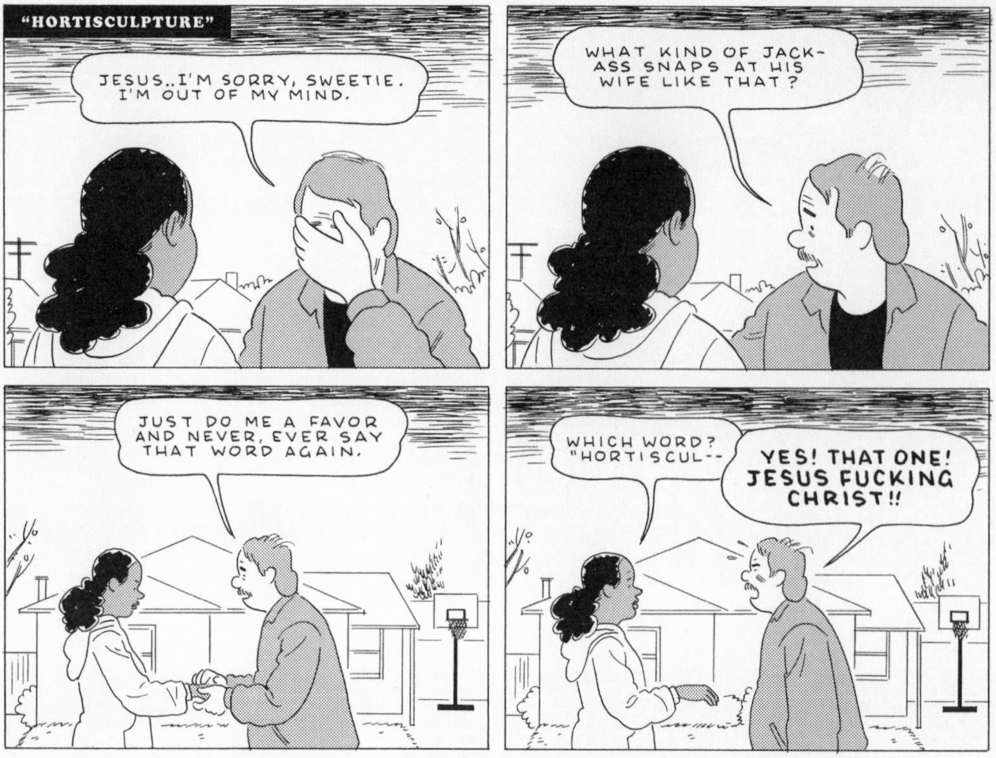
"HORTISCULPTURE"
JESUS..I'M SORRY, SWEETIE. I'M OUT OF MY MIND.
WHAT KIND OF JACK-ASS SNAPS AT HIS WIFE LIKE THAT?
JUST DO ME A FAVOR AND NEVER, EVER SAY THAT WORD AGAIN.
WHICH WORD? "HORTISCUL--
YES! THAT ONE! JESUS FUCKING CHRIST!!

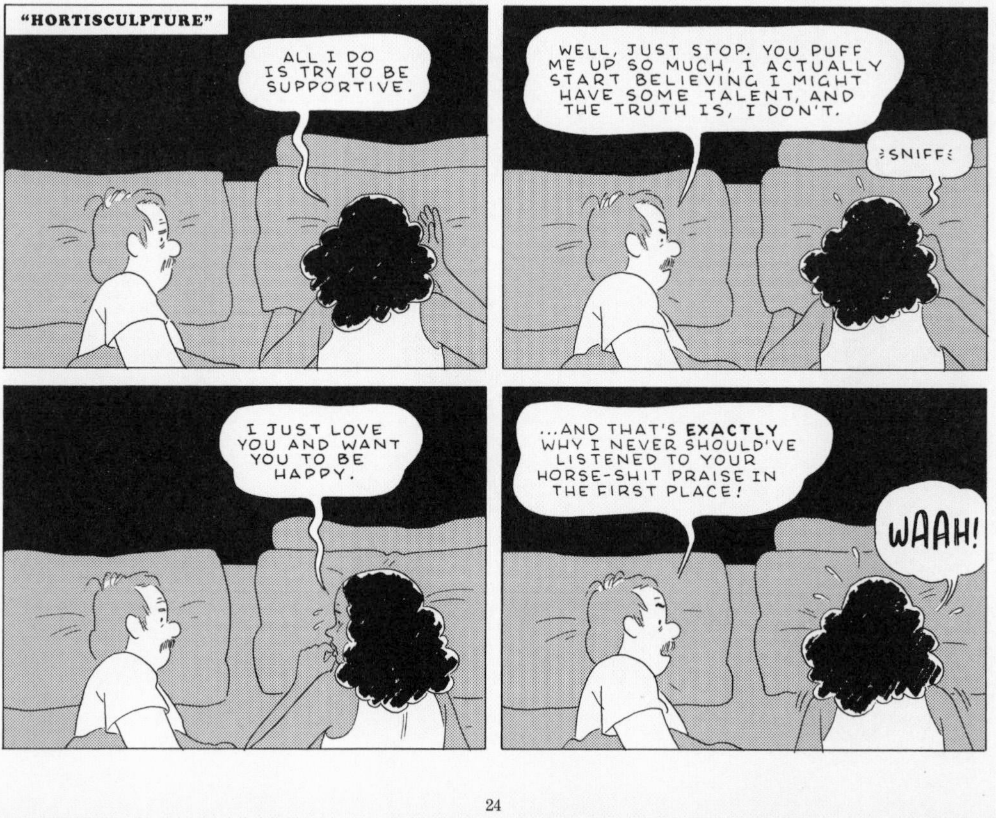
"HORTISCULPTURE"
ALL I DO IS TRY TO BE SUPPORTIVE.
WELL, JUST STOP. YOU PUFF ME UP SO MUCH, I ACTUALLY START BELIEVING I MIGHT HAVE SOME TALENT, AND THE TRUTH IS, I DON'T.
SNIFF
I JUST LOVE YOU AND WANT YOU TO BE HAPPY.
...AND THAT'S EXACTLY WHY I NEVER SHOULD'VE LISTENED TO YOUR HORSE-SHIT PRAISE IN THE FIRST PLACE!
WAAH!

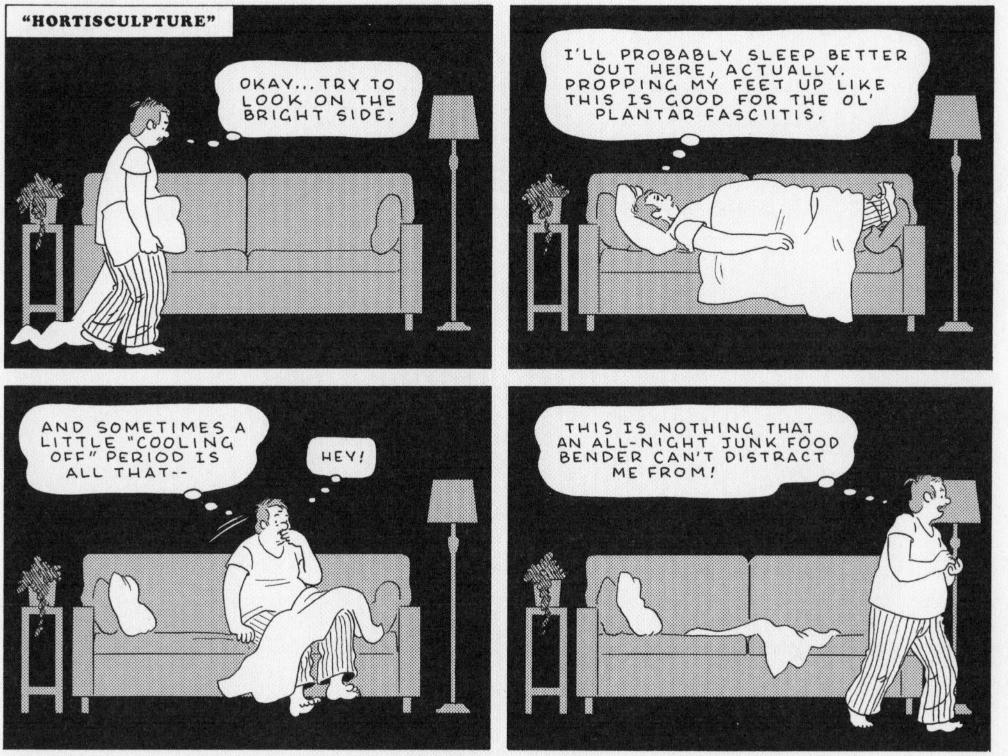
"HORTISCULPTURE"
OKAY... TRY TO LOOK ON THE BRIGHT SIDE.
I'LL PROBABLY SLEEP BETTER OUT HERE, ACTUALLY. PROPPING MY FEET UP LIKE THIS IS GOOD FOR THE OL' PLANTAR FASCIITIS.
AND SOMETIMES A LITTLE "COOLING OFF" PERIOD IS ALL THAT--
HEY!
THIS IS NOTHING THAT AN ALL-NIGHT JUNK FOOD BENDER CAN'T DISTRACT ME FROM!

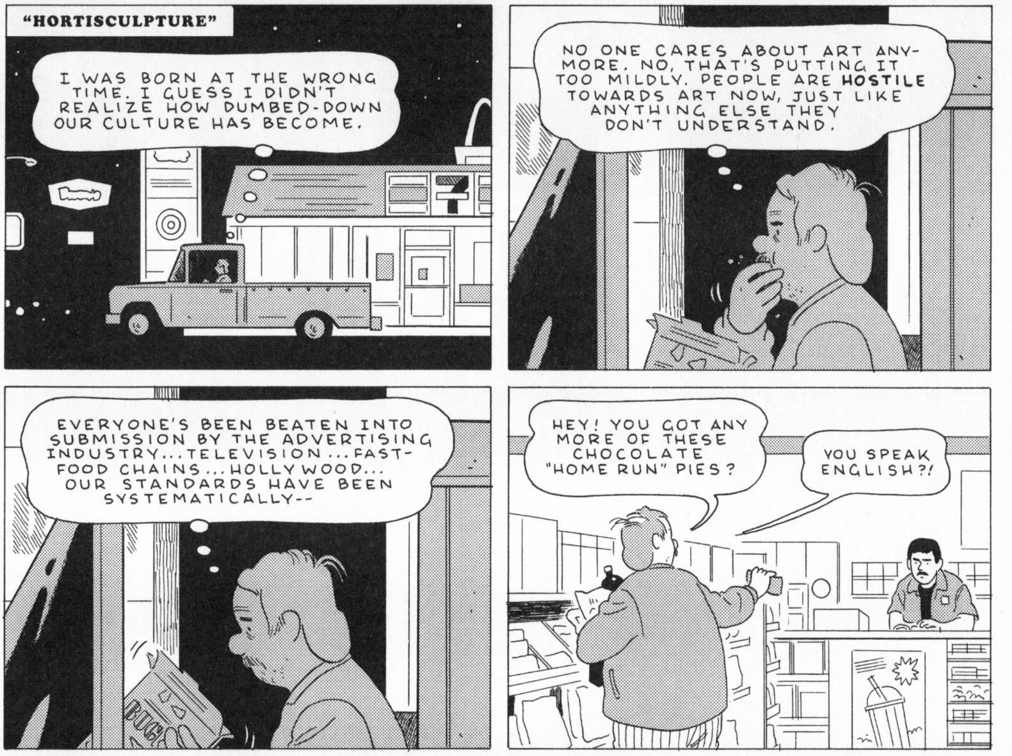
"HORTISCULPTURE"
I WAS BORN AT THE WRONG TIME. I GUESS I DIDN'T REALIZE HOW DUMBED-DOWN OUR CULTURE HAS BECOME.
NO ONE CARES ABOUT ART ANYMORE. NO, THAT'S PUTTING IT TOO MILDLY. PEOPLE ARE **HOSTILE** TOWARDS ART NOW, JUST LIKE ANYTHING ELSE THEY DON'T UNDERSTAND.
EVERYONE'S BEEN BEATEN INTO SUBMISSION BY THE ADVERTISING INDUSTRY... TELEVISION... FAST-FOOD CHAINS... HOLLYWOOD... OUR STANDARDS HAVE BEEN SYSTEMATICALLY--
HEY! YOU GOT ANY MORE OF THESE CHOCOLATE "HOME RUN" PIES?
YOU SPEAK ENGLISH?!

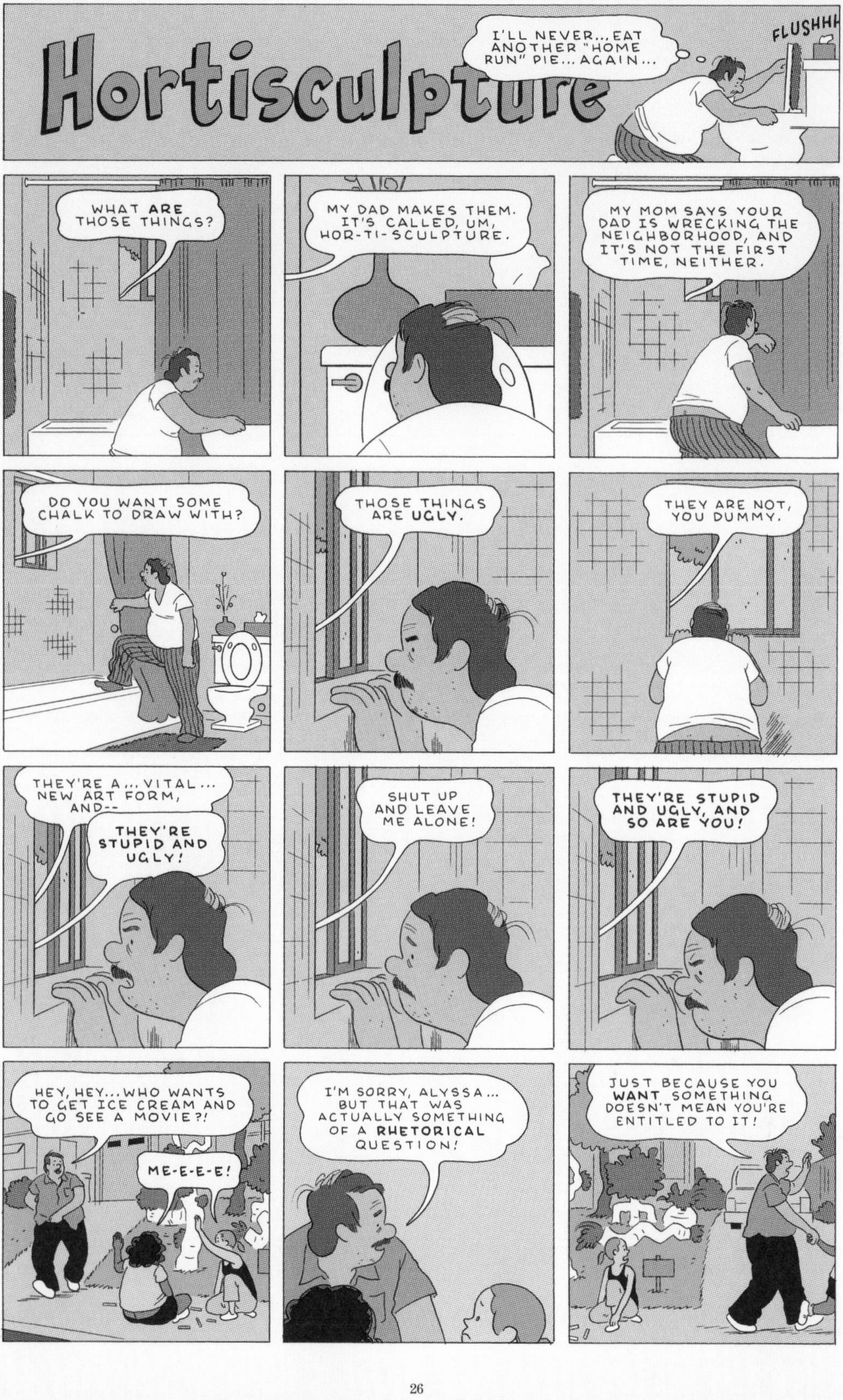
Hortisculpture
I'LL NEVER... EAT ANOTHER "HOME RUN" PIE... AGAIN...
FLUSHHH
WHAT ARE THOSE THINGS?
MY DAD MAKES THEM. IT'S CALLED, UM, HOR-TI-SCULPTURE.
MY MOM SAYS YOUR DAD IS WRECKING THE NEIGHBORHOOD, AND IT'S NOT THE FIRST TIME, NEITHER.
DO YOU WANT SOME CHALK TO DRAW WITH?
THOSE THINGS ARE UGLY.
THEY ARE NOT, YOU DUMMY.
THEY'RE A... VITAL... NEW ART FORM, AND--
THEY'RE STUPID AND UGLY!
SHUT UP AND LEAVE ME ALONE!
THEY'RE STUPID AND UGLY, AND SO ARE YOU!
HEY, HEY... WHO WANTS TO GET ICE CREAM AND GO SEE A MOVIE?!
ME-E-E-E!
I'M SORRY, ALYSSA... BUT THAT WAS ACTUALLY SOMETHING OF A RHETORICAL QUESTION!
JUST BECAUSE YOU WANT SOMETHING DOESN'T MEAN YOU'RE ENTITLED TO IT!

"HORTISCULPTURE"

SHE WAS DOING HER DAMNEDEST TO DEFEND ME, BUT I COULD TELL: SHE WAS EMBARRASSED!

DON'T BE SILLY, HONEY. YOU'LL HAVE PLENTY OF CHANCES TO EMBARRASS HER LATER ON, BUT RIGHT NOW SHE'S SIMPLY TOO YOUNG TO--

WHAT?

WHAT ARE YOU LOOKING AT?

SHE'S OUT IN THE YARD, AND IT LOOKS LIKE SHE'S... TRYING TO PUSH YOUR SCULPTURES OVER.

"HORTISCULPTURE"

OHH-H-H-H-H-H-H-H-H

WHAT IS IT? ARE YOU OKAY?

AAAH-H-H

HONEY, ARE YOU HAVING A HEART ATTACK?

NO-O-O-O-O

I'M CRINGING!

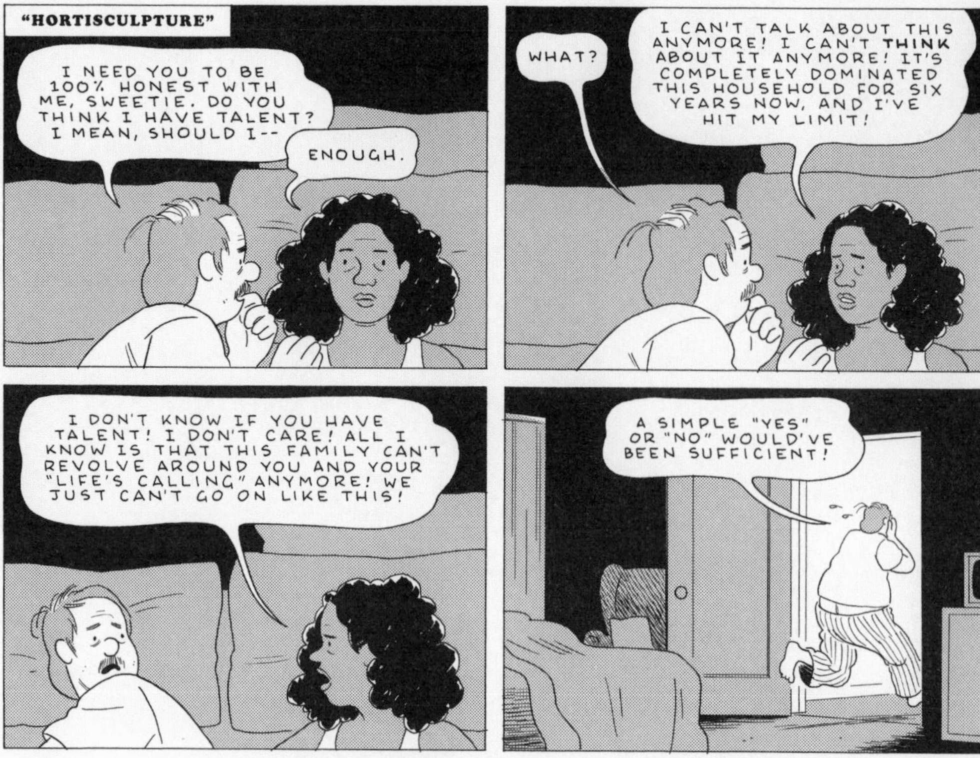
"HORTISCULPTURE"
I NEED YOU TO BE 100% HONEST WITH ME, SWEETIE. DO YOU THINK I HAVE TALENT? I MEAN, SHOULD I--
ENOUGH.
WHAT?
I CAN'T TALK ABOUT THIS ANYMORE! I CAN'T THINK ABOUT IT ANYMORE! IT'S COMPLETELY DOMINATED THIS HOUSEHOLD FOR SIX YEARS NOW, AND I'VE HIT MY LIMIT!
I DON'T KNOW IF YOU HAVE TALENT! I DON'T CARE! ALL I KNOW IS THAT THIS FAMILY CAN'T REVOLVE AROUND YOU AND YOUR "LIFE'S CALLING" ANYMORE! WE JUST CAN'T GO ON LIKE THIS!
A SIMPLE "YES" OR "NO" WOULD'VE BEEN SUFFICIENT!

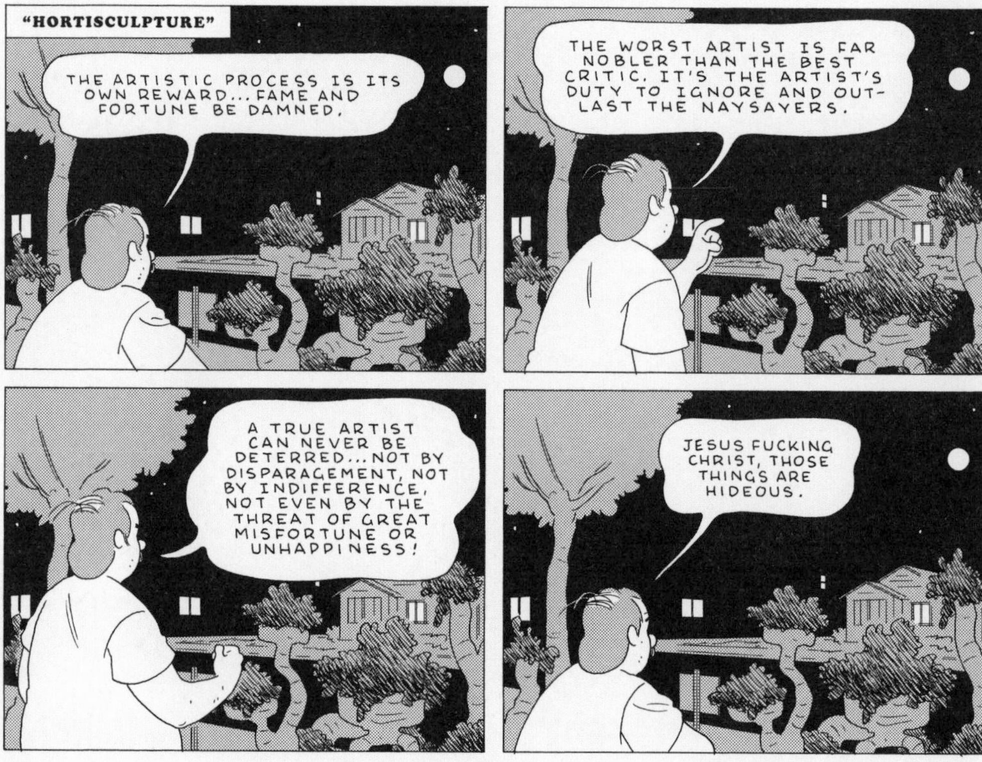
"HORTISCULPTURE"
THE ARTISTIC PROCESS IS ITS OWN REWARD... FAME AND FORTUNE BE DAMNED.
THE WORST ARTIST IS FAR NOBLER THAN THE BEST CRITIC. IT'S THE ARTIST'S DUTY TO IGNORE AND OUT-LAST THE NAYSAYERS.
A TRUE ARTIST CAN NEVER BE DETERRED... NOT BY DISPARAGEMENT, NOT BY INDIFFERENCE, NOT EVEN BY THE THREAT OF GREAT MISFORTUNE OR UNHAPPINESS!
JESUS FUCKING CHRIST, THOSE THINGS ARE HIDEOUS.

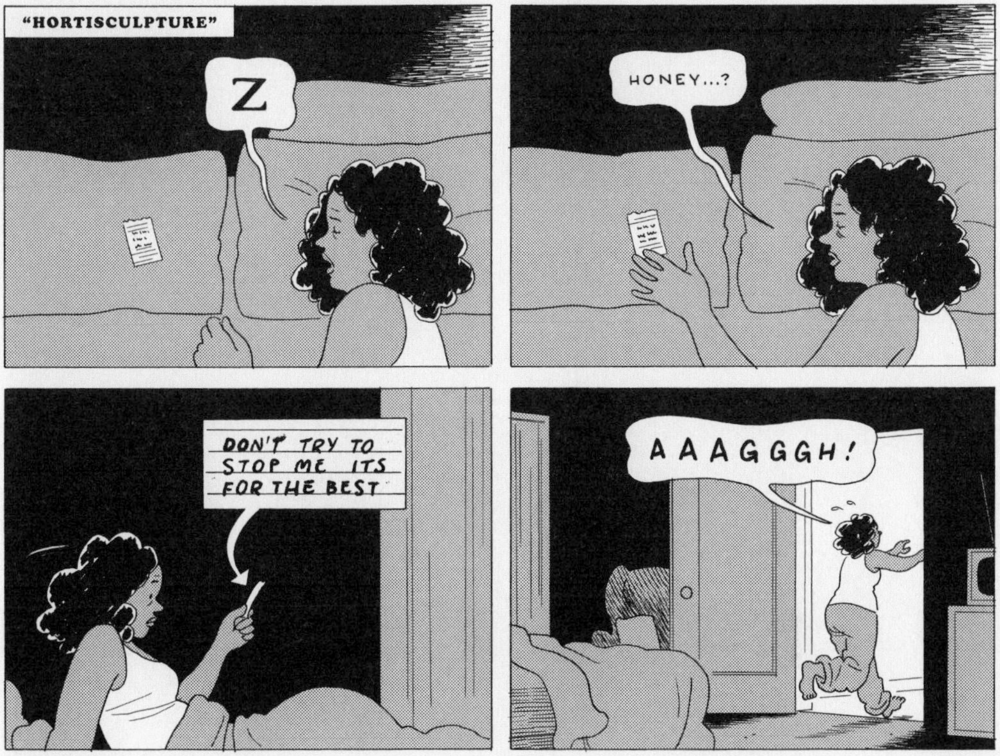
"HORTISCULPTURE"
Z
HONEY...?
DON'T TRY TO STOP ME ITS FOR THE BEST
AAAGGGH!

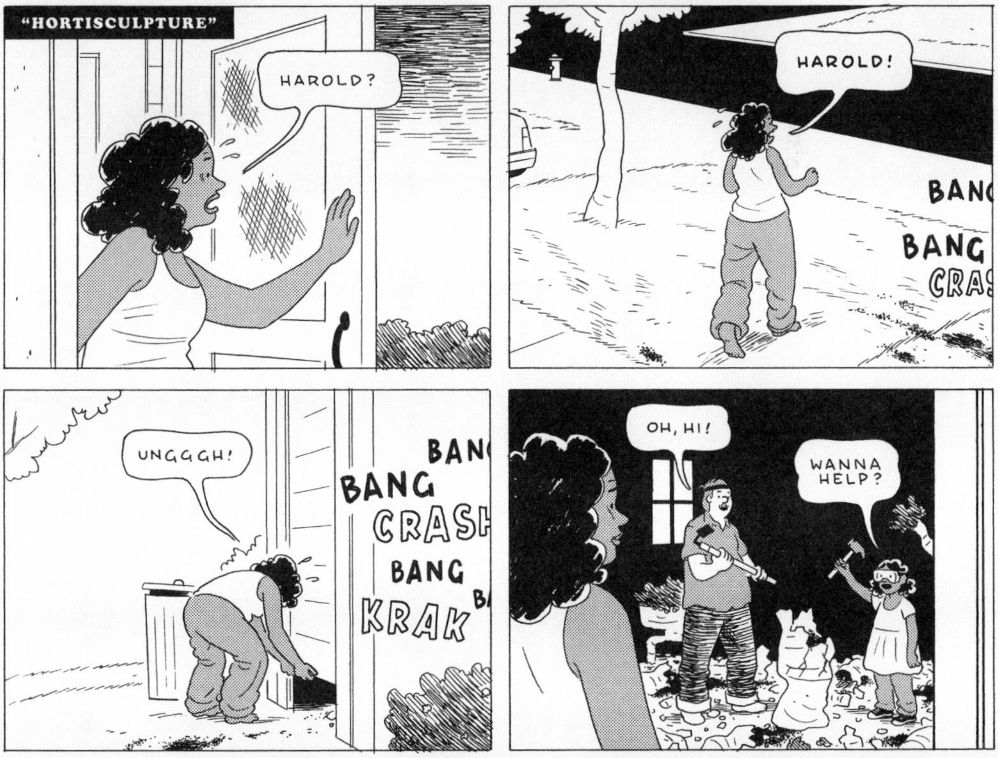
"HORTISCULPTURE"
HAROLD?
HAROLD!
BAN
BANG
CRAS
UNGGGH!
BAN
BANG
CRASH
BANG
KRAK
OH, HI!
WANNA HELP?

AMBER SWEET

AMBER SWEET

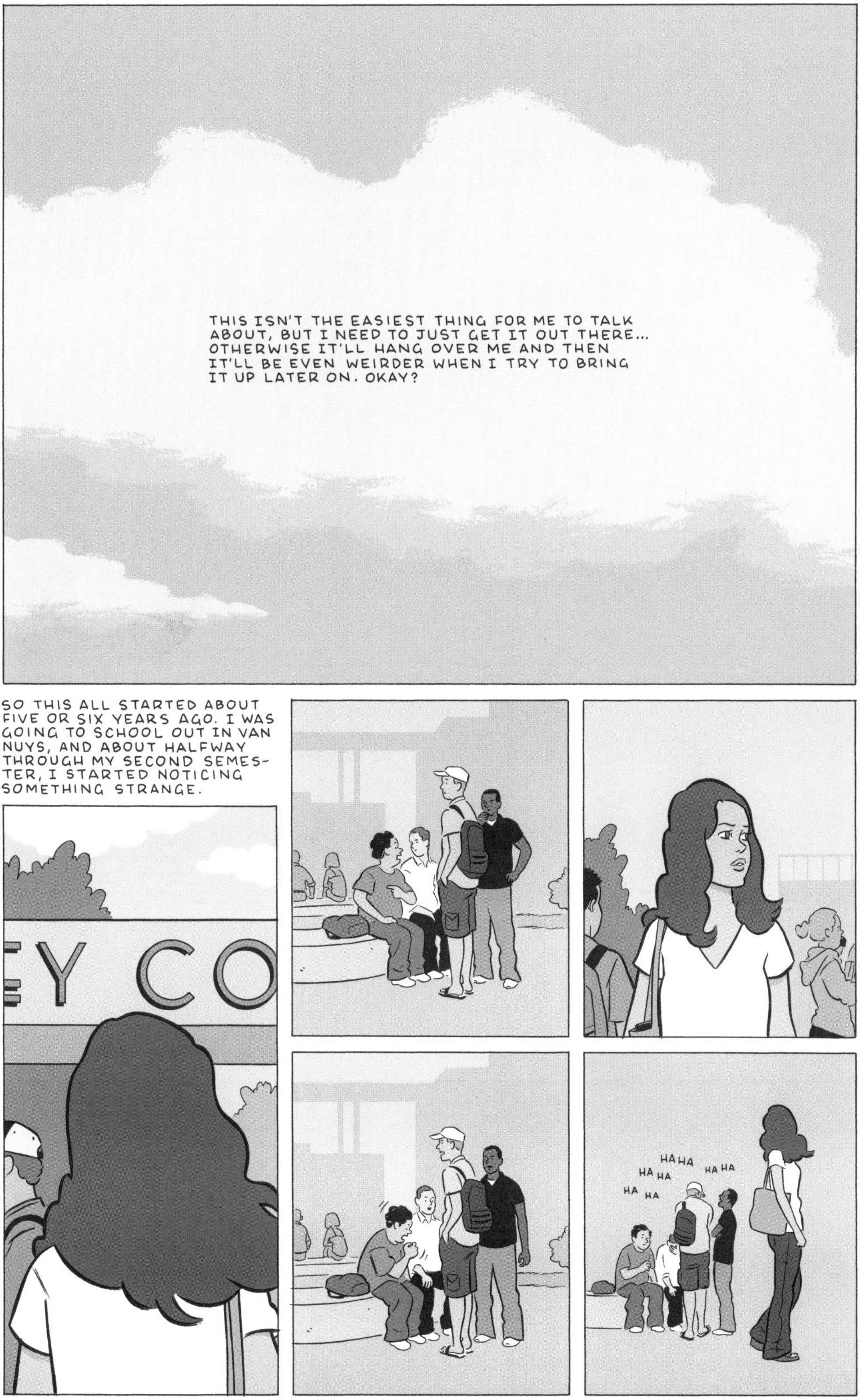
THIS ISN'T THE EASIEST THING FOR ME TO TALK ABOUT, BUT I NEED TO JUST GET IT OUT THERE... OTHERWISE IT'LL HANG OVER ME AND THEN IT'LL BE EVEN WEIRDER WHEN I TRY TO BRING IT UP LATER ON. OKAY?
SO THIS ALL STARTED ABOUT FIVE OR SIX YEARS AGO. I WAS GOING TO SCHOOL OUT IN VAN NUYS, AND ABOUT HALFWAY THROUGH MY SECOND SEMESTER, I STARTED NOTICING SOMETHING STRANGE.
EY CO
HA HA HA HA HA HA HA HA

IT WAS JUST LITTLE THINGS, LIKE PEOPLE LOOKING AT ME FUNNY OR WHISPERING WHEN I WALKED BY, BUT IT WAS TOO MUCH FOR ME TO IGNORE. IT GOT TO THE POINT WHERE I COULDN'T SET FOOT ON CAMPUS WITHOUT FEELING COMPLETELY SELF-CONSCIOUS.

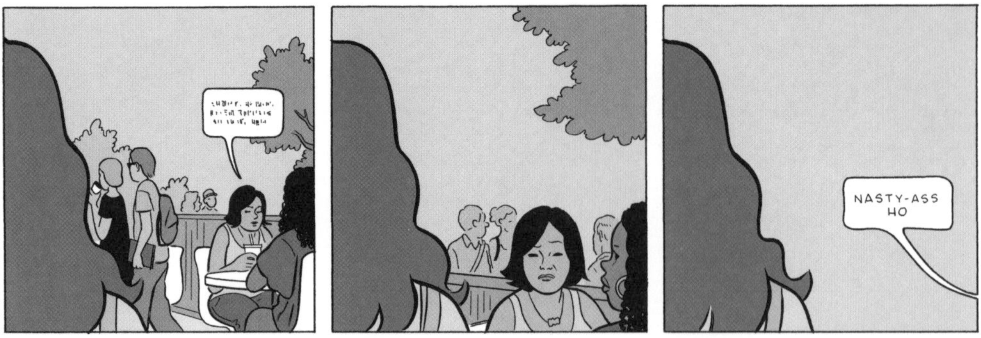
NASTY-ASS HO

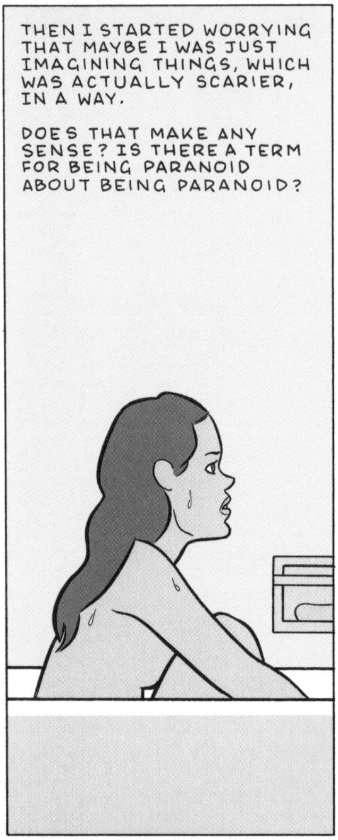
THEN I STARTED WORRYING THAT MAYBE I WAS JUST IMAGINING THINGS, WHICH WAS ACTUALLY SCARIER, IN A WAY.
DOES THAT MAKE ANY SENSE? IS THERE A TERM FOR BEING PARANOID ABOUT BEING PARANOID?

I TRIED TO PUT IT OUT OF MY MIND AND TOLD MYSELF TO JUST FOCUS ON MY STUDIES. THAT WAS THE IMPORTANT THING. BUT THERE'S ONLY SO MUCH YOU CAN BLOCK OUT, YOU KNOW?

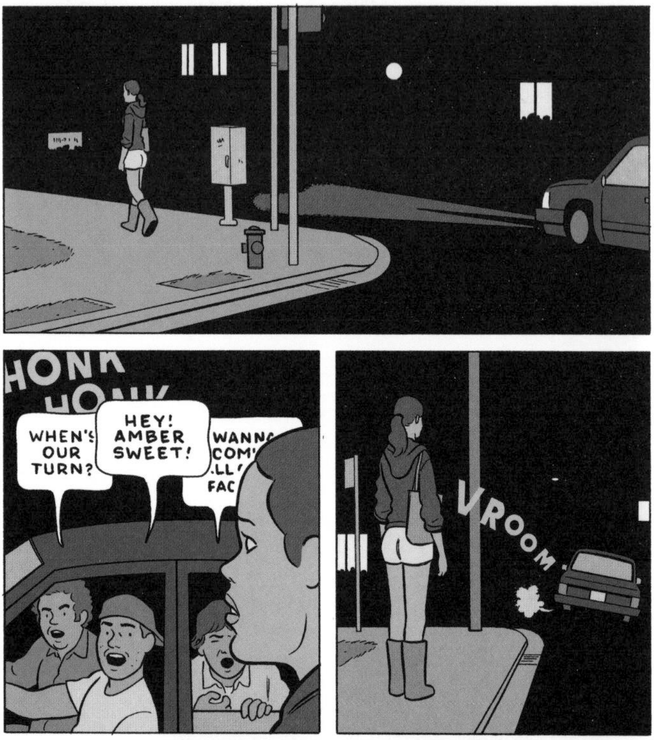
HONK
WHEN'S OUR TURN?
HEY! AMBER SWEET!
VROOM

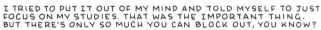

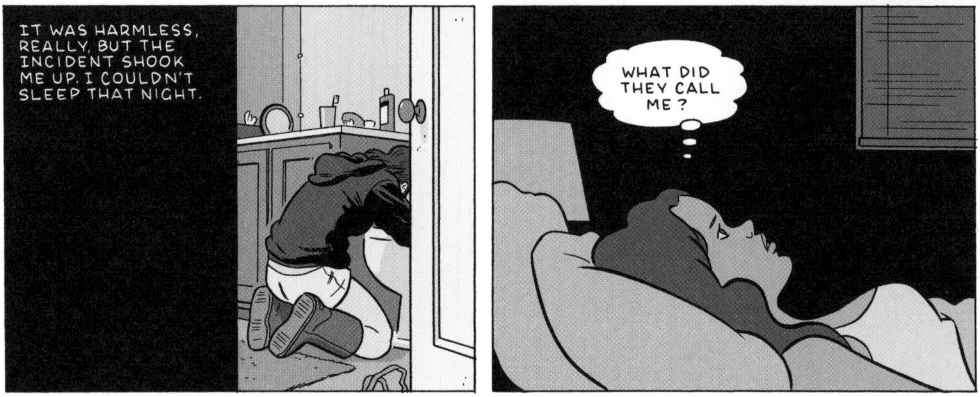
IT WAS HARMLESS, REALLY, BUT THE INCIDENT SHOOK ME UP. I COULDN'T SLEEP THAT NIGHT.
WHAT DID THEY CALL ME?

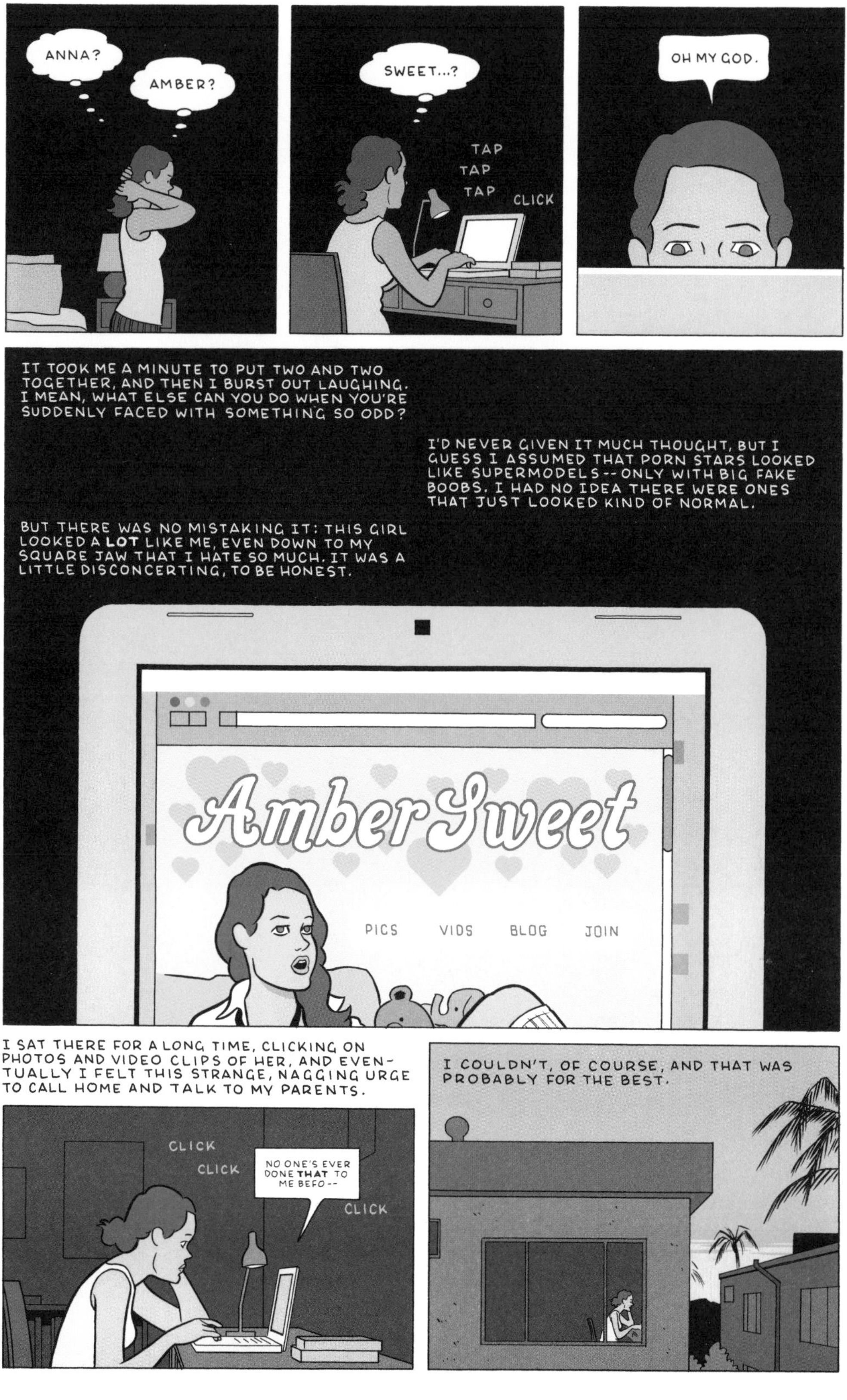
ANNA?
AMBER?
SWEET...?
TAP
TAP
TAP
CLICK
OH MY GOD.
IT TOOK ME A MINUTE TO PUT TWO AND TWO TOGETHER, AND THEN I BURST OUT LAUGHING. I MEAN, WHAT ELSE CAN YOU DO WHEN YOU'RE SUDDENLY FACED WITH SOMETHING SO ODD?
I'D NEVER GIVEN IT MUCH THOUGHT, BUT I GUESS I ASSUMED THAT PORN STARS LOOKED LIKE SUPERMODELS -- ONLY WITH BIG FAKE BOOBS. I HAD NO IDEA THERE WERE ONES THAT JUST LOOKED KIND OF NORMAL.
BUT THERE WAS NO MISTAKING IT: THIS GIRL LOOKED A **LOT** LIKE ME, EVEN DOWN TO MY SQUARE JAW THAT I HATE SO MUCH. IT WAS A LITTLE DISCONCERTING, TO BE HONEST.
AmberSweet
PICS
VIDS
BLOG
JOIN
I SAT THERE FOR A LONG TIME, CLICKING ON PHOTOS AND VIDEO CLIPS OF HER, AND EVENTUALLY I FELT THIS STRANGE, NAGGING URGE TO CALL HOME AND TALK TO MY PARENTS.
CLICK
CLICK
NO ONE'S EVER DONE **THAT** TO ME BEFO --
CLICK
I COULDN'T, OF COURSE, AND THAT WAS PROBABLY FOR THE BEST.

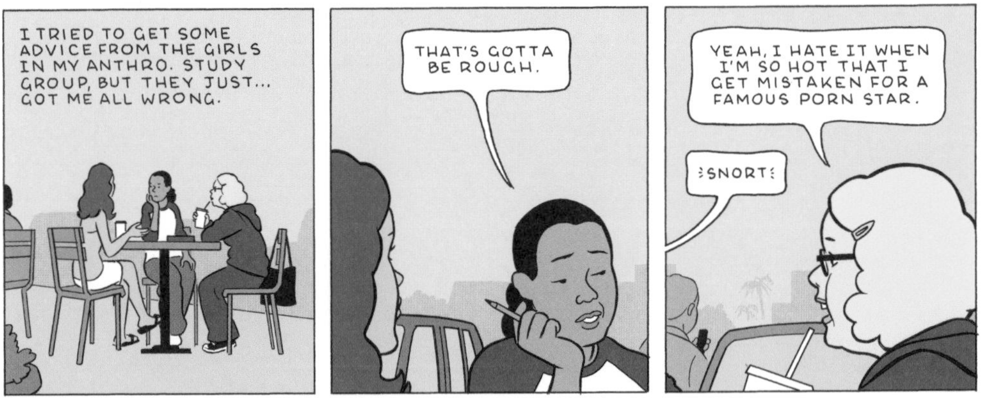
I TRIED TO GET SOME ADVICE FROM THE GIRLS IN MY ANTHRO. STUDY GROUP, BUT THEY JUST... GOT ME ALL WRONG.
THAT'S GOTTA BE ROUGH.
YEAH, I HATE IT WHEN I'M SO HOT THAT I GET MISTAKEN FOR A FAMOUS PORN STAR.
:SNORT:

AROUND THIS TIME A GUY FROM MY PSYCH. CLASS ASKED ME OUT. HE WASN'T REALLY MY TYPE PHYSICALLY, BUT HE SEEMED KIND OF SMART AND FUNNY, AND MORE IMPORTANTLY, OBLIVIOUS TO THE STUPID CAMPUS GOSSIP.

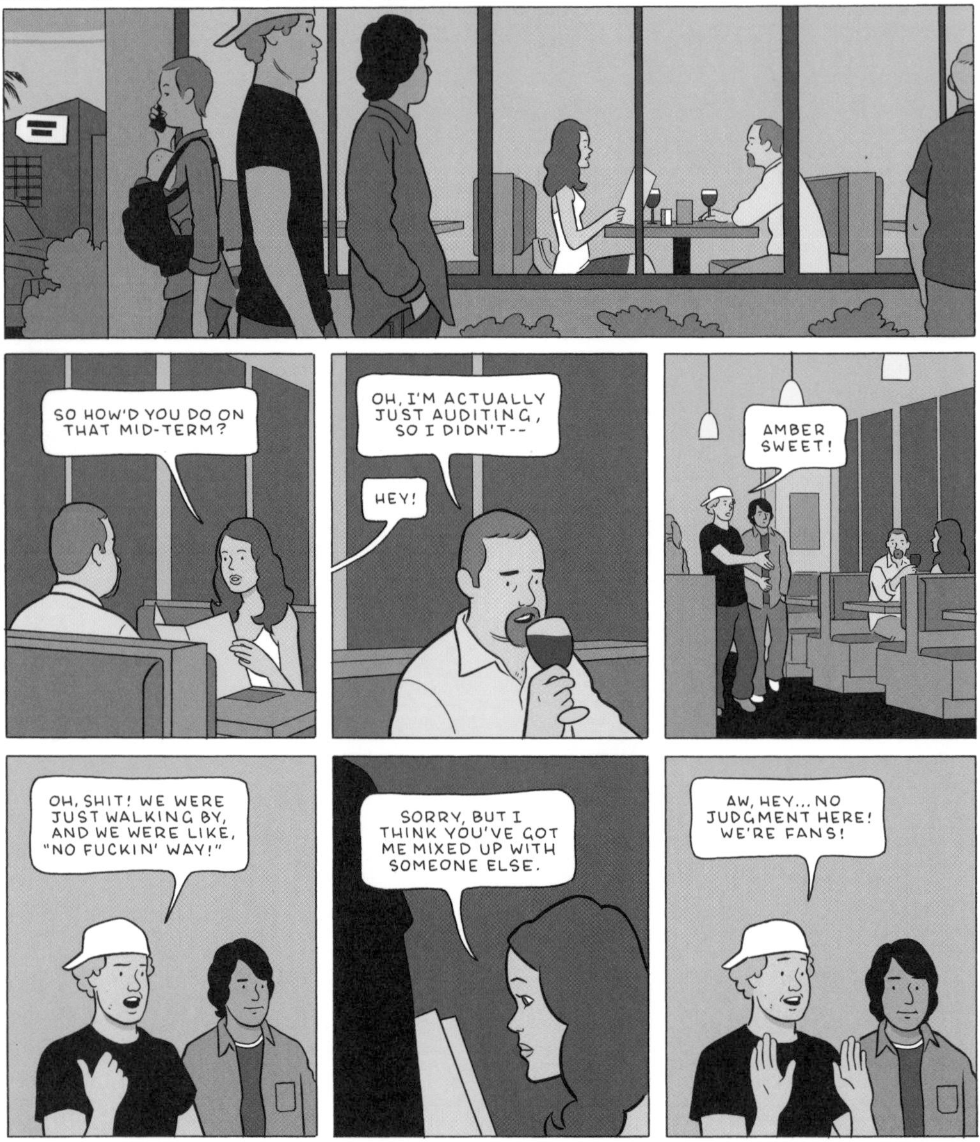
SO HOW'D YOU DO ON THAT MID-TERM?
OH, I'M ACTUALLY JUST AUDITING, SO I DIDN'T--
HEY!
AMBER SWEET!
OH, SHIT! WE WERE JUST WALKING BY, AND WE WERE LIKE, "NO FUCKIN' WAY!"
SORRY, BUT I THINK YOU'VE GOT ME MIXED UP WITH SOMEONE ELSE.
AW, HEY... NO JUDGMENT HERE! WE'RE FANS!

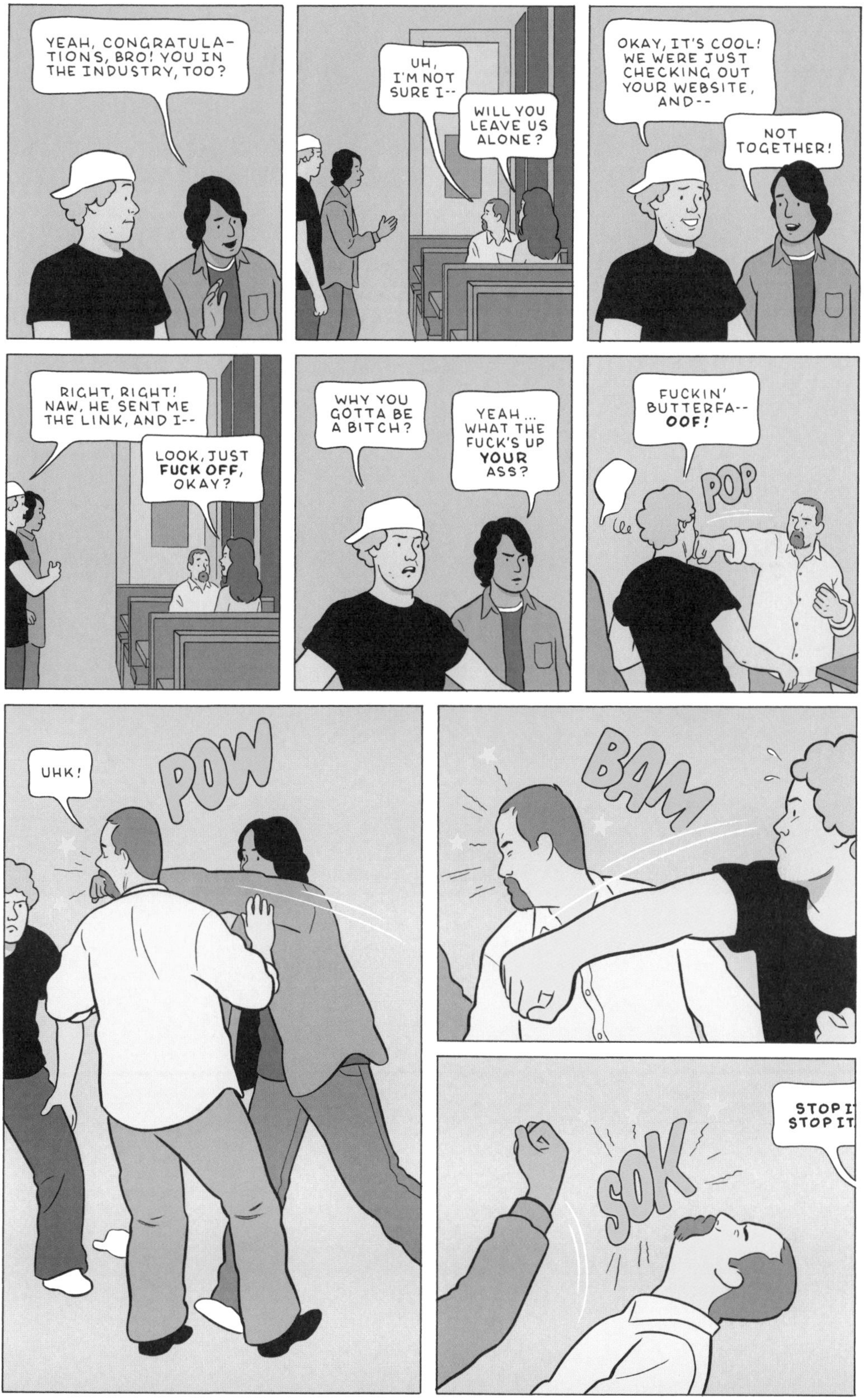
YEAH, CONGRATULATIONS, BRO! YOU IN THE INDUSTRY, TOO?
UH, I'M NOT SURE I--
WILL YOU LEAVE US ALONE?
OKAY, IT'S COOL! WE WERE JUST CHECKING OUT YOUR WEBSITE, AND--
NOT TOGETHER!
RIGHT, RIGHT! NAW, HE SENT ME THE LINK, AND I--
LOOK, JUST **FUCK OFF**, OKAY?
WHY YOU GOTTA BE A BITCH?
YEAH... WHAT THE FUCK'S UP **YOUR** ASS?
FUCKIN' BUTTERFA-- **OOF!**
POP
UHK!
POW
BAM
SOK
STOP IT
STOP IT

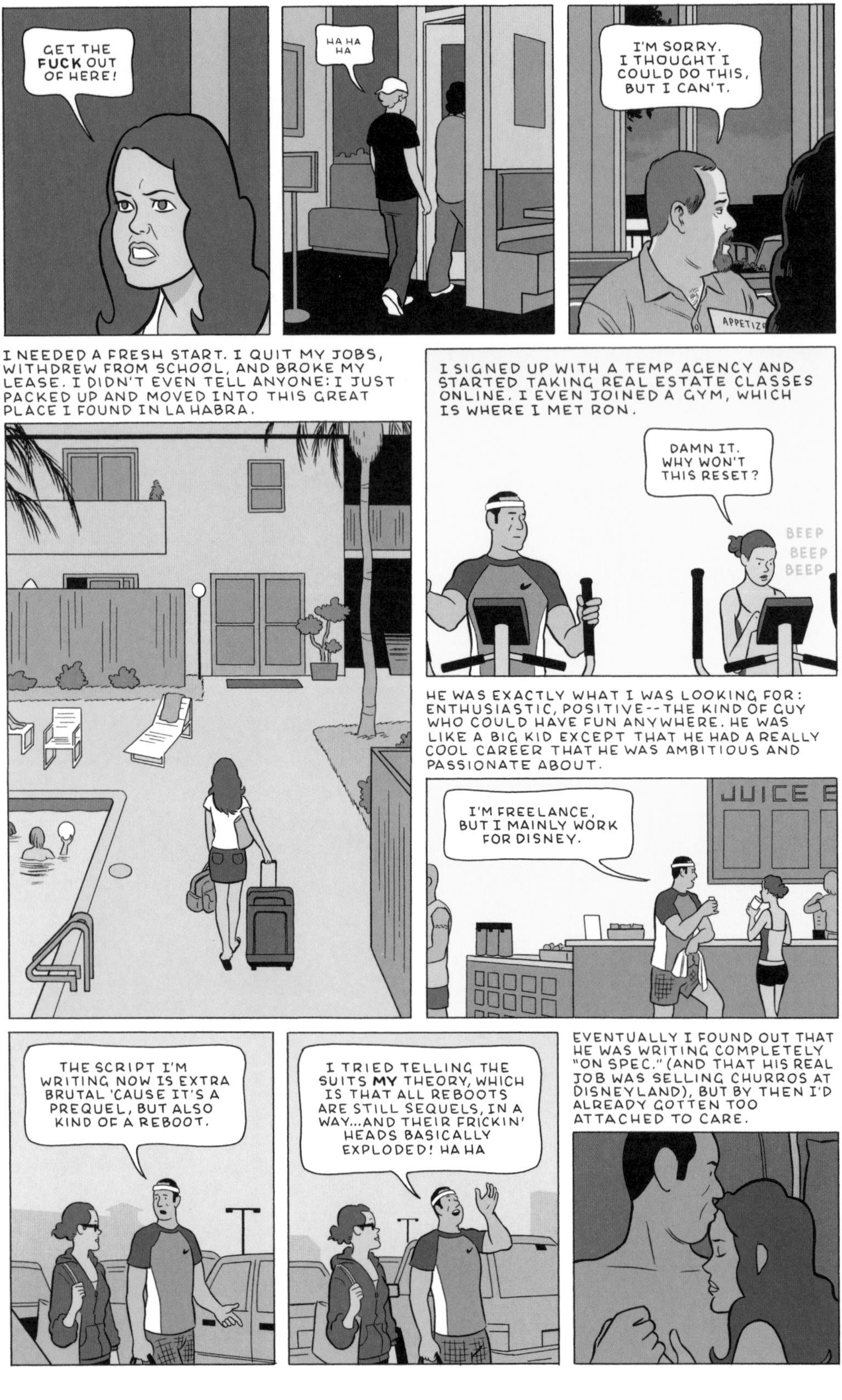

GET THE FUCK OUT OF HERE!
HA HA HA
I'M SORRY. I THOUGHT I COULD DO THIS, BUT I CAN'T.
APPETIZ
I NEEDED A FRESH START. I QUIT MY JOBS, WITHDREW FROM SCHOOL, AND BROKE MY LEASE. I DIDN'T EVEN TELL ANYONE: I JUST PACKED UP AND MOVED INTO THIS GREAT PLACE I FOUND IN LA HABRA.
I SIGNED UP WITH A TEMP AGENCY AND STARTED TAKING REAL ESTATE CLASSES ONLINE. I EVEN JOINED A GYM, WHICH IS WHERE I MET RON.
DAMN IT. WHY WON'T THIS RESET?
BEEP BEEP BEEP
HE WAS EXACTLY WHAT I WAS LOOKING FOR: ENTHUSIASTIC, POSITIVE--THE KIND OF GUY WHO COULD HAVE FUN ANYWHERE. HE WAS LIKE A BIG KID EXCEPT THAT HE HAD A REALLY COOL CAREER THAT HE WAS AMBITIOUS AND PASSIONATE ABOUT.
JUICE
I'M FREELANCE, BUT I MAINLY WORK FOR DISNEY.
THE SCRIPT I'M WRITING NOW IS EXTRA BRUTAL 'CAUSE IT'S A PREQUEL, BUT ALSO KIND OF A REBOOT.
I TRIED TELLING THE SUITS MY THEORY, WHICH IS THAT ALL REBOOTS ARE STILL SEQUELS, IN A WAY...AND THEIR FRICKIN' HEADS BASICALLY EXPLODED! HA HA
EVENTUALLY I FOUND OUT THAT HE WAS WRITING COMPLETELY "ON SPEC." (AND THAT HIS REAL JOB WAS SELLING CHURROS AT DISNEYLAND), BUT BY THEN I'D ALREADY GOTTEN TOO ATTACHED TO CARE.

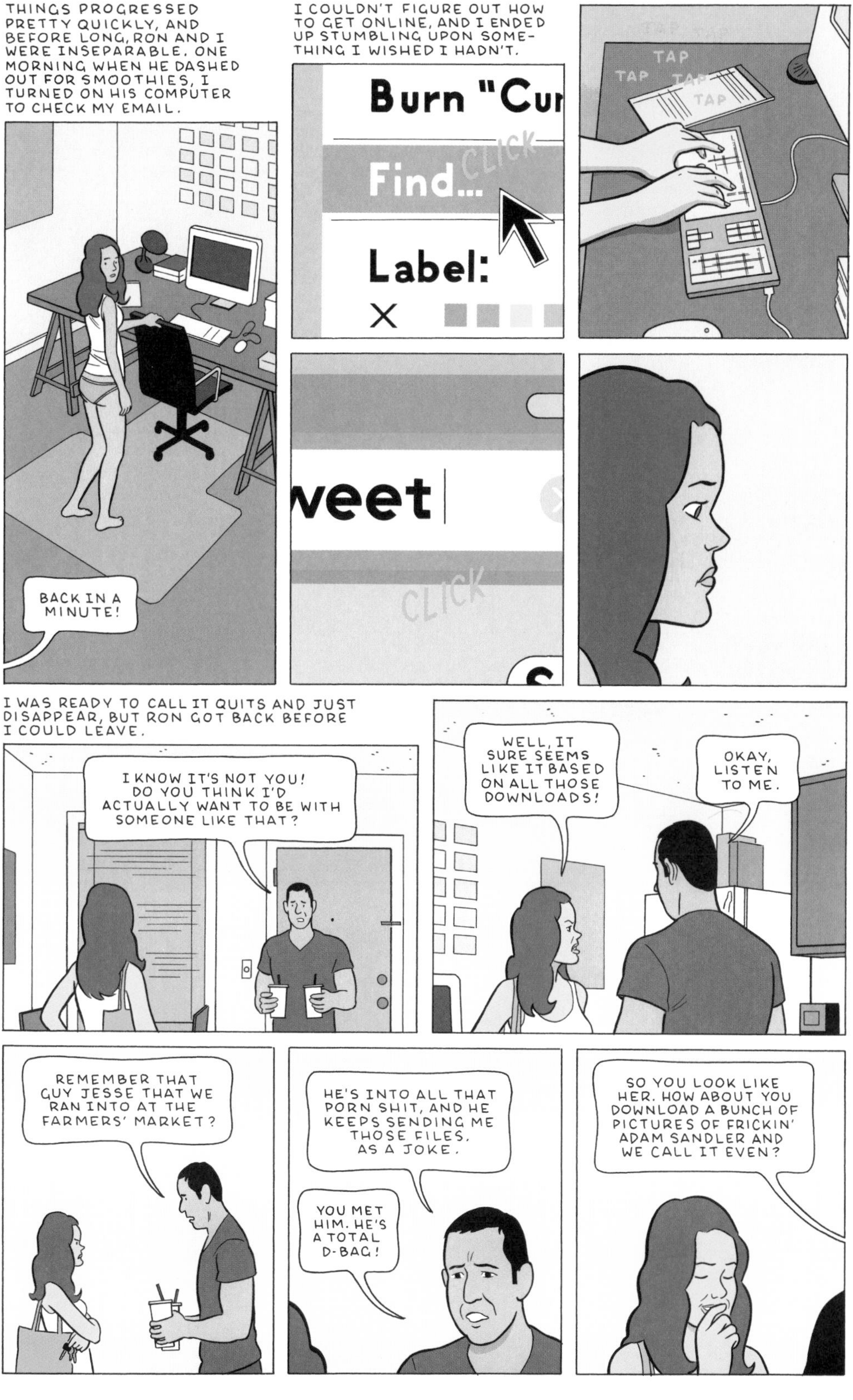
THINGS PROGRESSED PRETTY QUICKLY, AND BEFORE LONG, RON AND I WERE INSEPARABLE. ONE MORNING WHEN HE DASHED OUT FOR SMOOTHIES, I TURNED ON HIS COMPUTER TO CHECK MY EMAIL.
BACK IN A MINUTE!
I COULDN'T FIGURE OUT HOW TO GET ONLINE, AND I ENDED UP STUMBLING UPON SOMETHING I WISHED I HADN'T.
Burn "Cu
Find...
CLICK
Label:
TAP TAP TAP TAP
weet
CLICK
I WAS READY TO CALL IT QUITS AND JUST DISAPPEAR, BUT RON GOT BACK BEFORE I COULD LEAVE.
I KNOW IT'S NOT YOU! DO YOU THINK I'D ACTUALLY WANT TO BE WITH SOMEONE LIKE THAT?
WELL, IT SURE SEEMS LIKE IT BASED ON ALL THOSE DOWNLOADS!
OKAY, LISTEN TO ME.
REMEMBER THAT GUY JESSE THAT WE RAN INTO AT THE FARMERS' MARKET?
HE'S INTO ALL THAT PORN SHIT, AND HE KEEPS SENDING ME THOSE FILES. AS A JOKE.
YOU MET HIM. HE'S A TOTAL D-BAG!
SO YOU LOOK LIKE HER. HOW ABOUT YOU DOWNLOAD A BUNCH OF PICTURES OF FRICKIN' ADAM SANDLER AND WE CALL IT EVEN?

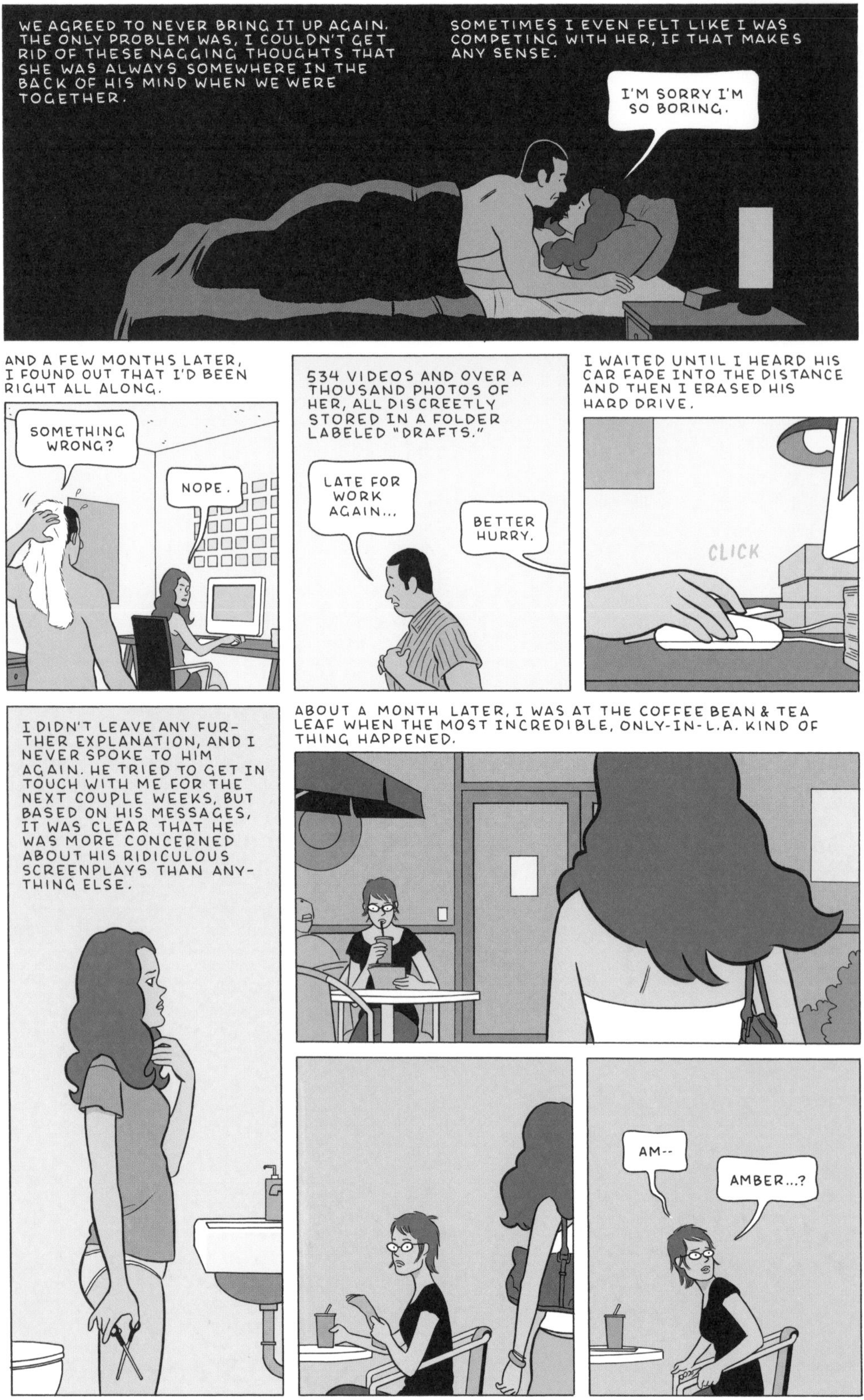
WE AGREED TO NEVER BRING IT UP AGAIN. THE ONLY PROBLEM WAS, I COULDN'T GET RID OF THESE NAGGING THOUGHTS THAT SHE WAS ALWAYS SOMEWHERE IN THE BACK OF HIS MIND WHEN WE WERE TOGETHER.
SOMETIMES I EVEN FELT LIKE I WAS COMPETING WITH HER, IF THAT MAKES ANY SENSE.
I'M SORRY I'M SO BORING.
AND A FEW MONTHS LATER, I FOUND OUT THAT I'D BEEN RIGHT ALL ALONG.
SOMETHING WRONG?
NOPE.
534 VIDEOS AND OVER A THOUSAND PHOTOS OF HER, ALL DISCREETLY STORED IN A FOLDER LABELED "DRAFTS."
LATE FOR WORK AGAIN...
BETTER HURRY.
I WAITED UNTIL I HEARD HIS CAR FADE INTO THE DISTANCE AND THEN I ERASED HIS HARD DRIVE.
CLICK
I DIDN'T LEAVE ANY FURTHER EXPLANATION, AND I NEVER SPOKE TO HIM AGAIN. HE TRIED TO GET IN TOUCH WITH ME FOR THE NEXT COUPLE WEEKS, BUT BASED ON HIS MESSAGES, IT WAS CLEAR THAT HE WAS MORE CONCERNED ABOUT HIS RIDICULOUS SCREENPLAYS THAN ANYTHING ELSE.
ABOUT A MONTH LATER, I WAS AT THE COFFEE BEAN & TEA LEAF WHEN THE MOST INCREDIBLE, ONLY-IN-L.A. KIND OF THING HAPPENED.
AM--
AMBER...?

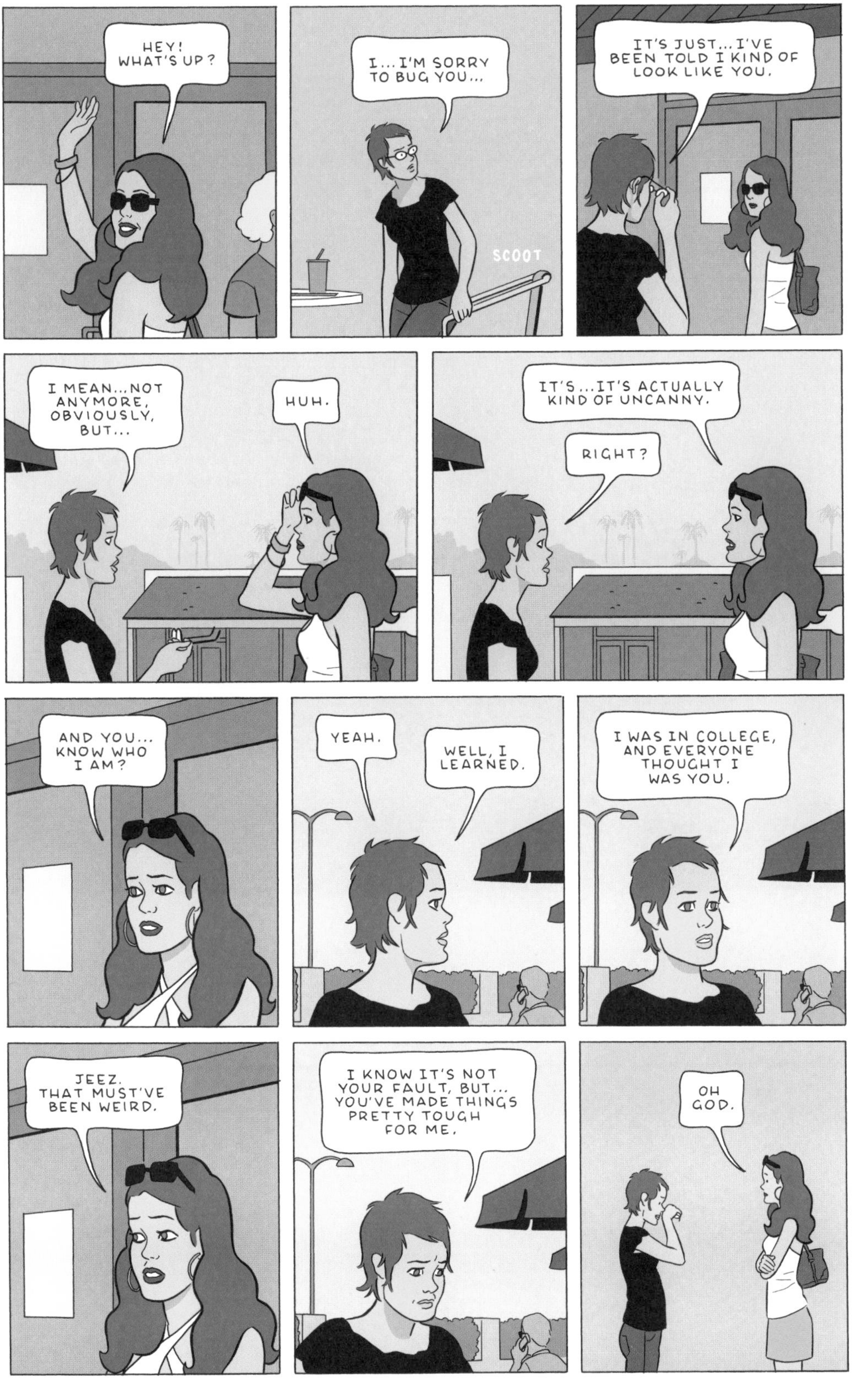
HEY! WHAT'S UP?
I... I'M SORRY TO BUG YOU...
SCOOT
IT'S JUST... I'VE BEEN TOLD I KIND OF LOOK LIKE YOU.
I MEAN... NOT ANYMORE, OBVIOUSLY, BUT...
HUH.
IT'S... IT'S ACTUALLY KIND OF UNCANNY.
RIGHT?
AND YOU... KNOW WHO I AM?
YEAH.
WELL, I LEARNED.
I WAS IN COLLEGE, AND EVERYONE THOUGHT I WAS YOU.
JEEZ. THAT MUST'VE BEEN WEIRD.
I KNOW IT'S NOT YOUR FAULT, BUT... YOU'VE MADE THINGS PRETTY TOUGH FOR ME.
OH GOD.

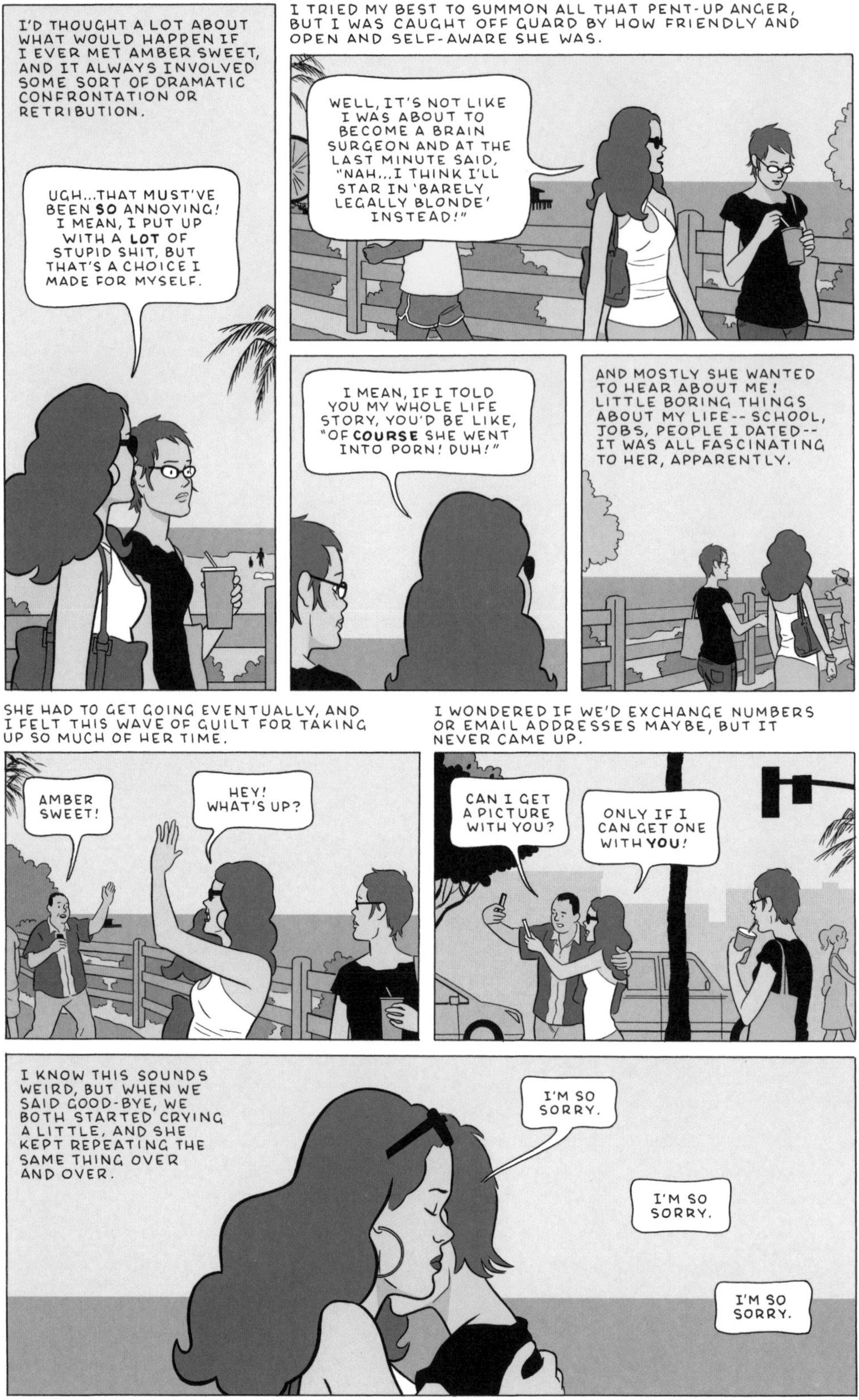
I'D THOUGHT A LOT ABOUT WHAT WOULD HAPPEN IF I EVER MET AMBER SWEET, AND IT ALWAYS INVOLVED SOME SORT OF DRAMATIC CONFRONTATION OR RETRIBUTION.
UGH...THAT MUST'VE BEEN **SO** ANNOYING! I MEAN, I PUT UP WITH A **LOT** OF STUPID SHIT, BUT THAT'S A CHOICE I MADE FOR MYSELF.
I TRIED MY BEST TO SUMMON ALL THAT PENT-UP ANGER, BUT I WAS CAUGHT OFF GUARD BY HOW FRIENDLY AND OPEN AND SELF-AWARE SHE WAS.
WELL, IT'S NOT LIKE I WAS ABOUT TO BECOME A BRAIN SURGEON AND AT THE LAST MINUTE SAID, "NAH...I THINK I'LL STAR IN 'BARELY LEGALLY BLONDE' INSTEAD!"
I MEAN, IF I TOLD YOU MY WHOLE LIFE STORY, YOU'D BE LIKE, "OF **COURSE** SHE WENT INTO PORN! DUH!"
AND MOSTLY SHE WANTED TO HEAR ABOUT ME! LITTLE BORING THINGS ABOUT MY LIFE--SCHOOL, JOBS, PEOPLE I DATED--IT WAS ALL FASCINATING TO HER, APPARENTLY.
SHE HAD TO GET GOING EVENTUALLY, AND I FELT THIS WAVE OF GUILT FOR TAKING UP SO MUCH OF HER TIME.
AMBER SWEET!
HEY! WHAT'S UP?
I WONDERED IF WE'D EXCHANGE NUMBERS OR EMAIL ADDRESSES MAYBE, BUT IT NEVER CAME UP.
CAN I GET A PICTURE WITH YOU?
ONLY IF I CAN GET ONE WITH **YOU**!
I KNOW THIS SOUNDS WEIRD, BUT WHEN WE SAID GOOD-BYE, WE BOTH STARTED CRYING A LITTLE, AND SHE KEPT REPEATING THE SAME THING OVER AND OVER.
I'M SO SORRY.
I'M SO SORRY.
I'M SO SORRY.

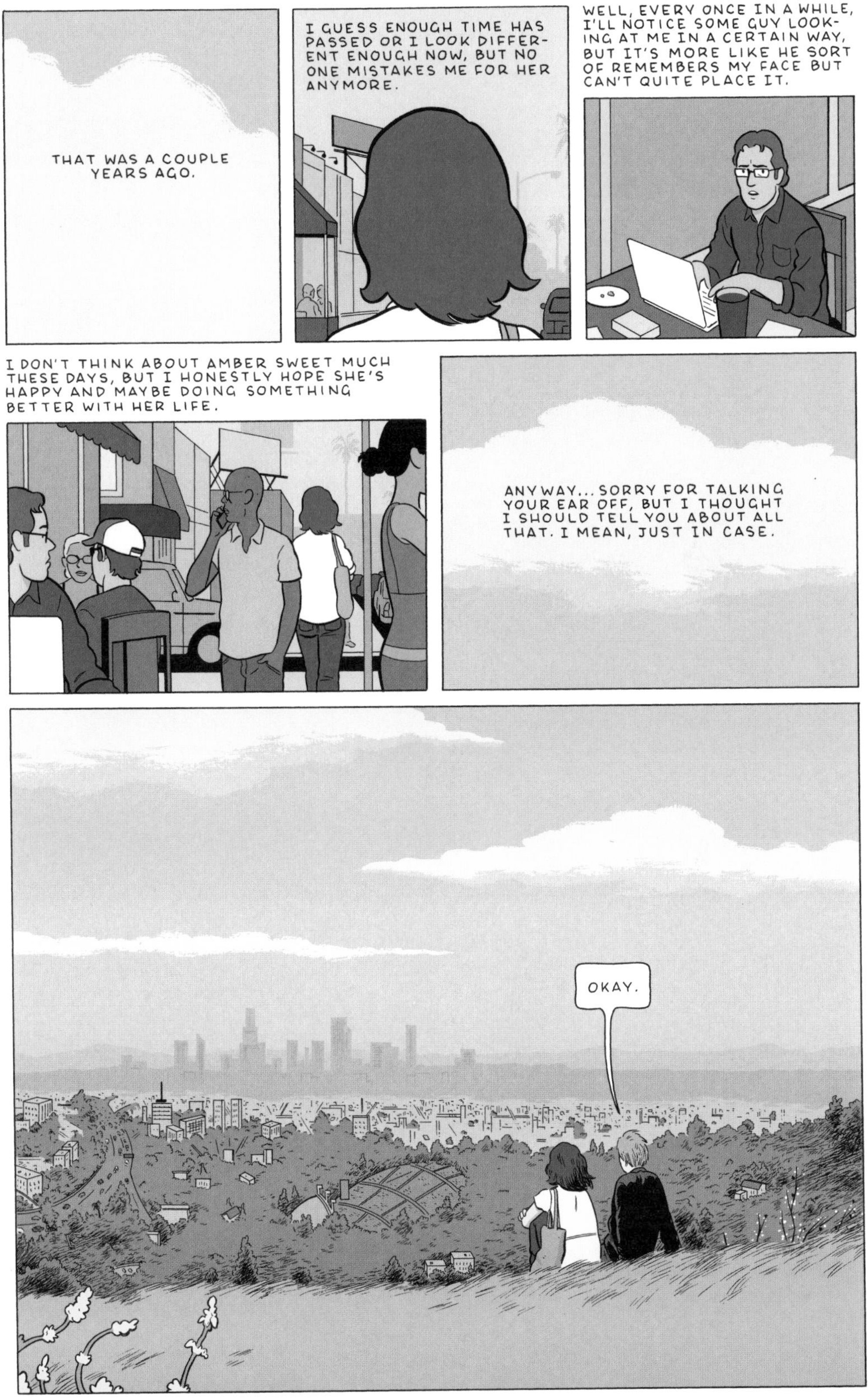
THAT WAS A COUPLE YEARS AGO.
I GUESS ENOUGH TIME HAS PASSED OR I LOOK DIFFERENT ENOUGH NOW, BUT NO ONE MISTAKES ME FOR HER ANYMORE.
WELL, EVERY ONCE IN A WHILE, I'LL NOTICE SOME GUY LOOKING AT ME IN A CERTAIN WAY, BUT IT'S MORE LIKE HE SORT OF REMEMBERS MY FACE BUT CAN'T QUITE PLACE IT.
I DON'T THINK ABOUT AMBER SWEET MUCH THESE DAYS, BUT I HONESTLY HOPE SHE'S HAPPY AND MAYBE DOING SOMETHING BETTER WITH HER LIFE.
ANYWAY... SORRY FOR TALKING YOUR EAR OFF, BUT I THOUGHT I SHOULD TELL YOU ABOUT ALL THAT. I MEAN, JUST IN CASE.
OKAY.

GO OWLS

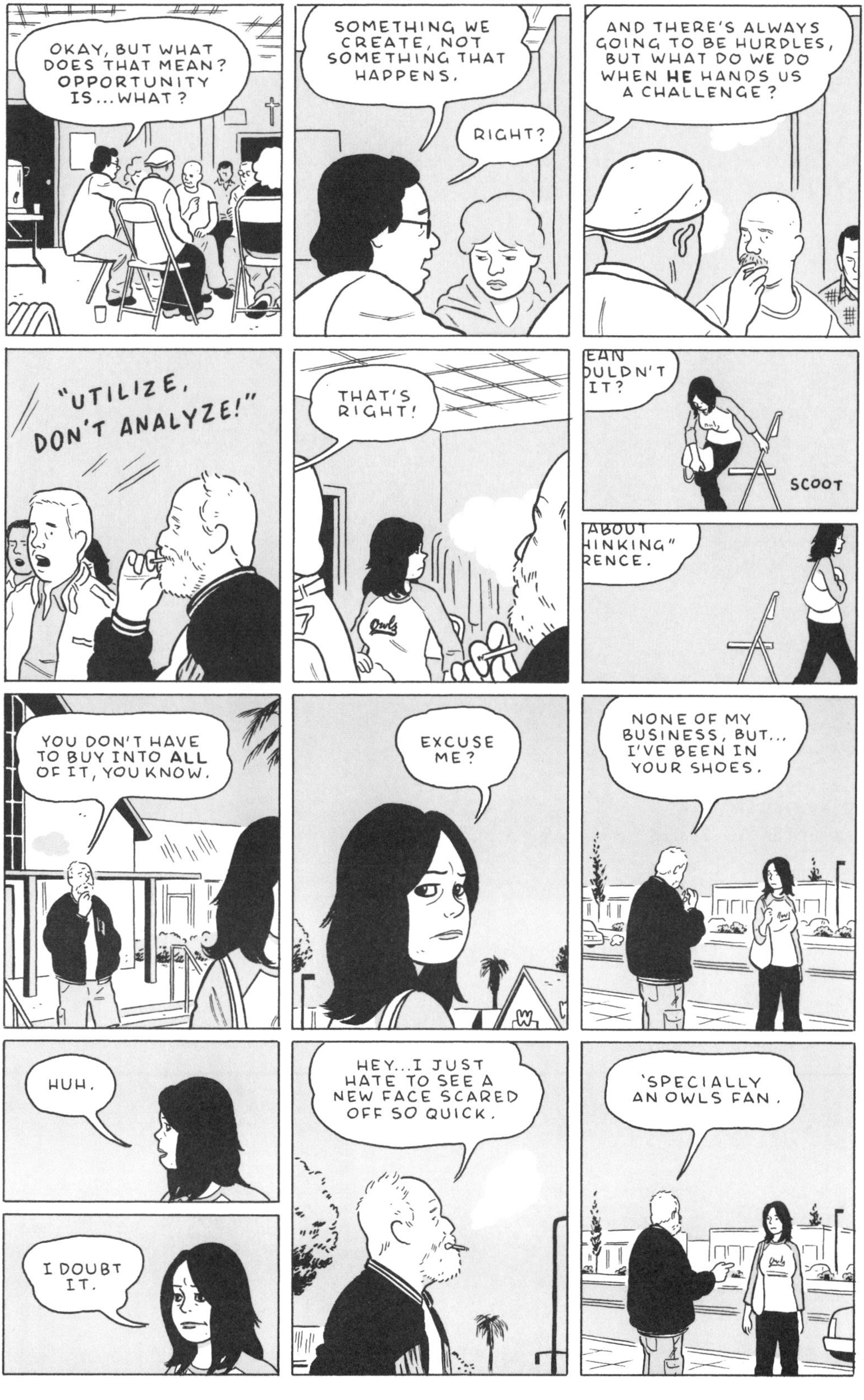

OKAY, BUT WHAT DOES THAT MEAN? OPPORTUNITY IS... WHAT?
SOMETHING WE CREATE, NOT SOMETHING THAT HAPPENS.
RIGHT?
AND THERE'S ALWAYS GOING TO BE HURDLES, BUT WHAT DO WE DO WHEN **HE** HANDS US A CHALLENGE?
"UTILIZE, DON'T ANALYZE!"
THAT'S RIGHT!
EAN
OULDN'T
IT?
SCOOT
ABOUT
HINKING"
RENCE.
YOU DON'T HAVE TO BUY INTO **ALL** OF IT, YOU KNOW.
EXCUSE ME?
NONE OF MY BUSINESS, BUT... I'VE BEEN IN YOUR SHOES.
HUH.
I DOUBT IT.
HEY...I JUST HATE TO SEE A NEW FACE SCARED OFF SO QUICK.
'SPECIALLY AN OWLS FAN.

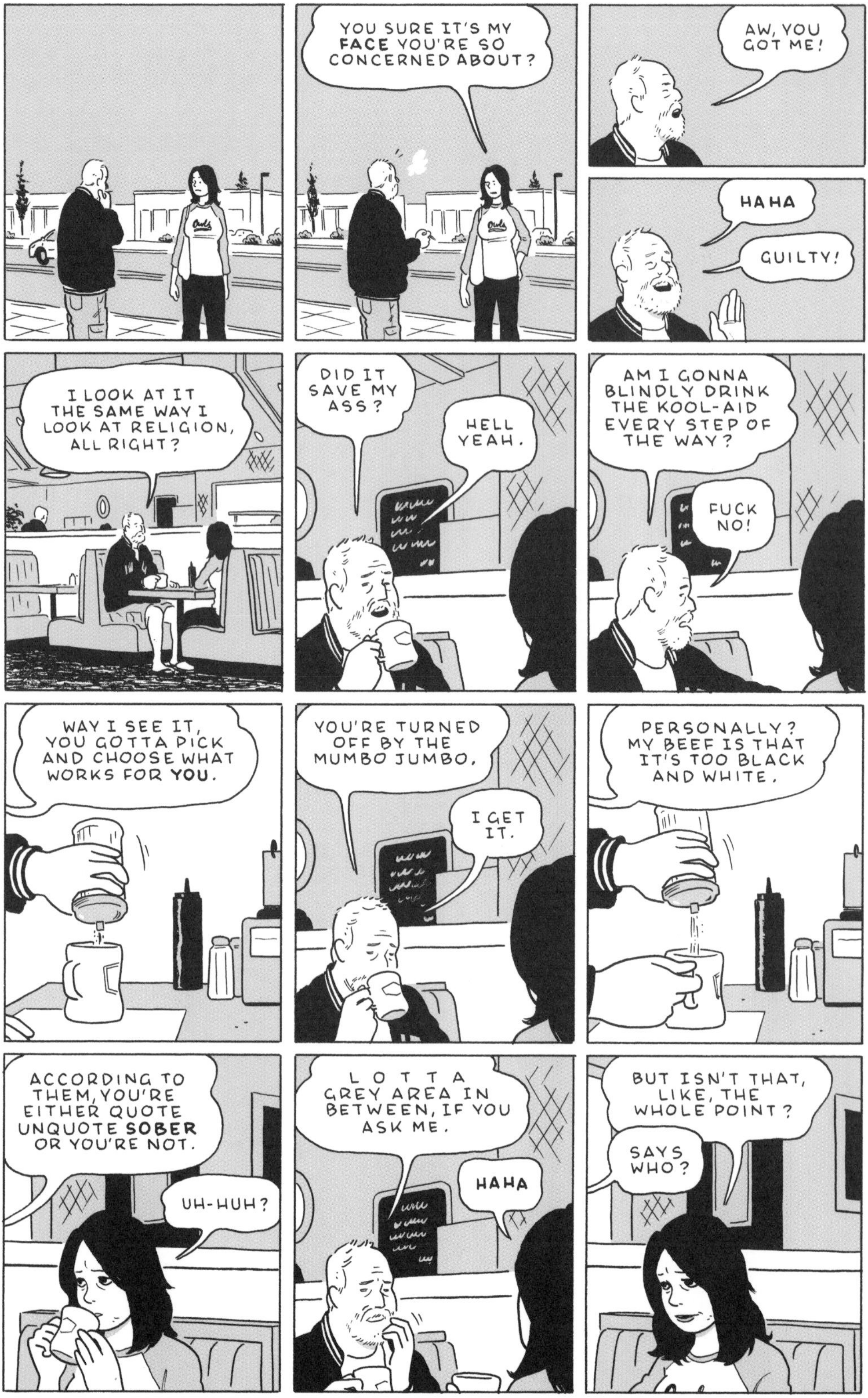
YOU SURE IT'S MY FACE YOU'RE SO CONCERNED ABOUT?
AW, YOU GOT ME!
HAHA
GUILTY!
I LOOK AT IT THE SAME WAY I LOOK AT RELIGION, ALL RIGHT?
DID IT SAVE MY ASS?
HELL YEAH.
AM I GONNA BLINDLY DRINK THE KOOL-AID EVERY STEP OF THE WAY?
FUCK NO!
WAY I SEE IT, YOU GOTTA PICK AND CHOOSE WHAT WORKS FOR YOU.
YOU'RE TURNED OFF BY THE MUMBO JUMBO.
I GET IT.
PERSONALLY? MY BEEF IS THAT IT'S TOO BLACK AND WHITE.
ACCORDING TO THEM, YOU'RE EITHER QUOTE UNQUOTE SOBER OR YOU'RE NOT.
UH-HUH?
L O T T A GREY AREA IN BETWEEN, IF YOU ASK ME.
HAHA
BUT ISN'T THAT, LIKE, THE WHOLE POINT?
SAYS WHO?

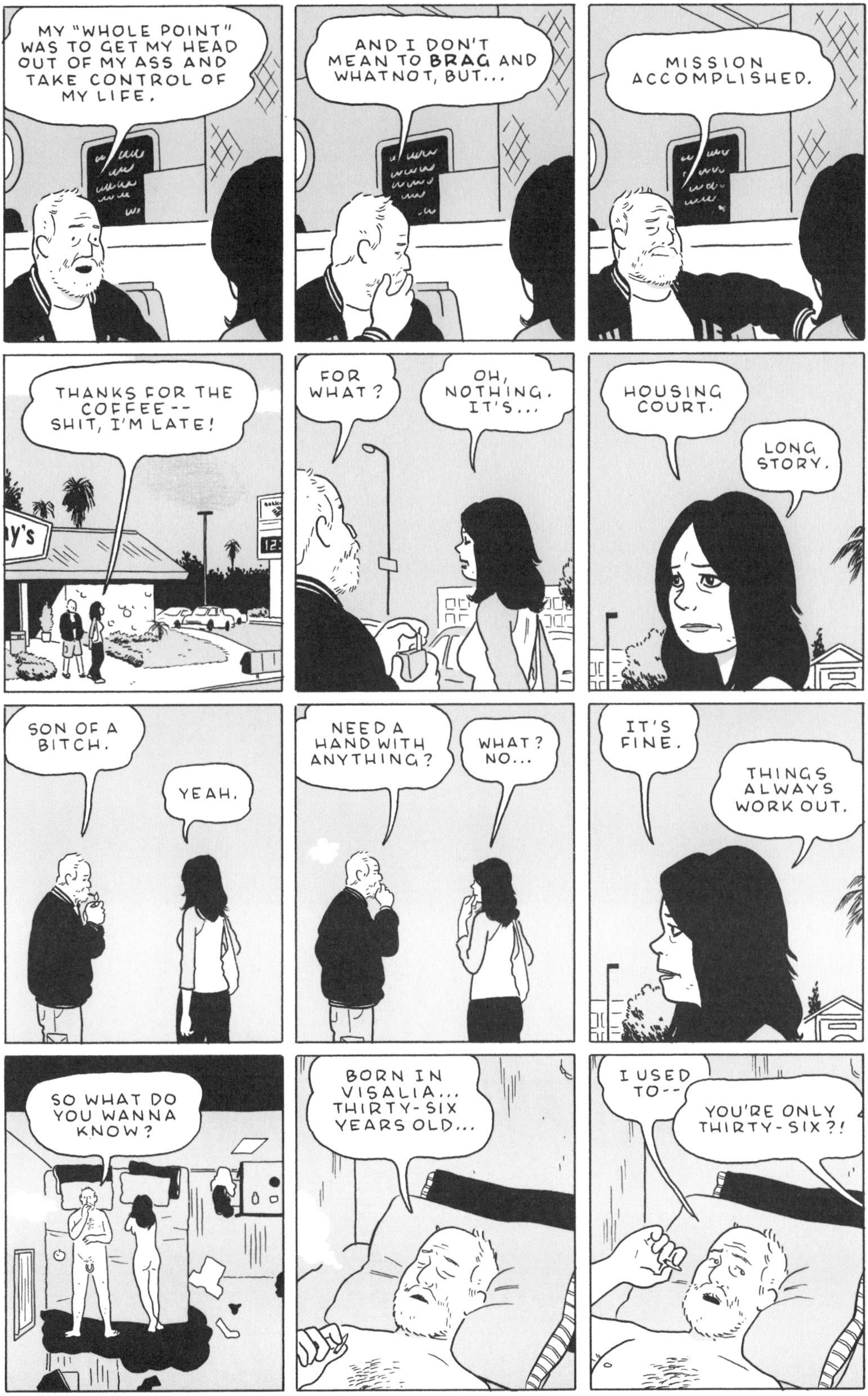
MY "WHOLE POINT" WAS TO GET MY HEAD OUT OF MY ASS AND TAKE CONTROL OF MY LIFE.
AND I DON'T MEAN TO BRAG AND WHATNOT, BUT...
MISSION ACCOMPLISHED.
THANKS FOR THE COFFEE -- SHIT, I'M LATE!
FOR WHAT?
OH, NOTHING. IT'S...
HOUSING COURT.
LONG STORY.
SON OF A BITCH.
YEAH.
NEED A HAND WITH ANYTHING?
WHAT? NO...
IT'S FINE.
THINGS ALWAYS WORK OUT.
SO WHAT DO YOU WANNA KNOW?
BORN IN VISALIA... THIRTY-SIX YEARS OLD...
I USED TO--
YOU'RE ONLY THIRTY-SIX?!

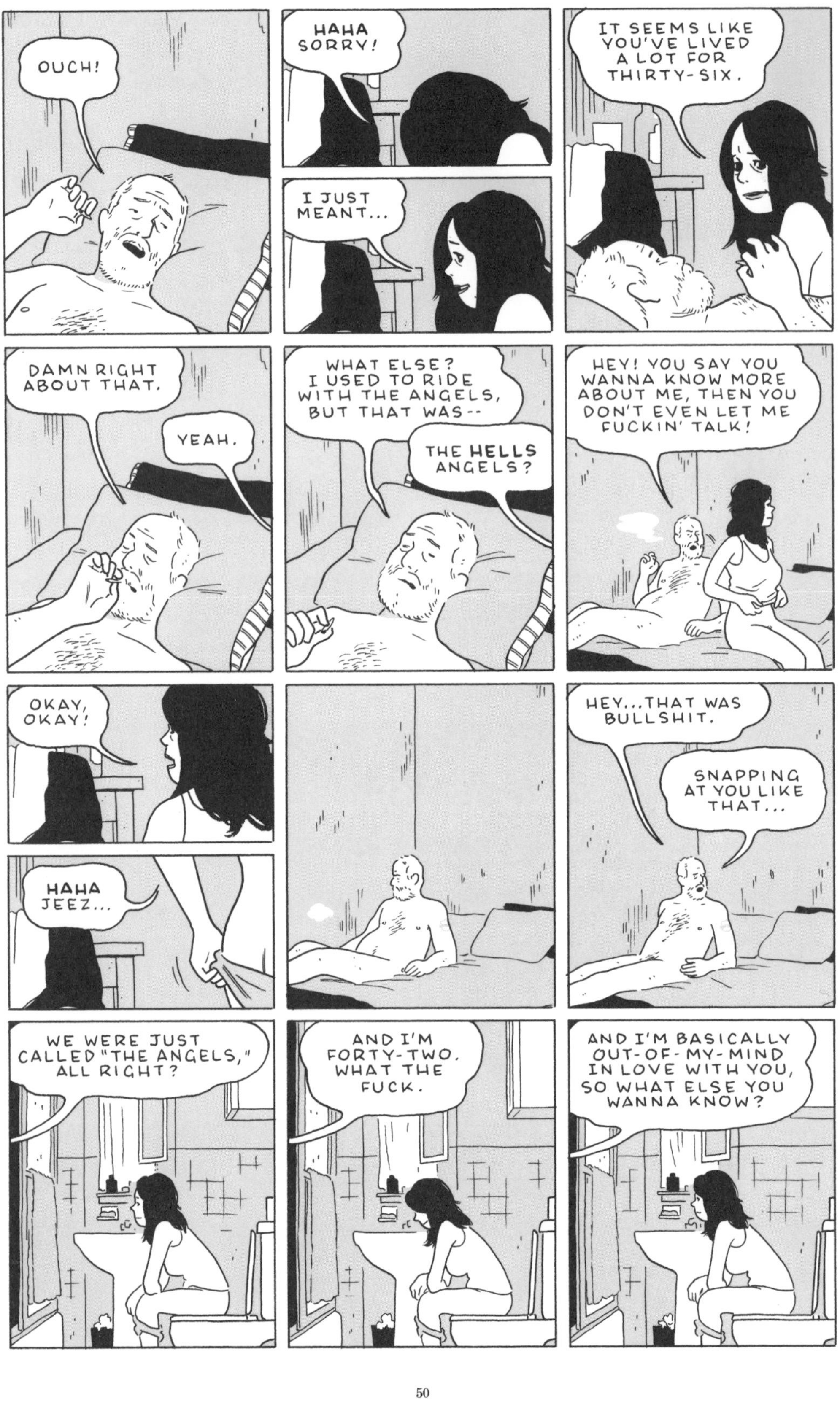
OUCH!
HAHA SORRY!
I JUST MEANT...
IT SEEMS LIKE YOU'VE LIVED A LOT FOR THIRTY-SIX.
DAMN RIGHT ABOUT THAT.
YEAH.
WHAT ELSE? I USED TO RIDE WITH THE ANGELS, BUT THAT WAS--
THE HELLS ANGELS?
HEY! YOU SAY YOU WANNA KNOW MORE ABOUT ME, THEN YOU DON'T EVEN LET ME FUCKIN' TALK!
OKAY, OKAY!
HAHA JEEZ...
HEY...THAT WAS BULLSHIT.
SNAPPING AT YOU LIKE THAT...
WE WERE JUST CALLED "THE ANGELS," ALL RIGHT?
AND I'M FORTY-TWO. WHAT THE FUCK.
AND I'M BASICALLY OUT-OF-MY-MIND IN LOVE WITH YOU, SO WHAT ELSE YOU WANNA KNOW?

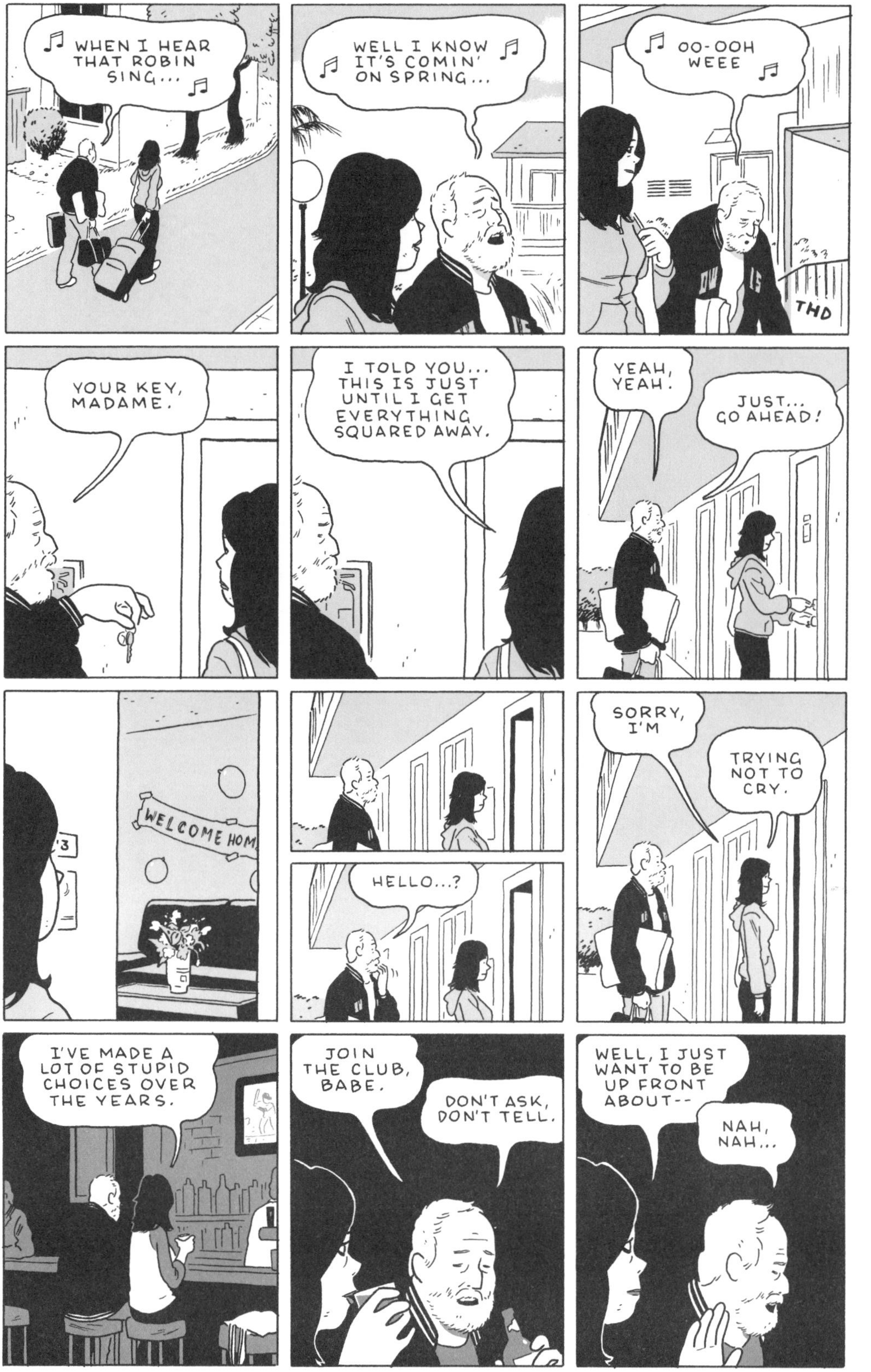
♫ WHEN I HEAR THAT ROBIN SING... ♫
♫ WELL I KNOW IT'S COMIN' ON SPRING... ♫
♫ OO-OOH WEEE ♫
THD
YOUR KEY, MADAME.
I TOLD YOU... THIS IS JUST UNTIL I GET EVERYTHING SQUARED AWAY.
YEAH, YEAH.
JUST... GO AHEAD!
WELCOME HOM
HELLO...?
SORRY, I'M
TRYING NOT TO CRY.
I'VE MADE A LOT OF STUPID CHOICES OVER THE YEARS.
JOIN THE CLUB, BABE.
DON'T ASK, DON'T TELL.
WELL, I JUST WANT TO BE UP FRONT ABOUT--
NAH, NAH...

LISTEN: YOU CAN'T DRIVE FORWARD IF YOU'RE ALWAYS LOOKING IN THE REAR-VIEW MIRROR.

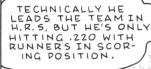

WHAT?

OH! OKAY, NOW SEE THIS JOKER?

TECHNICALLY HE LEADS THE TEAM IN H.R.S, BUT HE'S ONLY HITTING .220 WITH RUNNERS IN SCORING POSITION.

WE DON'T NEED A CLEAN-UP HITTER LAUNCHING SOLO SHOTS INTO THE UPPER DECK...

WE NEED HIM DRIVING IN RUNS IN KEY SITUATIONS!

HEY ASS-WIPE! STRANDING TEAM-MATES ON THE BASES IS WHAT WE PAY OUR FUCKIN' 9-SLOT FOR!

ASSHOLES WERE GETTING AWAY WITH HIGHWAY ROBBERY WITH WHAT THEY WERE PAYING YOU, SO FUCK 'EM!

I PASSED OUT IN A ROOM I WAS SUPPOSED TO BE CLEANING.

THAT'S WHAT THEY GET FOR WORKING YOU LIKE THAT!

I'LL FIND SOMETHING ELSE.

HOW MANY TIMES DO I HAVE TO TELL YOU? I GOT US COVERED, BABE.

TOLDJA I'D TAKE CARE OF YOU, AND I MEAN IT.

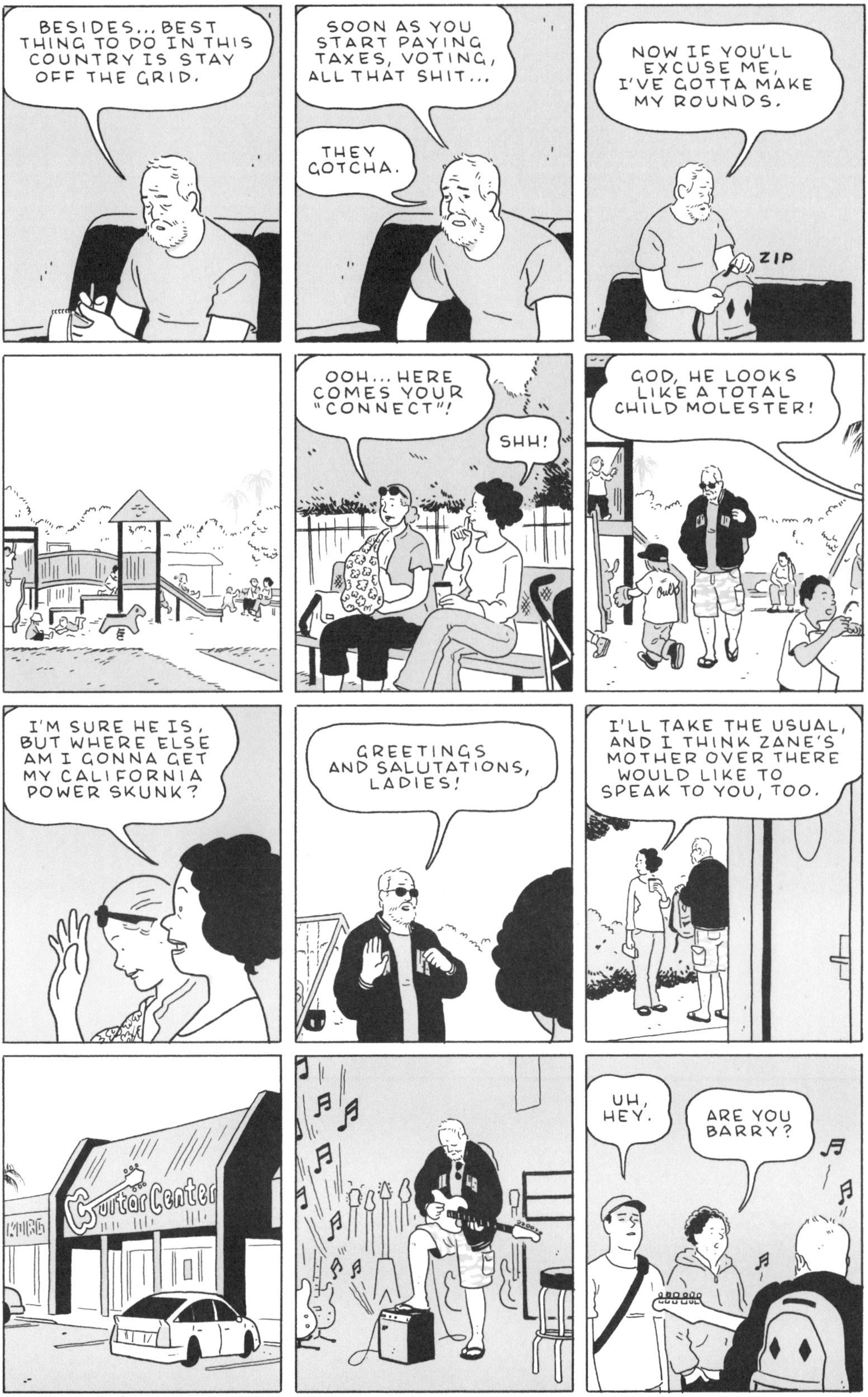
BESIDES... BEST THING TO DO IN THIS COUNTRY IS STAY OFF THE GRID.
SOON AS YOU START PAYING TAXES, VOTING, ALL THAT SHIT...
THEY GOTCHA.
NOW IF YOU'LL EXCUSE ME, I'VE GOTTA MAKE MY ROUNDS.
ZIP
OOH... HERE COMES YOUR "CONNECT"!
SHH!
GOD, HE LOOKS LIKE A TOTAL CHILD MOLESTER!
I'M SURE HE IS, BUT WHERE ELSE AM I GONNA GET MY CALIFORNIA POWER SKUNK?
GREETINGS AND SALUTATIONS, LADIES!
I'LL TAKE THE USUAL, AND I THINK ZANE'S MOTHER OVER THERE WOULD LIKE TO SPEAK TO YOU, TOO.
Guitar Center
UH, HEY.
ARE YOU BARRY?

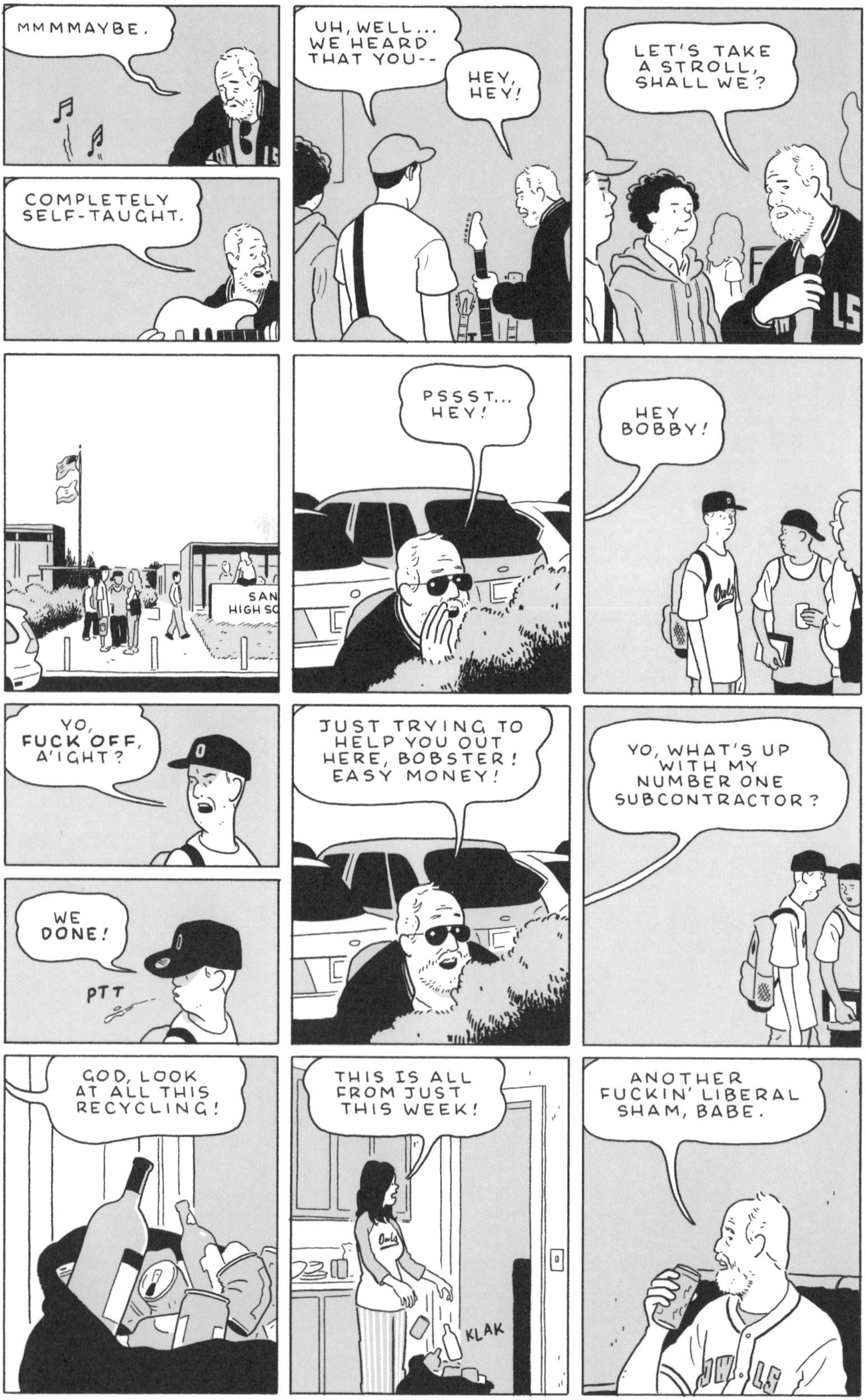
MMMMAYBE.
COMPLETELY SELF-TAUGHT.
UH, WELL... WE HEARD THAT YOU--
HEY, HEY!
LET'S TAKE A STROLL, SHALL WE?
SAN HIGH SC
PSSST... HEY!
HEY BOBBY!
YO, FUCK OFF, A'IGHT?
WE DONE!
PTT
JUST TRYING TO HELP YOU OUT HERE, BOBSTER! EASY MONEY!
YO, WHAT'S UP WITH MY NUMBER ONE SUBCONTRACTOR?
GOD, LOOK AT ALL THIS RECYCLING!
THIS IS ALL FROM JUST THIS WEEK!
KLAK
ANOTHER FUCKIN' LIBERAL SHAM, BABE.

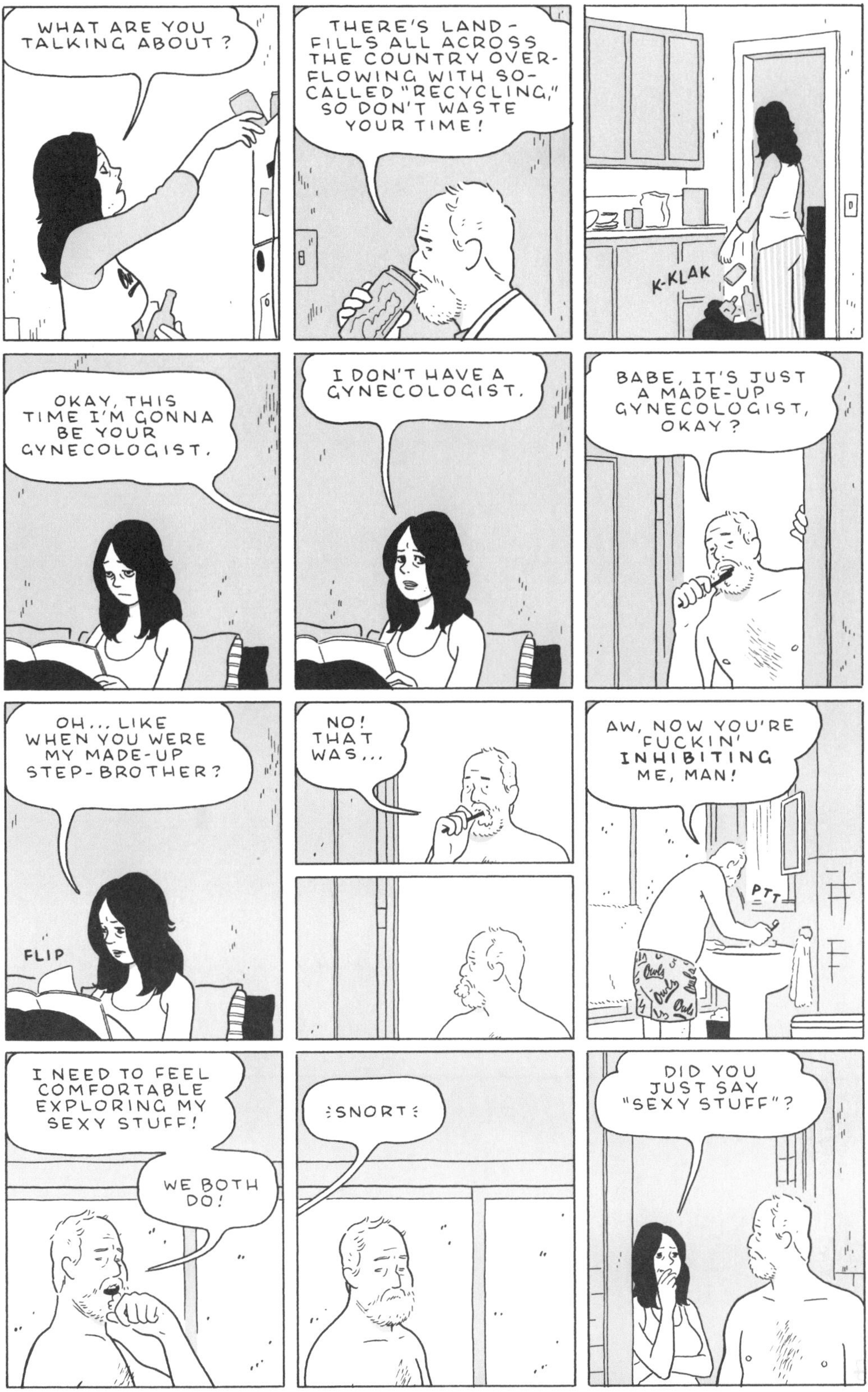
WHAT ARE YOU TALKING ABOUT?
THERE'S LAND-FILLS ALL ACROSS THE COUNTRY OVER-FLOWING WITH SO-CALLED "RECYCLING," SO DON'T WASTE YOUR TIME!
K-KLAK
OKAY, THIS TIME I'M GONNA BE YOUR GYNECOLOGIST.
I DON'T HAVE A GYNECOLOGIST.
BABE, IT'S JUST A MADE-UP GYNECOLOGIST, OKAY?
OH... LIKE WHEN YOU WERE MY MADE-UP STEP-BROTHER?
FLIP
NO! THAT WAS...
AW, NOW YOU'RE FUCKIN' INHIBITING ME, MAN!
PTT
I NEED TO FEEL COMFORTABLE EXPLORING MY SEXY STUFF!
WE BOTH DO!
SNORT
DID YOU JUST SAY "SEXY STUFF"?

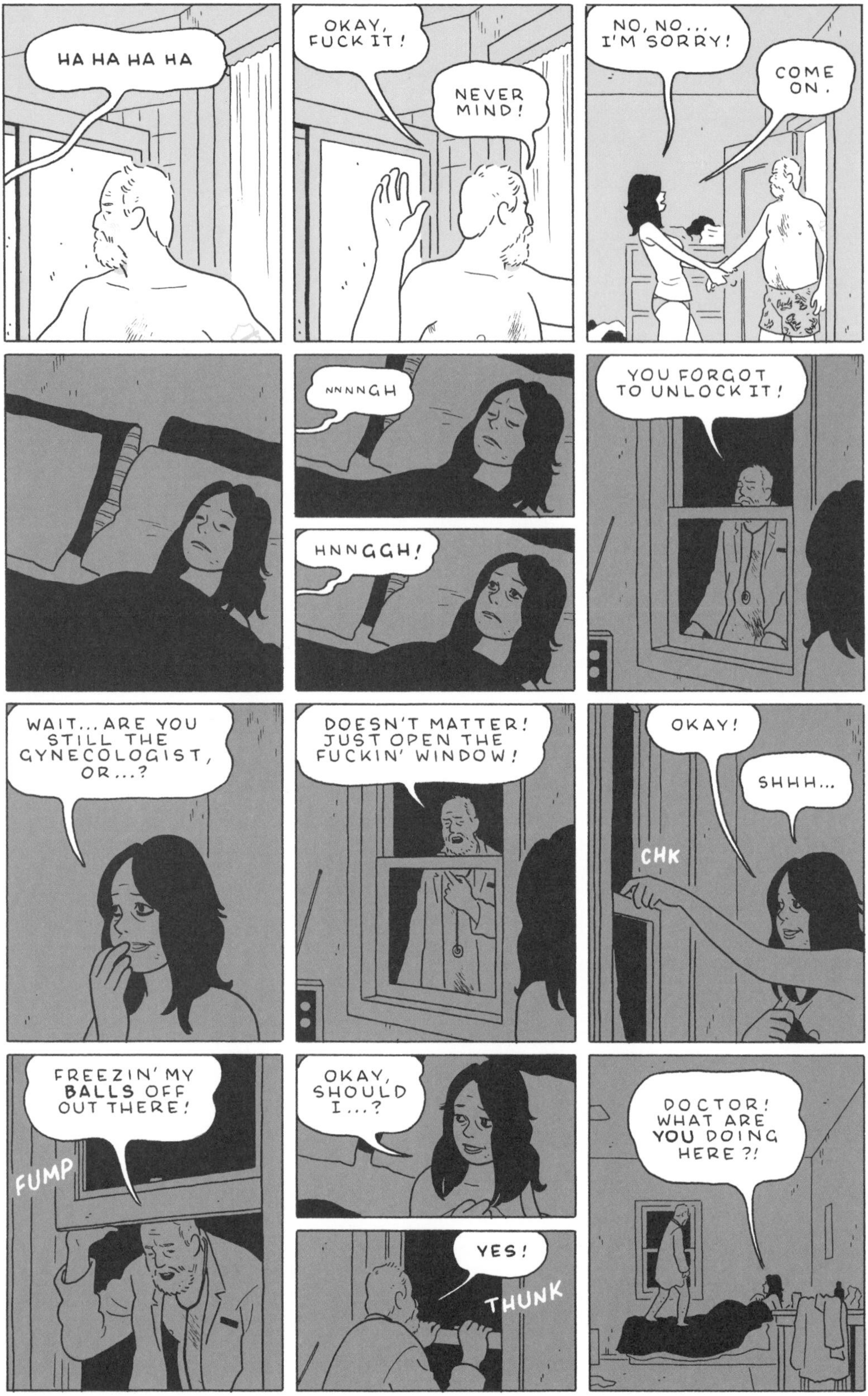

HA HA HA HA
OKAY, FUCK IT!
NEVER MIND!
NO, NO... I'M SORRY!
COME ON.
NNNNGH
HNNGGH!
YOU FORGOT TO UNLOCK IT!
WAIT... ARE YOU STILL THE GYNECOLOGIST, OR...?
DOESN'T MATTER! JUST OPEN THE FUCKIN' WINDOW!
OKAY!
SHHH...
CHK
FREEZIN' MY BALLS OFF OUT THERE!
FUMP
OKAY, SHOULD I...?
YES!
THUNK
DOCTOR! WHAT ARE YOU DOING HERE?!

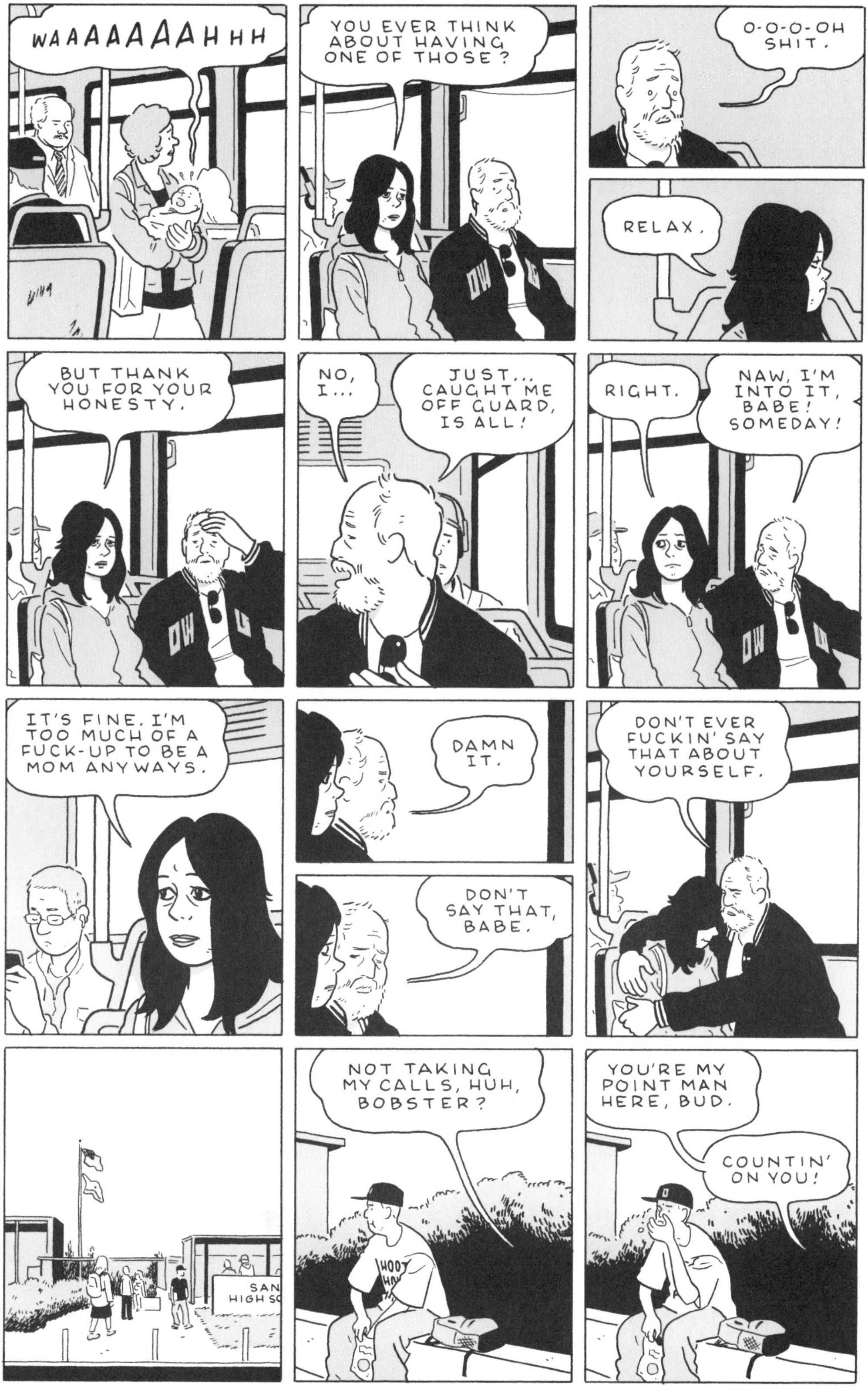
WAAAAAAAHHH
YOU EVER THINK ABOUT HAVING ONE OF THOSE?
O-O-O-OH SHIT.
RELAX.
BUT THANK YOU FOR YOUR HONESTY.
NO, I...
JUST... CAUGHT ME OFF GUARD, IS ALL!
RIGHT.
NAW, I'M INTO IT, BABE! SOMEDAY!
IT'S FINE. I'M TOO MUCH OF A FUCK-UP TO BE A MOM ANYWAYS.
DAMN IT.
DON'T SAY THAT, BABE.
DON'T EVER FUCKIN' SAY THAT ABOUT YOURSELF.
NOT TAKING MY CALLS, HUH, BOBSTER?
YOU'RE MY POINT MAN HERE, BUD.
COUNTIN' ON YOU!

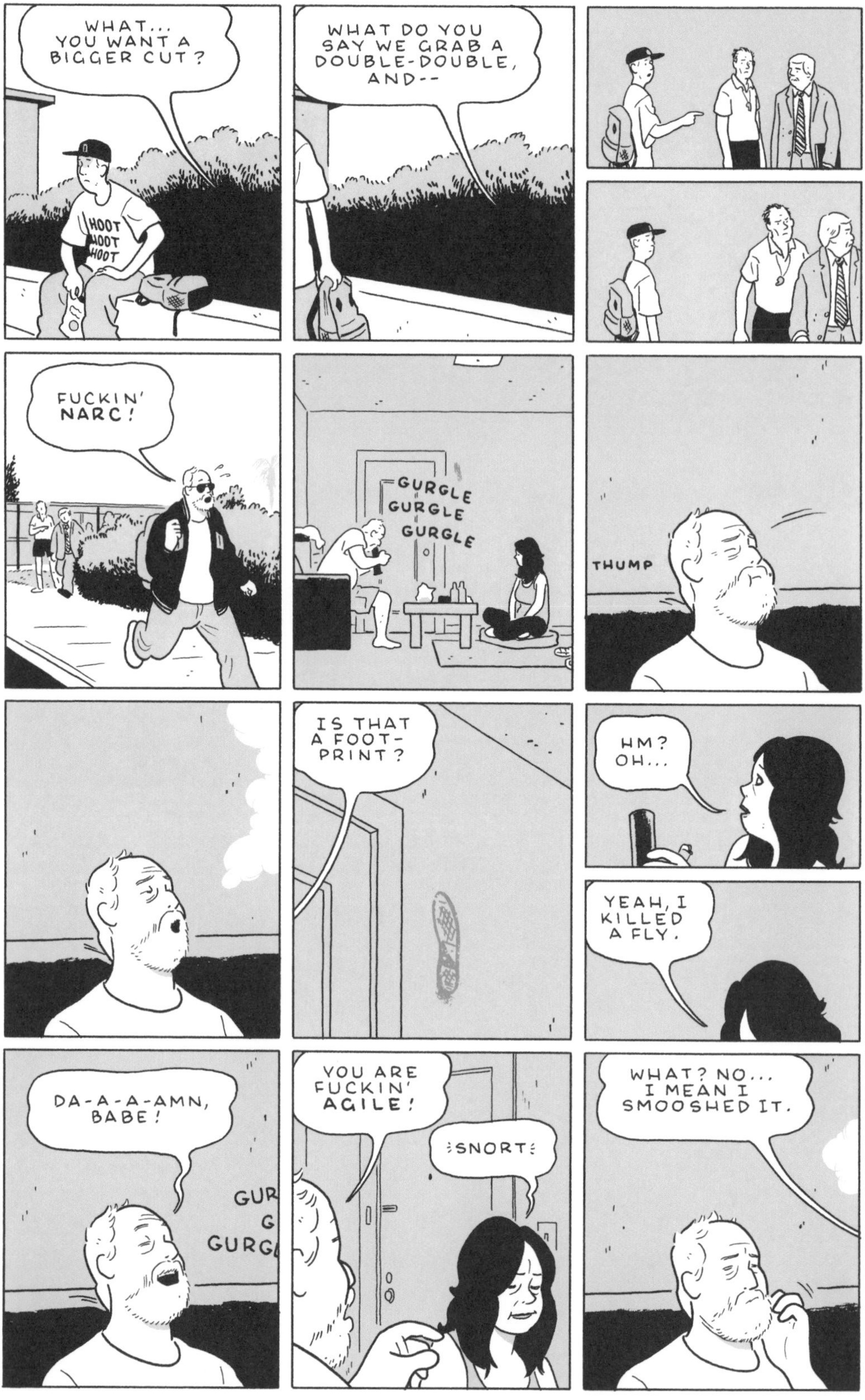
WHAT... YOU WANT A BIGGER CUT?
HOOT HOOT HOOT
WHAT DO YOU SAY WE GRAB A DOUBLE-DOUBLE, AND--
FUCKIN' NARC!
GURGLE GURGLE GURGLE
THUMP
IS THAT A FOOT-PRINT?
HM? OH...
YEAH, I KILLED A FLY.
DA-A-A-AMN, BABE!
YOU ARE FUCKIN' AGILE!
SNORT
WHAT? NO... I MEAN I SMOOSHED IT.

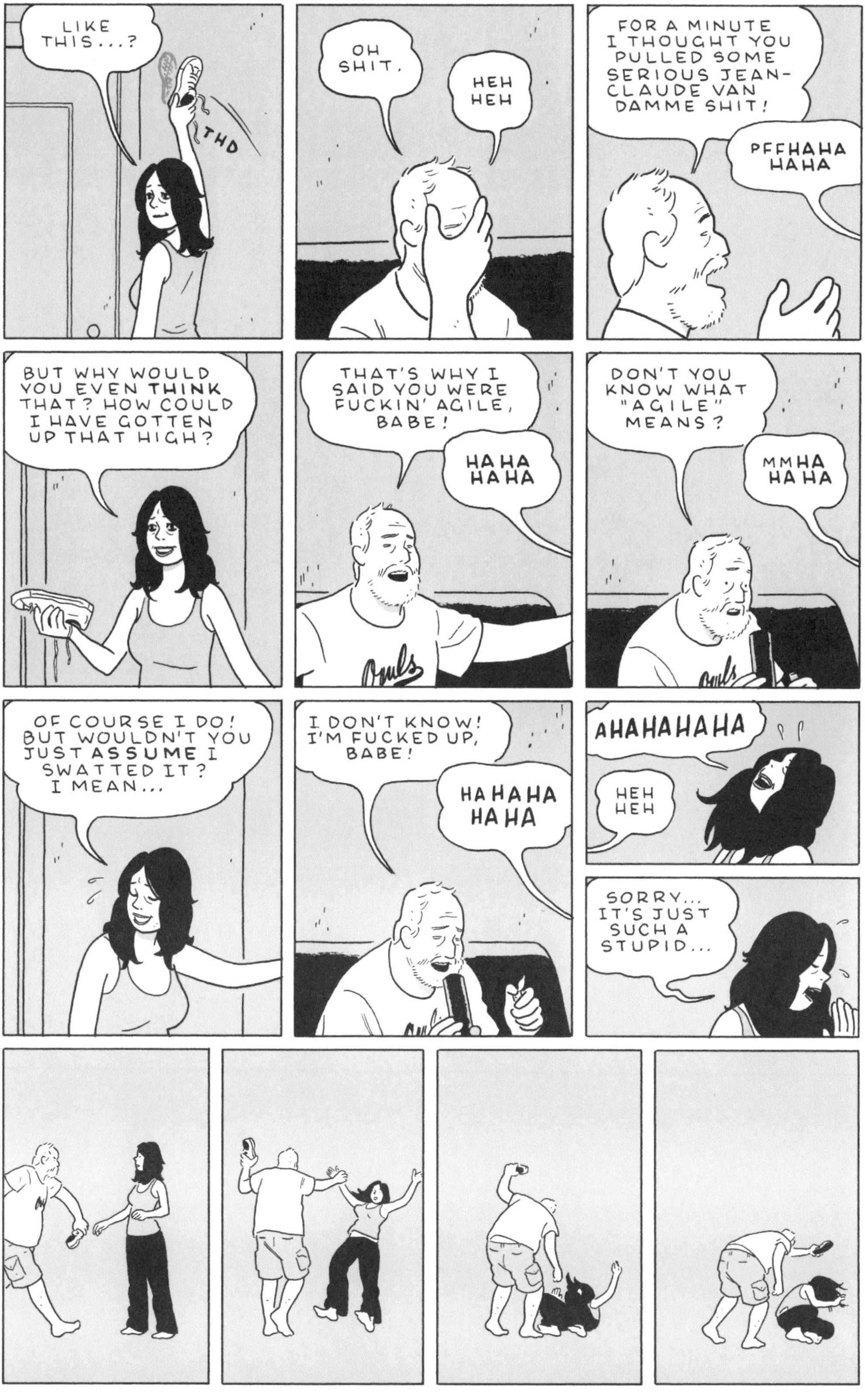
LIKE THIS...?
THD
OH SHIT.
HEH HEH
FOR A MINUTE I THOUGHT YOU PULLED SOME SERIOUS JEAN-CLAUDE VAN DAMME SHIT!
PFFHAHA HAHA
BUT WHY WOULD YOU EVEN THINK THAT? HOW COULD I HAVE GOTTEN UP THAT HIGH?
THAT'S WHY I SAID YOU WERE FUCKIN' AGILE, BABE!
HAHA HAHA
DON'T YOU KNOW WHAT "AGILE" MEANS?
MMHA HAHA
OF COURSE I DO! BUT WOULDN'T YOU JUST ASSUME I SWATTED IT? I MEAN...
I DON'T KNOW! I'M FUCKED UP, BABE!
HAHAHA HAHA
AHAHAHAHA
HEH HEH
SORRY... IT'S JUST SUCH A STUPID...

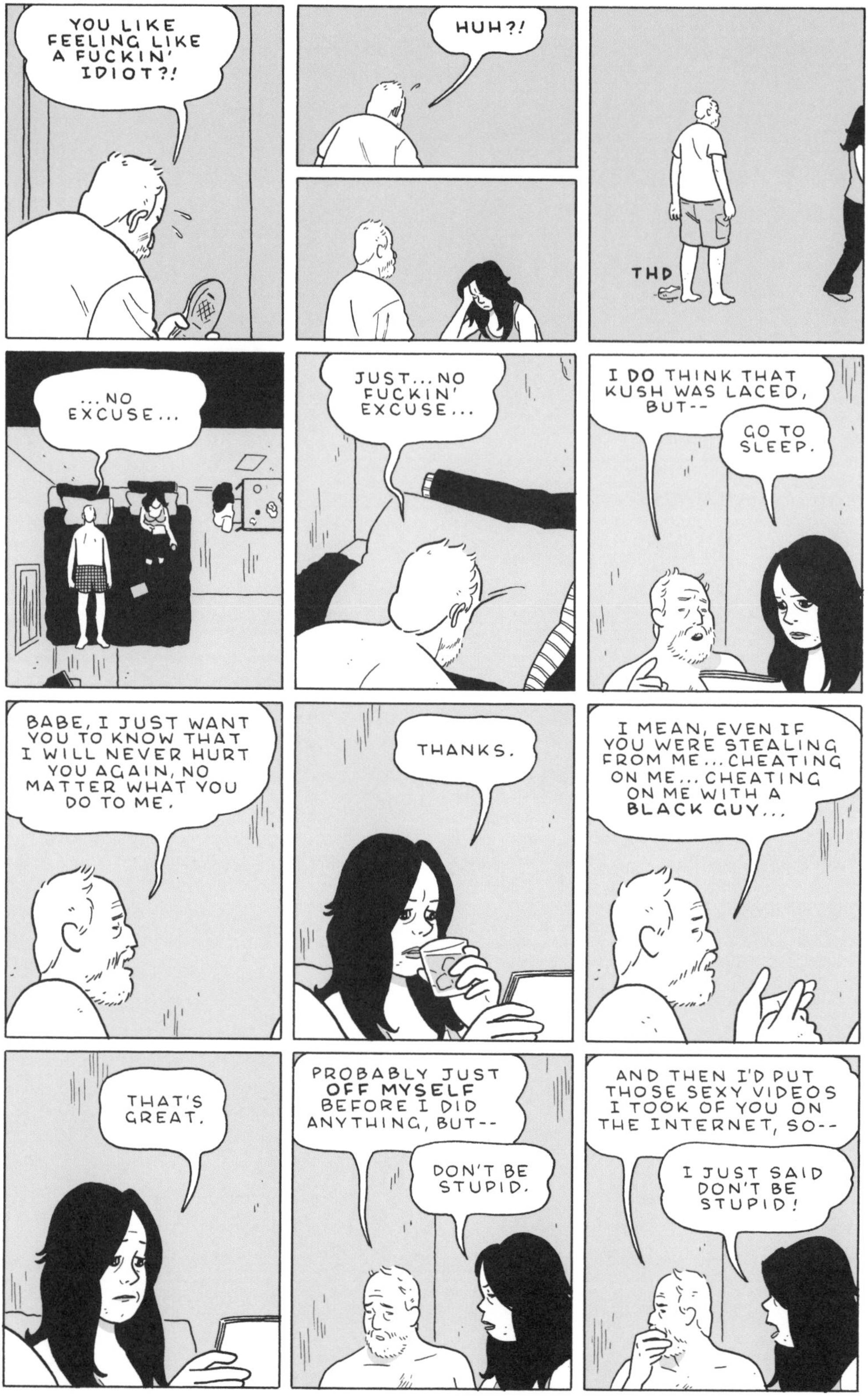
YOU LIKE FEELING LIKE A FUCKIN' IDIOT?!
HUH?!
THD
...NO EXCUSE...
JUST...NO FUCKIN' EXCUSE...
I DO THINK THAT KUSH WAS LACED, BUT--
GO TO SLEEP.
BABE, I JUST WANT YOU TO KNOW THAT I WILL NEVER HURT YOU AGAIN, NO MATTER WHAT YOU DO TO ME.
THANKS.
I MEAN, EVEN IF YOU WERE STEALING FROM ME...CHEATING ON ME...CHEATING ON ME WITH A BLACK GUY...
THAT'S GREAT.
PROBABLY JUST OFF MYSELF BEFORE I DID ANYTHING, BUT--
DON'T BE STUPID.
AND THEN I'D PUT THOSE SEXY VIDEOS I TOOK OF YOU ON THE INTERNET, SO--
I JUST SAID DON'T BE STUPID!

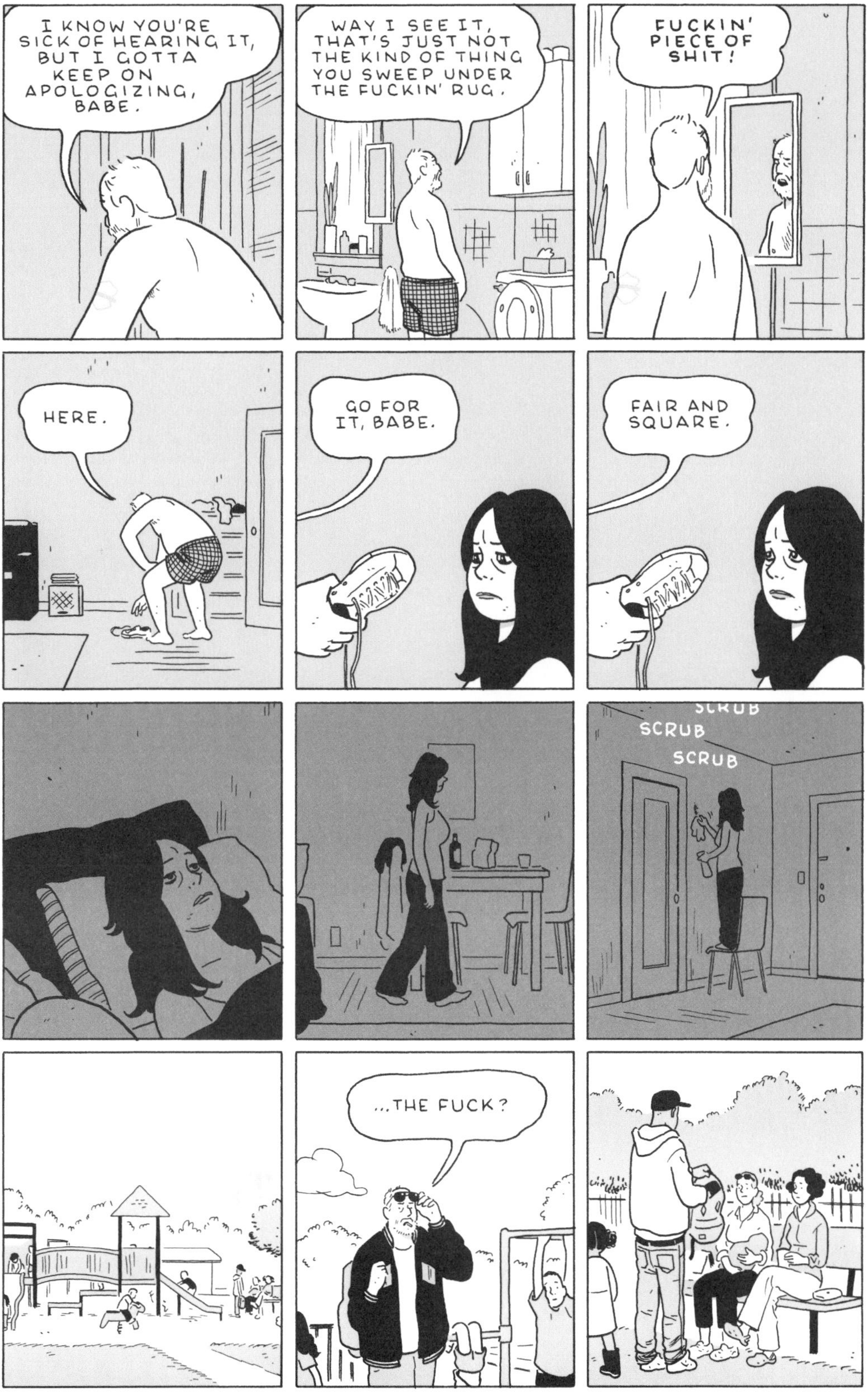
I KNOW YOU'RE SICK OF HEARING IT, BUT I GOTTA KEEP ON APOLOGIZING, BABE.
WAY I SEE IT, THAT'S JUST NOT THE KIND OF THING YOU SWEEP UNDER THE FUCKIN' RUG.
FUCKIN' PIECE OF SHIT!
HERE.
GO FOR IT, BABE.
FAIR AND SQUARE.
SCRUB
SCRUB
SCRUB
...THE FUCK?

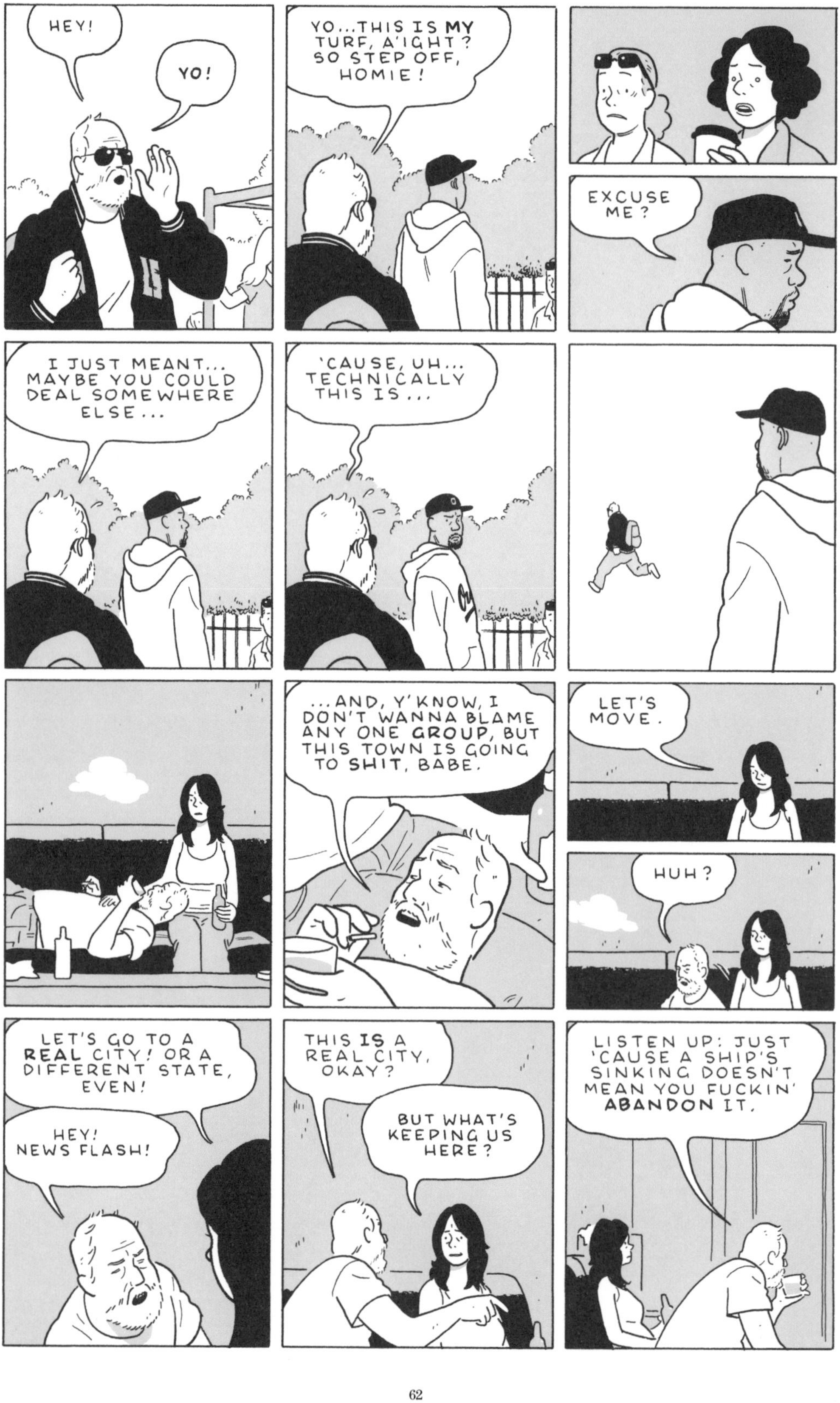
HEY!
YO!
YO...THIS IS MY TURF, A'IGHT? SO STEP OFF, HOMIE!
EXCUSE ME?
I JUST MEANT... MAYBE YOU COULD DEAL SOMEWHERE ELSE...
'CAUSE, UH... TECHNICALLY THIS IS...
...AND, Y'KNOW, I DON'T WANNA BLAME ANY ONE GROUP, BUT THIS TOWN IS GOING TO SHIT, BABE.
LET'S MOVE.
HUH?
LET'S GO TO A REAL CITY! OR A DIFFERENT STATE, EVEN!
HEY! NEWS FLASH!
THIS IS A REAL CITY, OKAY?
BUT WHAT'S KEEPING US HERE?
LISTEN UP: JUST 'CAUSE A SHIP'S SINKING DOESN'T MEAN YOU FUCKIN' ABANDON IT.

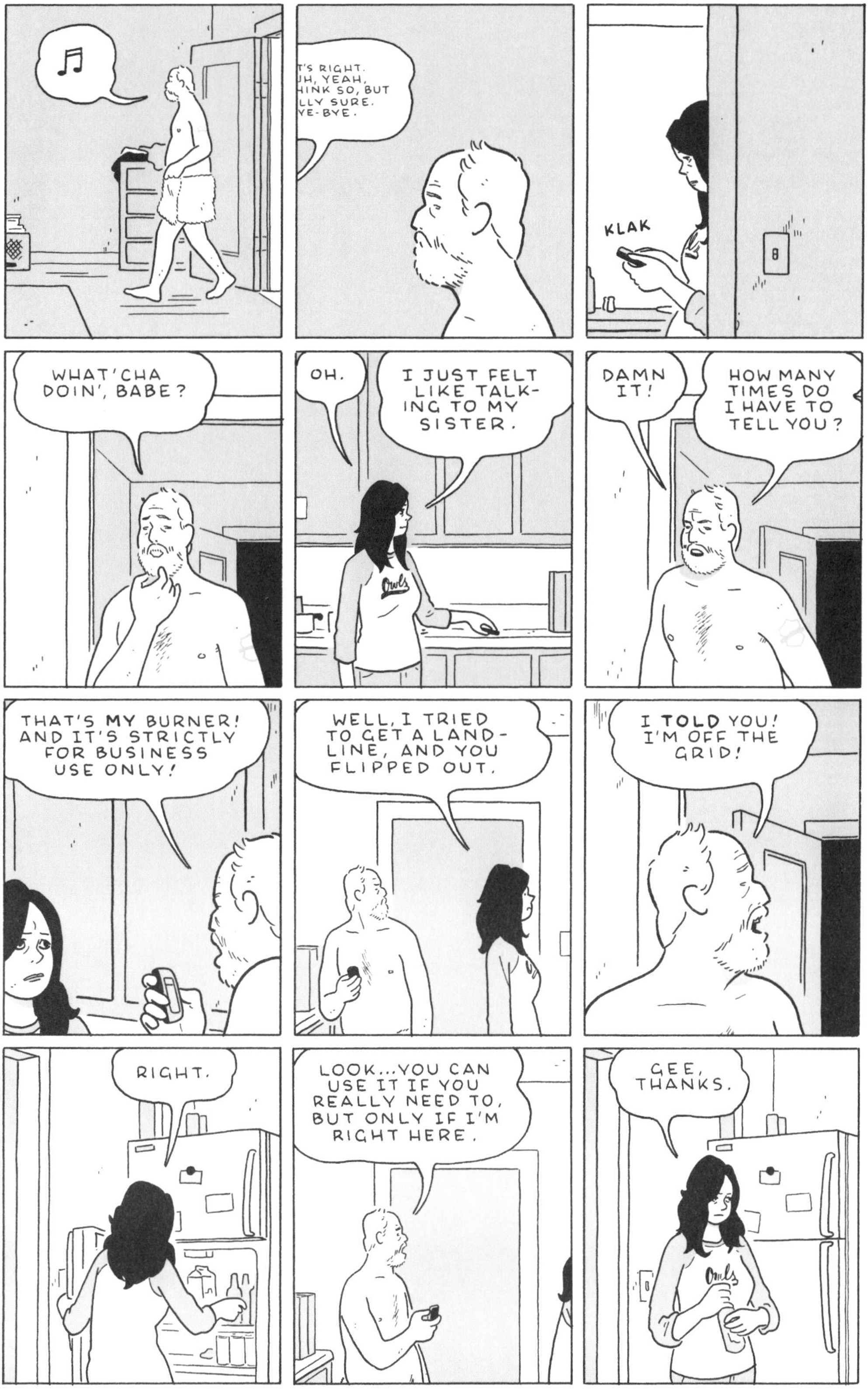
♫
'S RIGHT.
H, YEAH,
HINK SO, BUT
LLY SURE.
YE-BYE.
KLAK
WHAT'CHA DOIN', BABE?
OH.
I JUST FELT LIKE TALKING TO MY SISTER.
DAMN IT!
HOW MANY TIMES DO I HAVE TO TELL YOU?
THAT'S MY BURNER! AND IT'S STRICTLY FOR BUSINESS USE ONLY!
WELL, I TRIED TO GET A LAND-LINE, AND YOU FLIPPED OUT.
I TOLD YOU! I'M OFF THE GRID!
RIGHT.
LOOK... YOU CAN USE IT IF YOU REALLY NEED TO, BUT ONLY IF I'M RIGHT HERE.
GEE, THANKS.

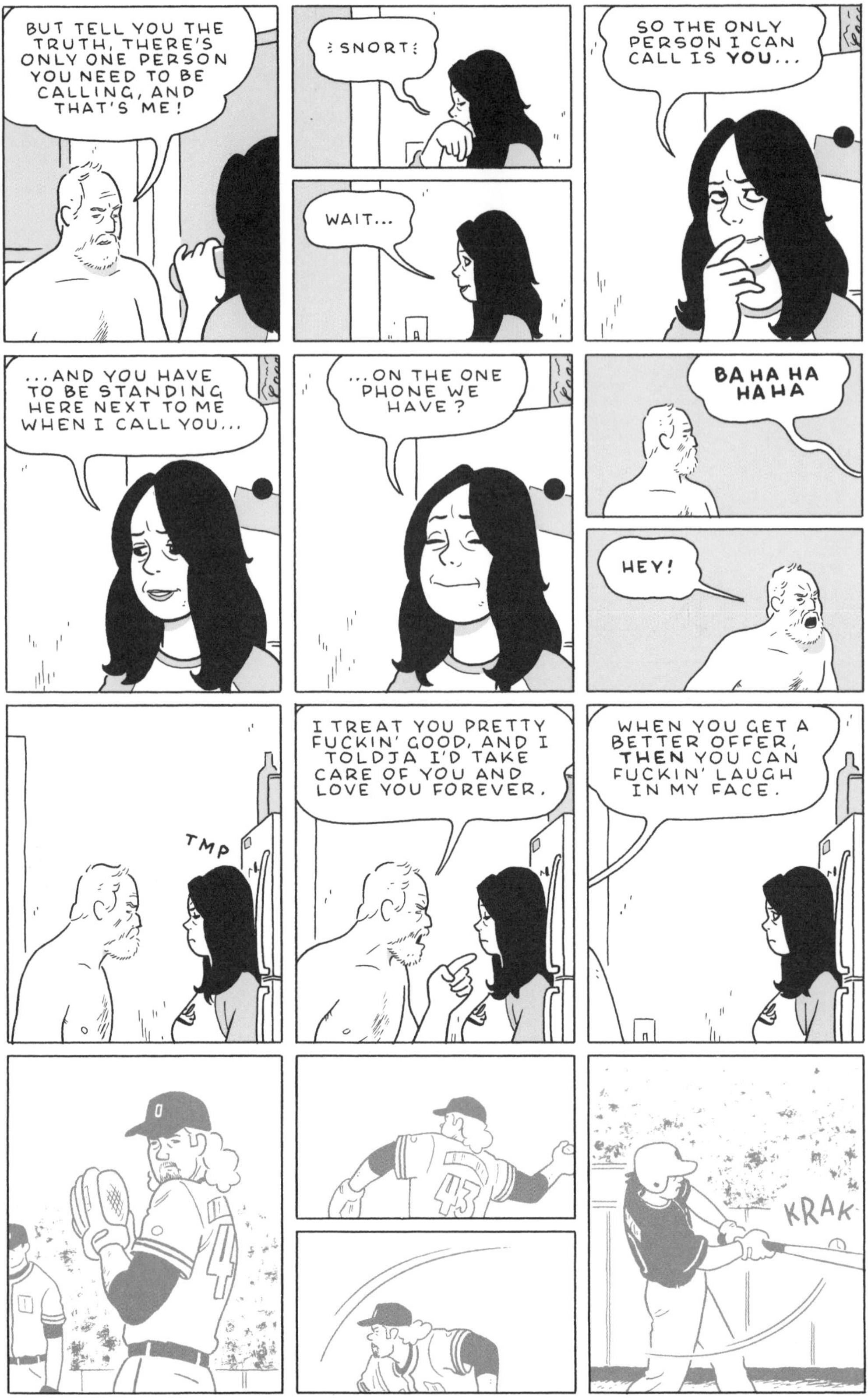
BUT TELL YOU THE TRUTH, THERE'S ONLY ONE PERSON YOU NEED TO BE CALLING, AND THAT'S ME!
SNORT
WAIT...
SO THE ONLY PERSON I CAN CALL IS YOU...
...AND YOU HAVE TO BE STANDING HERE NEXT TO ME WHEN I CALL YOU...
...ON THE ONE PHONE WE HAVE?
BA HA HA HA HA
HEY!
TMP
I TREAT YOU PRETTY FUCKIN' GOOD, AND I TOLDJA I'D TAKE CARE OF YOU AND LOVE YOU FOREVER.
WHEN YOU GET A BETTER OFFER, THEN YOU CAN FUCKIN' LAUGH IN MY FACE.
KRAK

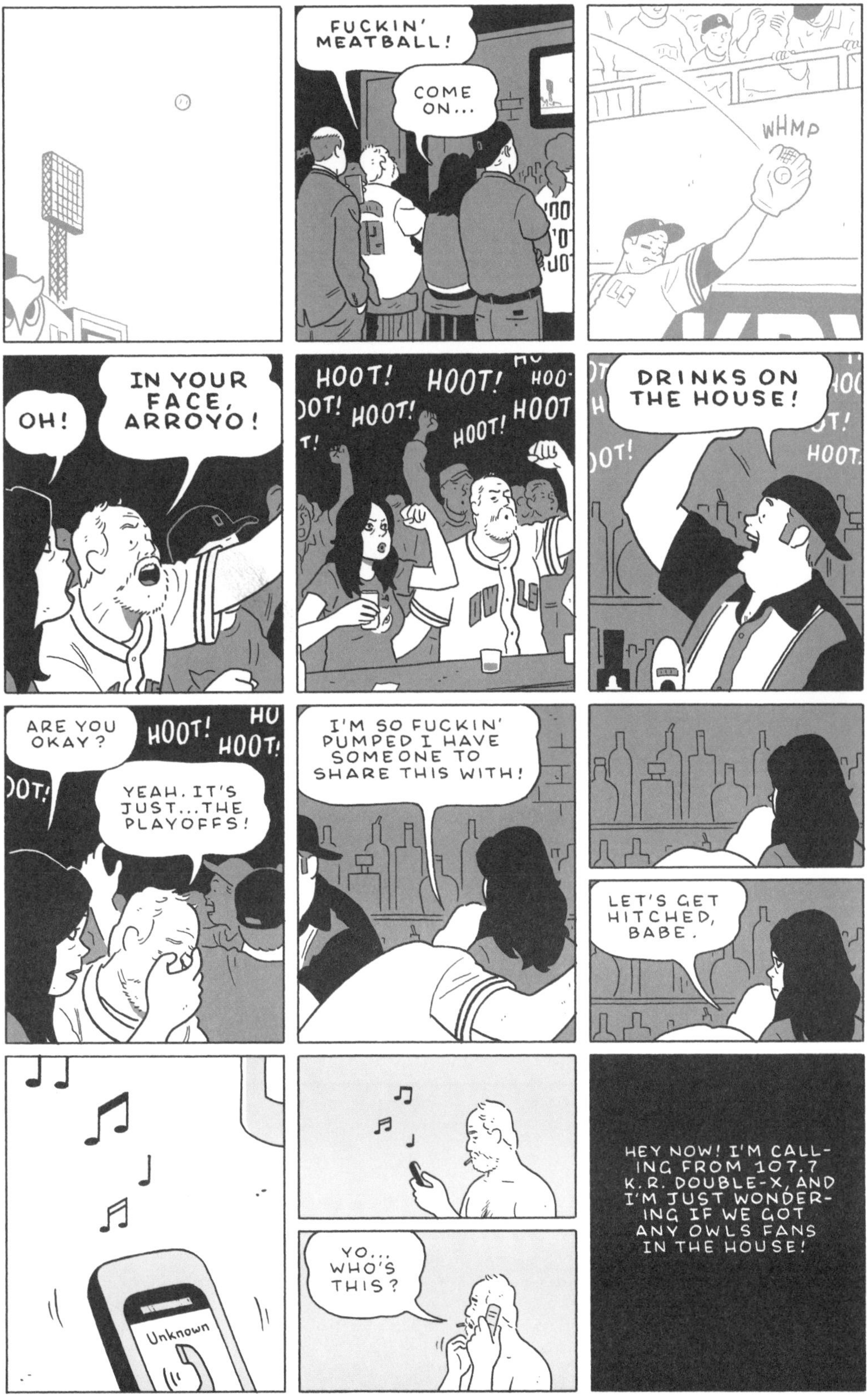
FUCKIN' MEATBALL!
COME ON...
WHMP
OH!
IN YOUR FACE, ARROYO!
HOOT! HOOT! HOOT! HOOT! HOOT!
DRINKS ON THE HOUSE!
HOOT!
ARE YOU OKAY?
HOOT! HOOT!
YEAH. IT'S JUST... THE PLAYOFFS!
I'M SO FUCKIN' PUMPED I HAVE SOMEONE TO SHARE THIS WITH!
LET'S GET HITCHED, BABE.
Unknown
YO... WHO'S THIS?
HEY NOW! I'M CALLING FROM 107.7 K.R. DOUBLE-X, AND I'M JUST WONDERING IF WE GOT ANY OWLS FANS IN THE HOUSE!

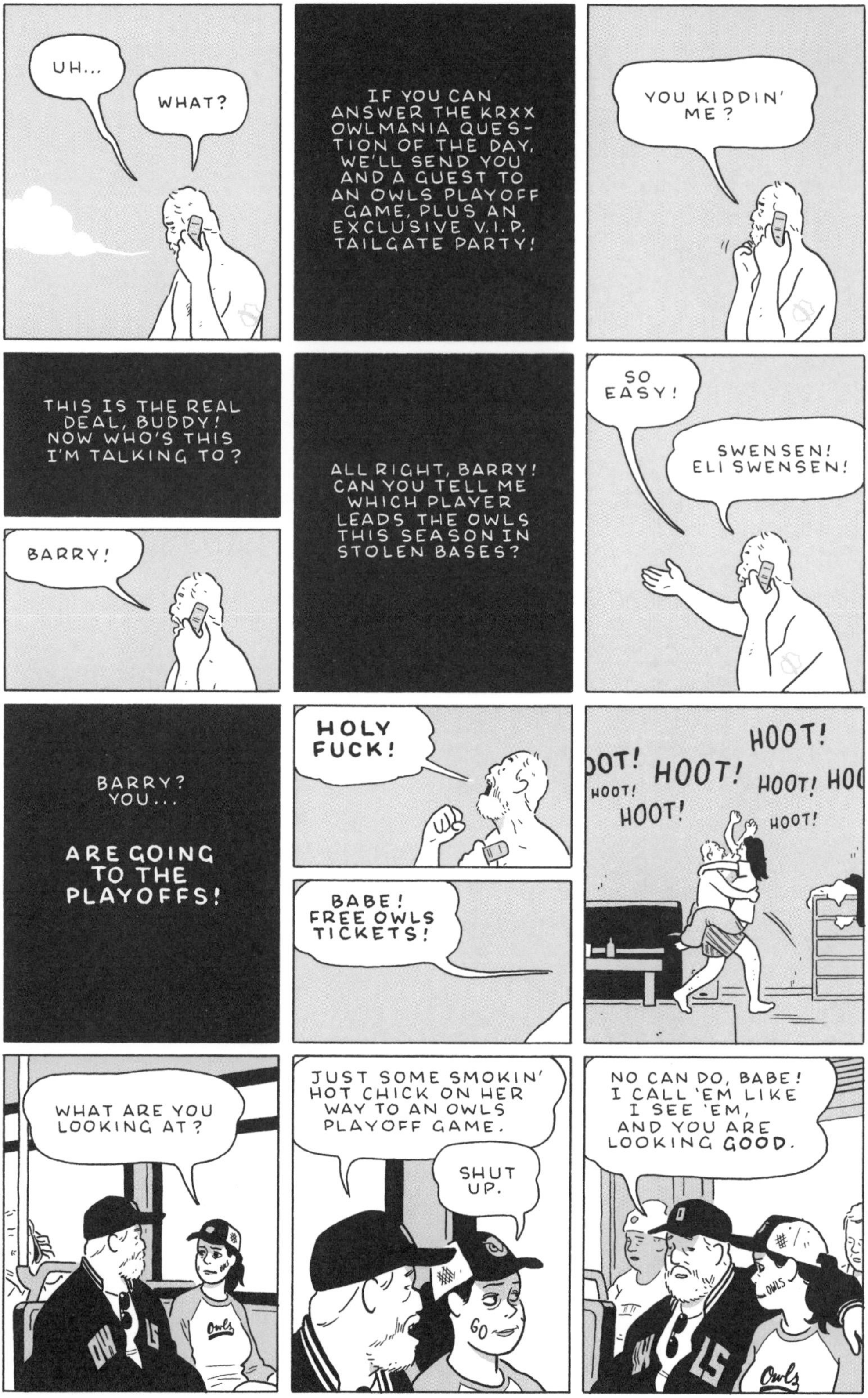
UH...
WHAT?
IF YOU CAN ANSWER THE KRXX OWLMANIA QUESTION OF THE DAY, WE'LL SEND YOU AND A GUEST TO AN OWLS PLAYOFF GAME, PLUS AN EXCLUSIVE V.I.P. TAILGATE PARTY!
YOU KIDDIN' ME?
THIS IS THE REAL DEAL, BUDDY! NOW WHO'S THIS I'M TALKING TO?
BARRY!
ALL RIGHT, BARRY! CAN YOU TELL ME WHICH PLAYER LEADS THE OWLS THIS SEASON IN STOLEN BASES?
SO EASY!
SWENSEN! ELI SWENSEN!
BARRY? YOU...
ARE GOING TO THE PLAYOFFS!
HOLY FUCK!
BABE! FREE OWLS TICKETS!
HOOT! HOOT! HOOT! HOOT! HOOT! HOOT! HOOT!
WHAT ARE YOU LOOKING AT?
JUST SOME SMOKIN' HOT CHICK ON HER WAY TO AN OWLS PLAYOFF GAME.
SHUT UP.
NO CAN DO, BABE! I CALL 'EM LIKE I SEE 'EM, AND YOU ARE LOOKING **GOOD**.

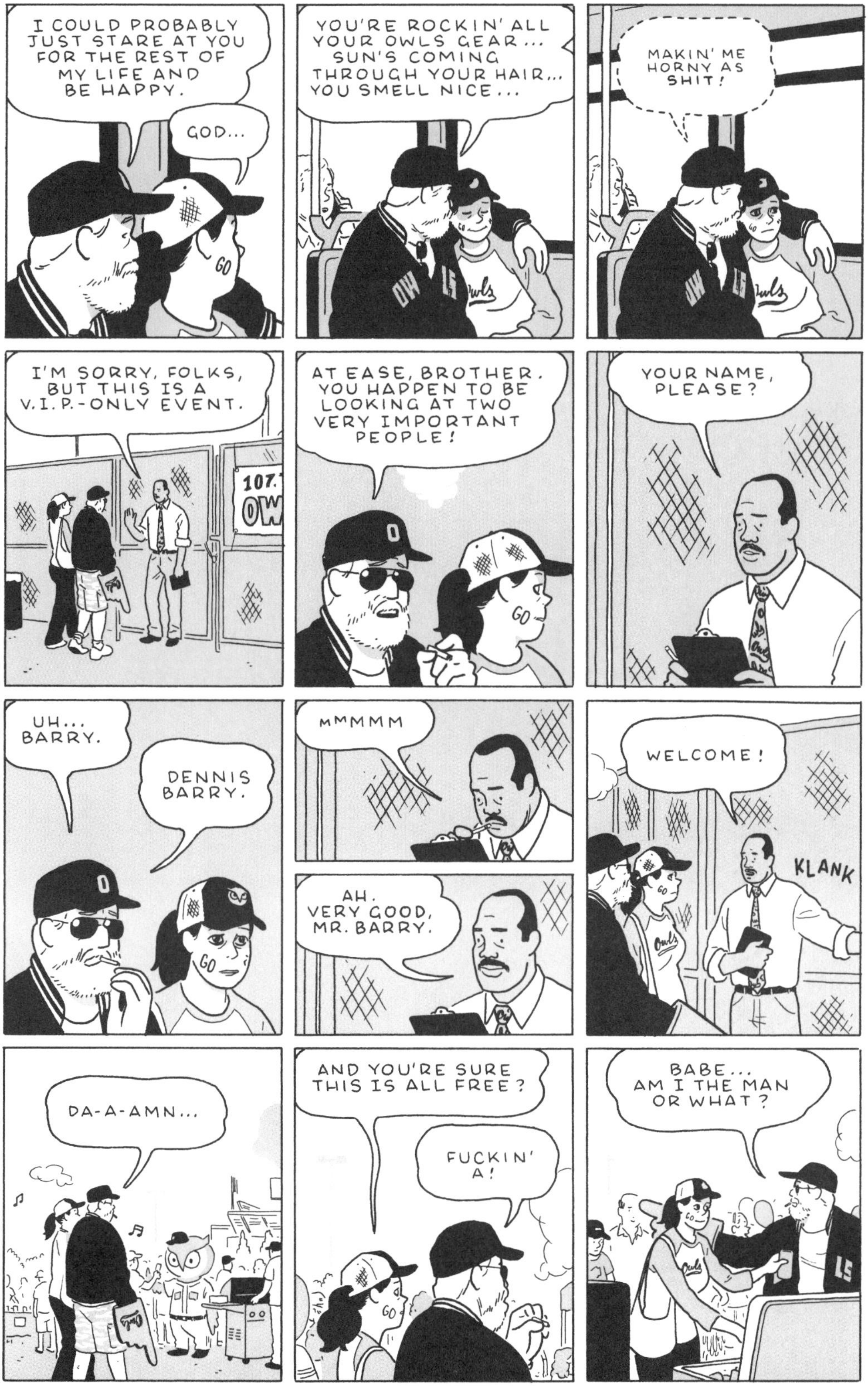

I COULD PROBABLY JUST STARE AT YOU FOR THE REST OF MY LIFE AND BE HAPPY.
GOD...
YOU'RE ROCKIN' ALL YOUR OWLS GEAR... SUN'S COMING THROUGH YOUR HAIR... YOU SMELL NICE...
MAKIN' ME HORNY AS SHIT!
I'M SORRY, FOLKS, BUT THIS IS A V.I.P.-ONLY EVENT.
AT EASE, BROTHER. YOU HAPPEN TO BE LOOKING AT TWO VERY IMPORTANT PEOPLE!
YOUR NAME, PLEASE?
UH... BARRY.
DENNIS BARRY.
MMMMM
AH. VERY GOOD, MR. BARRY.
WELCOME!
KLANK
DA-A-AMN...
AND YOU'RE SURE THIS IS ALL FREE?
FUCKIN' A!
BABE... AM I THE MAN OR WHAT?

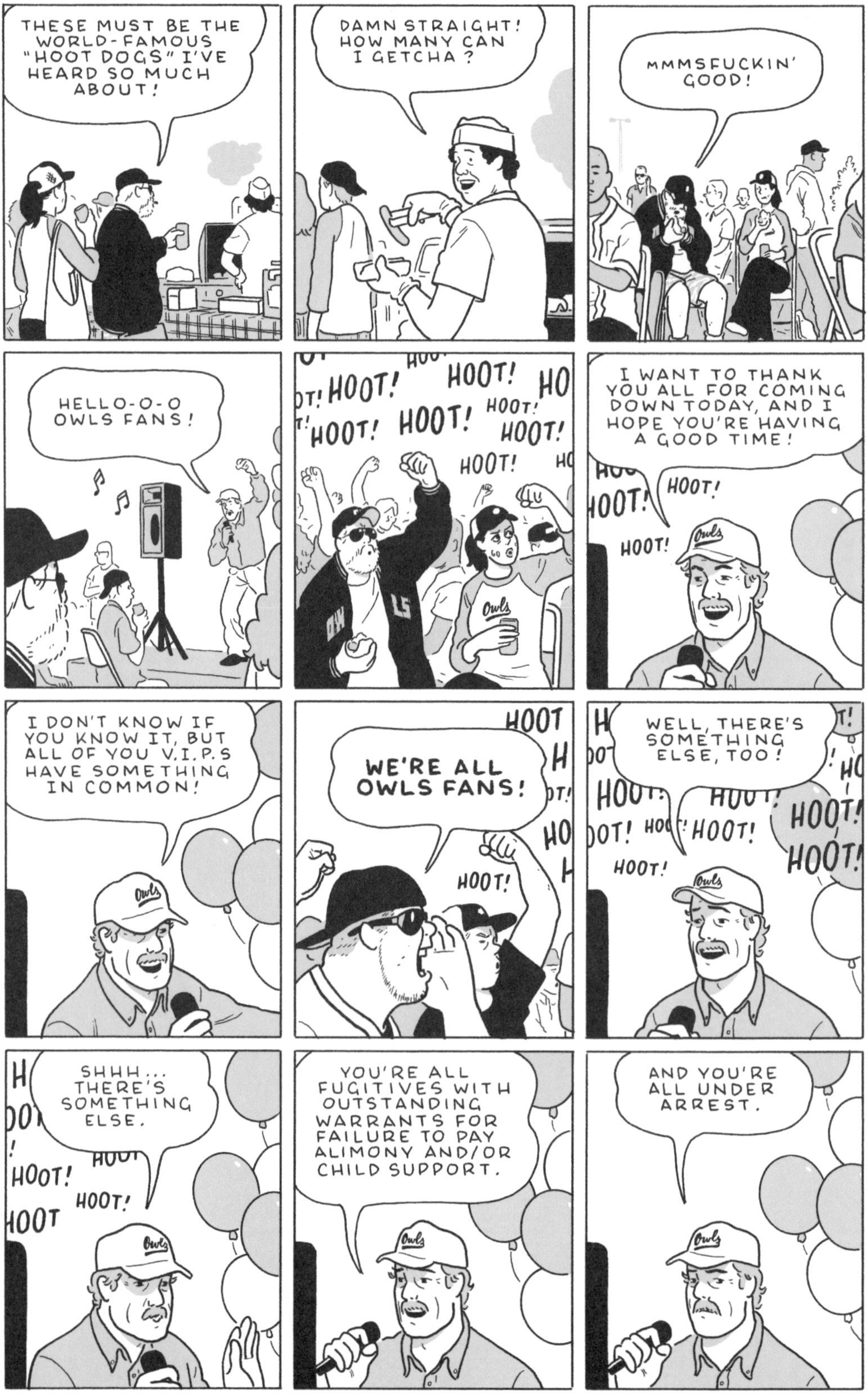
THESE MUST BE THE WORLD-FAMOUS "HOOT DOGS" I'VE HEARD SO MUCH ABOUT!
DAMN STRAIGHT! HOW MANY CAN I GETCHA?
MMMSFUCKIN' GOOD!
HELLO-O-O OWLS FANS!
HOOT! HOOT! HOOT! HOOT! HOOT! HOOT! HOOT!
I WANT TO THANK YOU ALL FOR COMING DOWN TODAY, AND I HOPE YOU'RE HAVING A GOOD TIME!
HOOT! HOOT!
I DON'T KNOW IF YOU KNOW IT, BUT ALL OF YOU V.I.P.S HAVE SOMETHING IN COMMON!
WE'RE ALL OWLS FANS!
HOOT!
WELL, THERE'S SOMETHING ELSE, TOO!
HOOT! HOOT! HOOT! HOOT!
SHHH... THERE'S SOMETHING ELSE.
HOOT! HOOT!
YOU'RE ALL FUGITIVES WITH OUTSTANDING WARRANTS FOR FAILURE TO PAY ALIMONY AND/OR CHILD SUPPORT.
AND YOU'RE ALL UNDER ARREST.

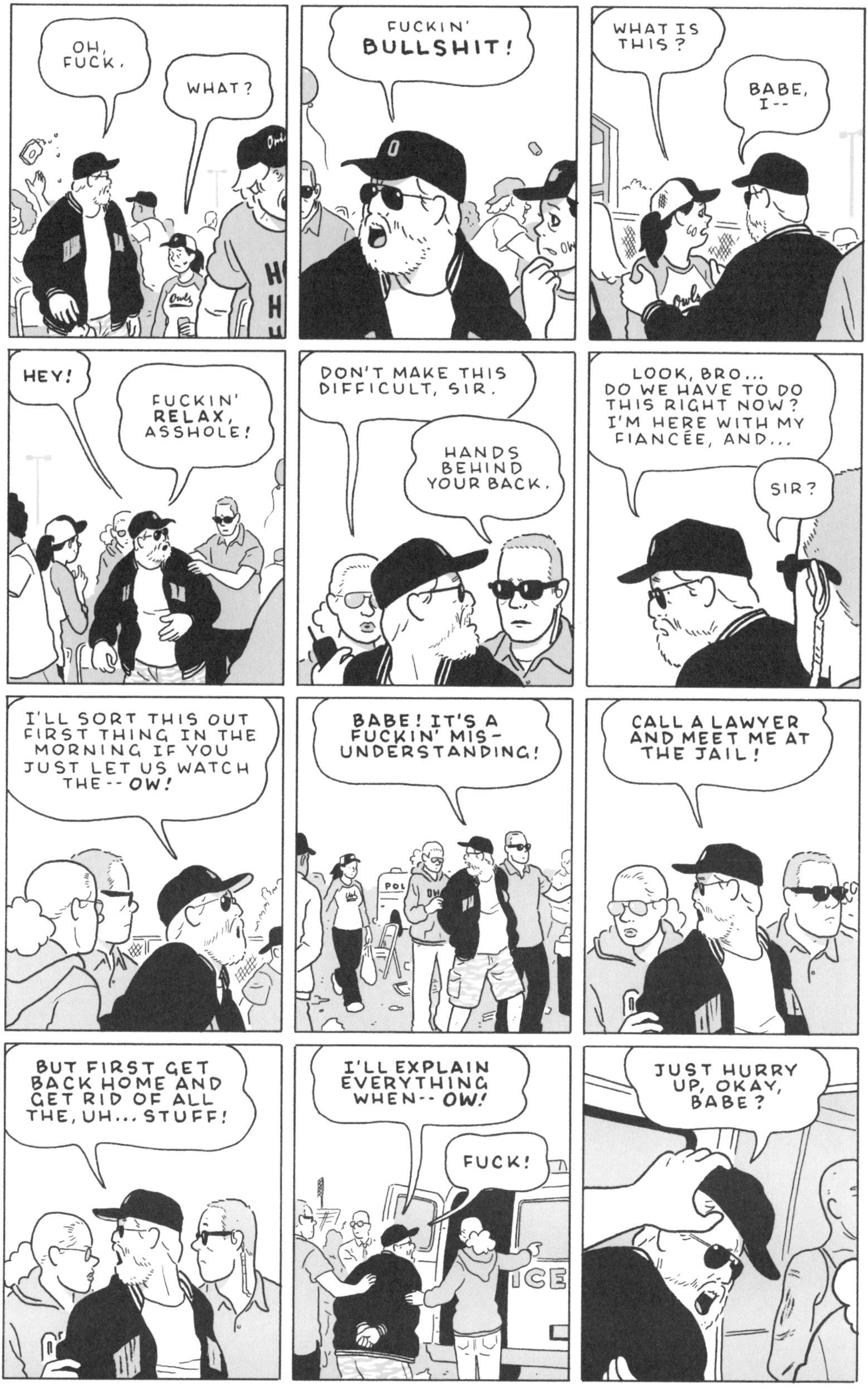
OH, FUCK.
WHAT?
FUCKIN' BULLSHIT!
WHAT IS THIS?
BABE, I--
HEY!
FUCKIN' RELAX, ASSHOLE!
DON'T MAKE THIS DIFFICULT, SIR.
HANDS BEHIND YOUR BACK.
LOOK, BRO... DO WE HAVE TO DO THIS RIGHT NOW? I'M HERE WITH MY FIANCÉE, AND...
SIR?
I'LL SORT THIS OUT FIRST THING IN THE MORNING IF YOU JUST LET US WATCH THE--OW!
BABE! IT'S A FUCKIN' MIS-UNDERSTANDING!
CALL A LAWYER AND MEET ME AT THE JAIL!
BUT FIRST GET BACK HOME AND GET RID OF ALL THE, UH... STUFF!
I'LL EXPLAIN EVERYTHING WHEN--OW!
FUCK!
JUST HURRY UP, OKAY, BABE?

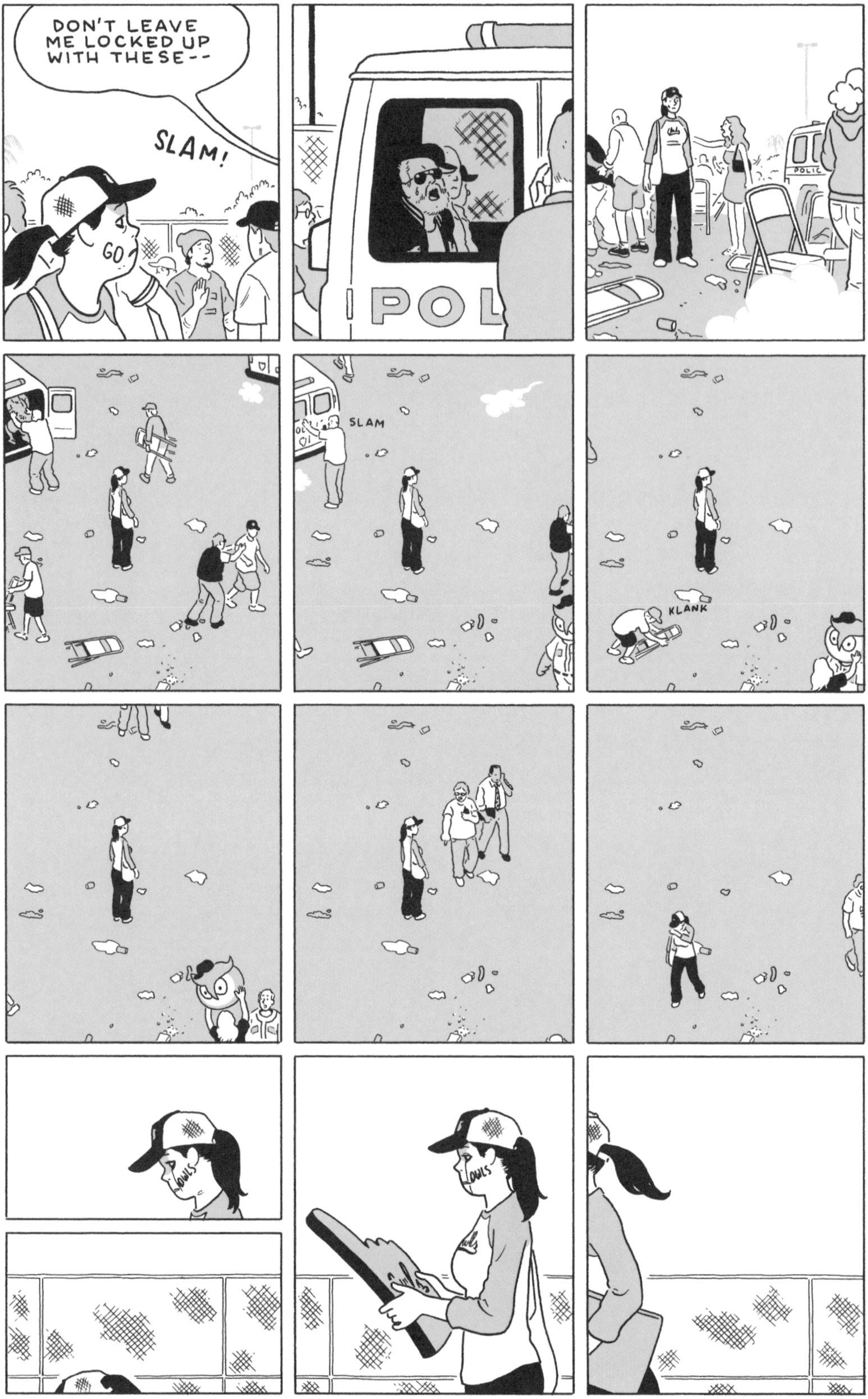
DON'T LEAVE ME LOCKED UP WITH THESE--
SLAM!
GO
POL
POLIC
SLAM
KLANK
OWLS

二月に気持ちの整理がついて全てを良く
考えられる様になった時には、カリフォルニア
に帰る事に決めました。あなたのお婆さん
と伯母さんと伯父さん達は皆この選択
には反対で、お互いに気まずいまま別れ
ました。でもそれは仕方のない事でした。

TRANSLATED,

from the JAPANESE,

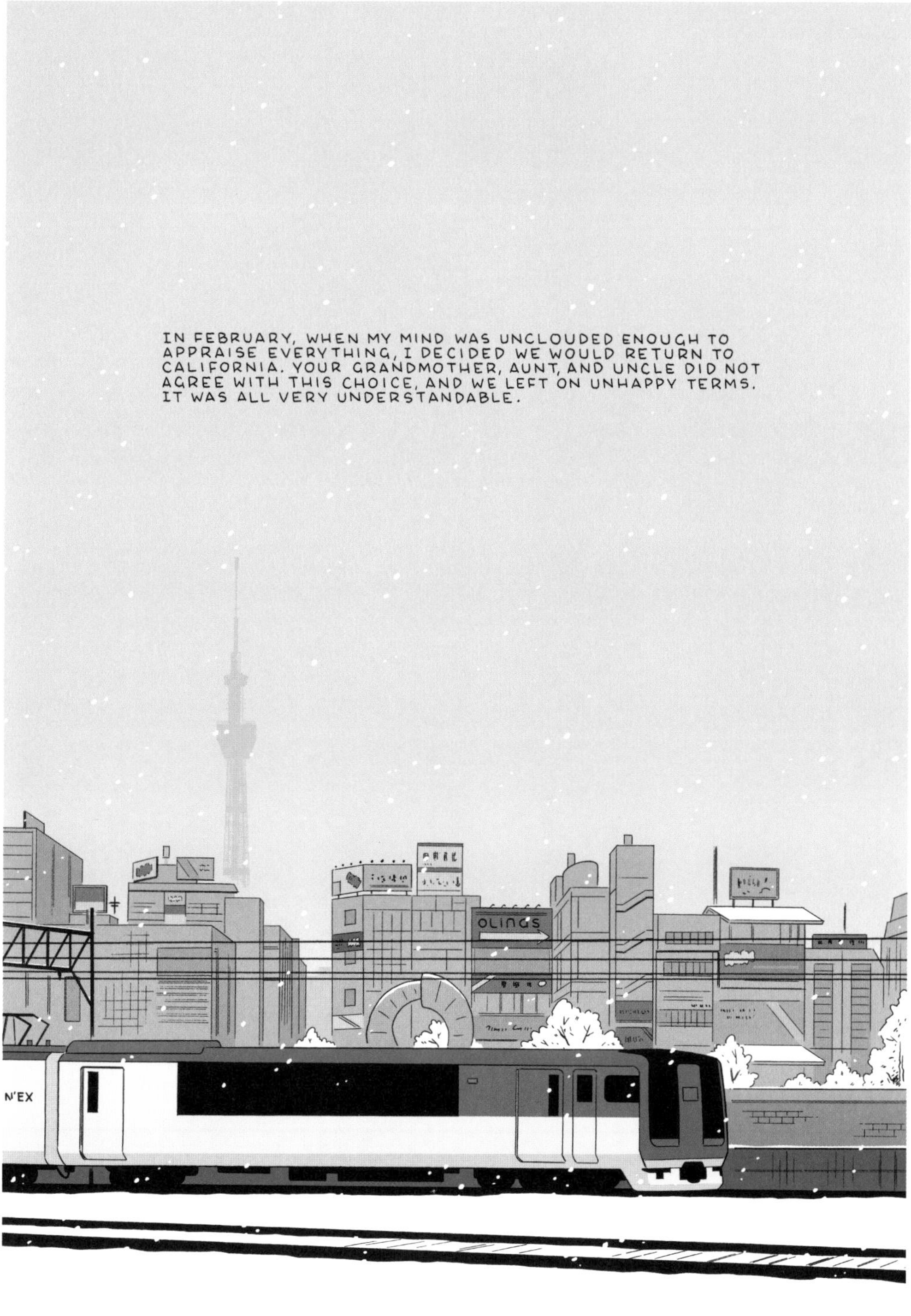
IN FEBRUARY, WHEN MY MIND WAS UNCLOUDED ENOUGH TO APPRAISE EVERYTHING, I DECIDED WE WOULD RETURN TO CALIFORNIA. YOUR GRANDMOTHER, AUNT, AND UNCLE DID NOT AGREE WITH THIS CHOICE, AND WE LEFT ON UNHAPPY TERMS. IT WAS ALL VERY UNDERSTANDABLE.
OLINGS
N'EX

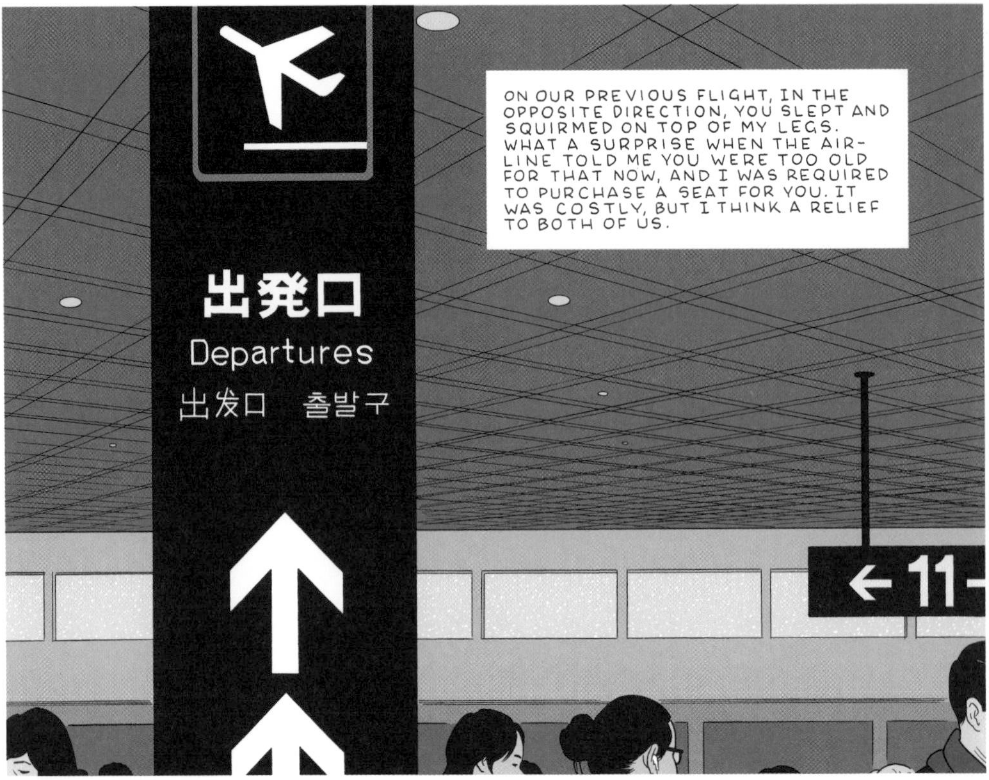
ON OUR PREVIOUS FLIGHT, IN THE OPPOSITE DIRECTION, YOU SLEPT AND SQUIRMED ON TOP OF MY LEGS. WHAT A SURPRISE WHEN THE AIR-LINE TOLD ME YOU WERE TOO OLD FOR THAT NOW, AND I WAS REQUIRED TO PURCHASE A SEAT FOR YOU. IT WAS COSTLY, BUT I THINK A RELIEF TO BOTH OF US.
出発口
Departures
出发口 출발구
← 11

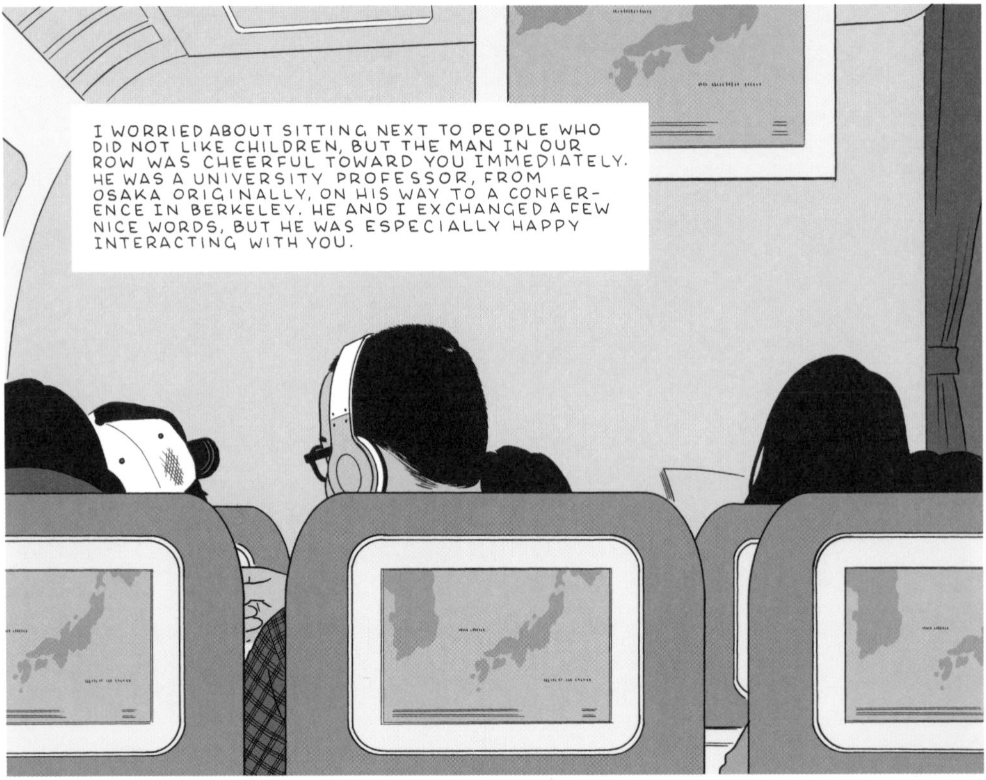
I WORRIED ABOUT SITTING NEXT TO PEOPLE WHO DID NOT LIKE CHILDREN, BUT THE MAN IN OUR ROW WAS CHEERFUL TOWARD YOU IMMEDIATELY. HE WAS A UNIVERSITY PROFESSOR, FROM OSAKA ORIGINALLY, ON HIS WAY TO A CONFER-ENCE IN BERKELEY. HE AND I EXCHANGED A FEW NICE WORDS, BUT HE WAS ESPECIALLY HAPPY INTERACTING WITH YOU.

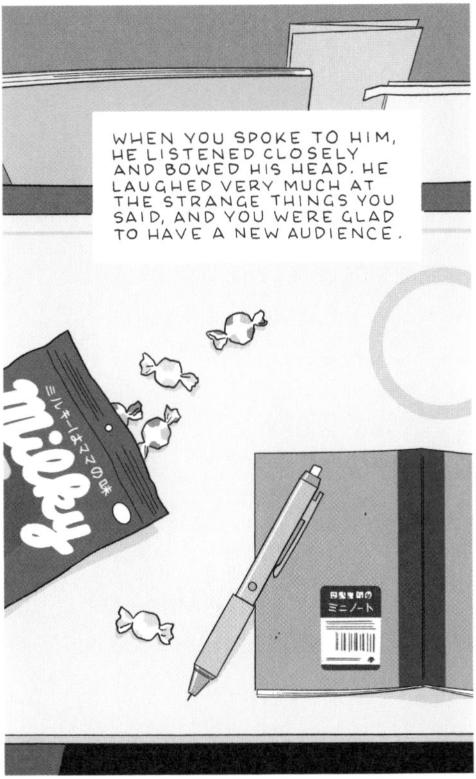
WHEN YOU SPOKE TO HIM, HE LISTENED CLOSELY AND BOWED HIS HEAD. HE LAUGHED VERY MUCH AT THE STRANGE THINGS YOU SAID, AND YOU WERE GLAD TO HAVE A NEW AUDIENCE.
Milky
ミルキーはママの味

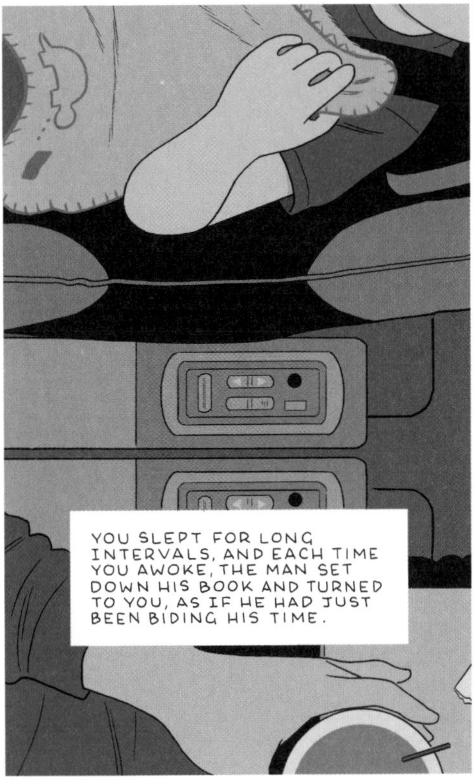
YOU SLEPT FOR LONG INTERVALS, AND EACH TIME YOU AWOKE, THE MAN SET DOWN HIS BOOK AND TURNED TO YOU, AS IF HE HAD JUST BEEN BIDING HIS TIME.

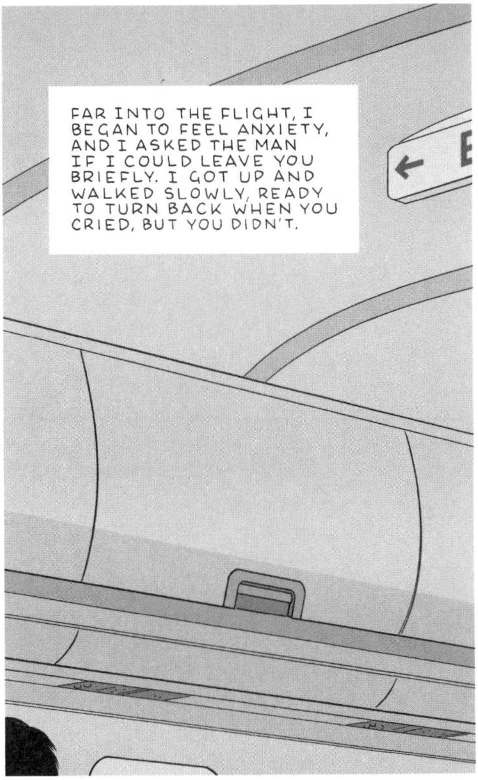
FAR INTO THE FLIGHT, I BEGAN TO FEEL ANXIETY, AND I ASKED THE MAN IF I COULD LEAVE YOU BRIEFLY. I GOT UP AND WALKED SLOWLY, READY TO TURN BACK WHEN YOU CRIED, BUT YOU DIDN'T.

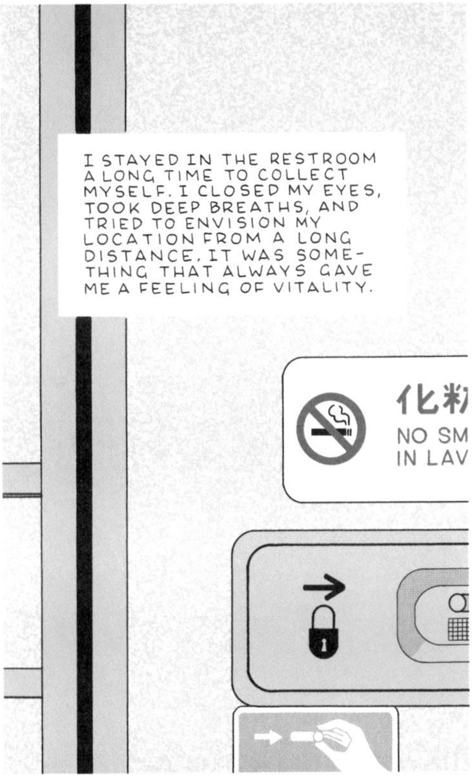
I STAYED IN THE RESTROOM A LONG TIME TO COLLECT MYSELF. I CLOSED MY EYES, TOOK DEEP BREATHS, AND TRIED TO ENVISION MY LOCATION FROM A LONG DISTANCE. IT WAS SOMETHING THAT ALWAYS GAVE ME A FEELING OF VITALITY.

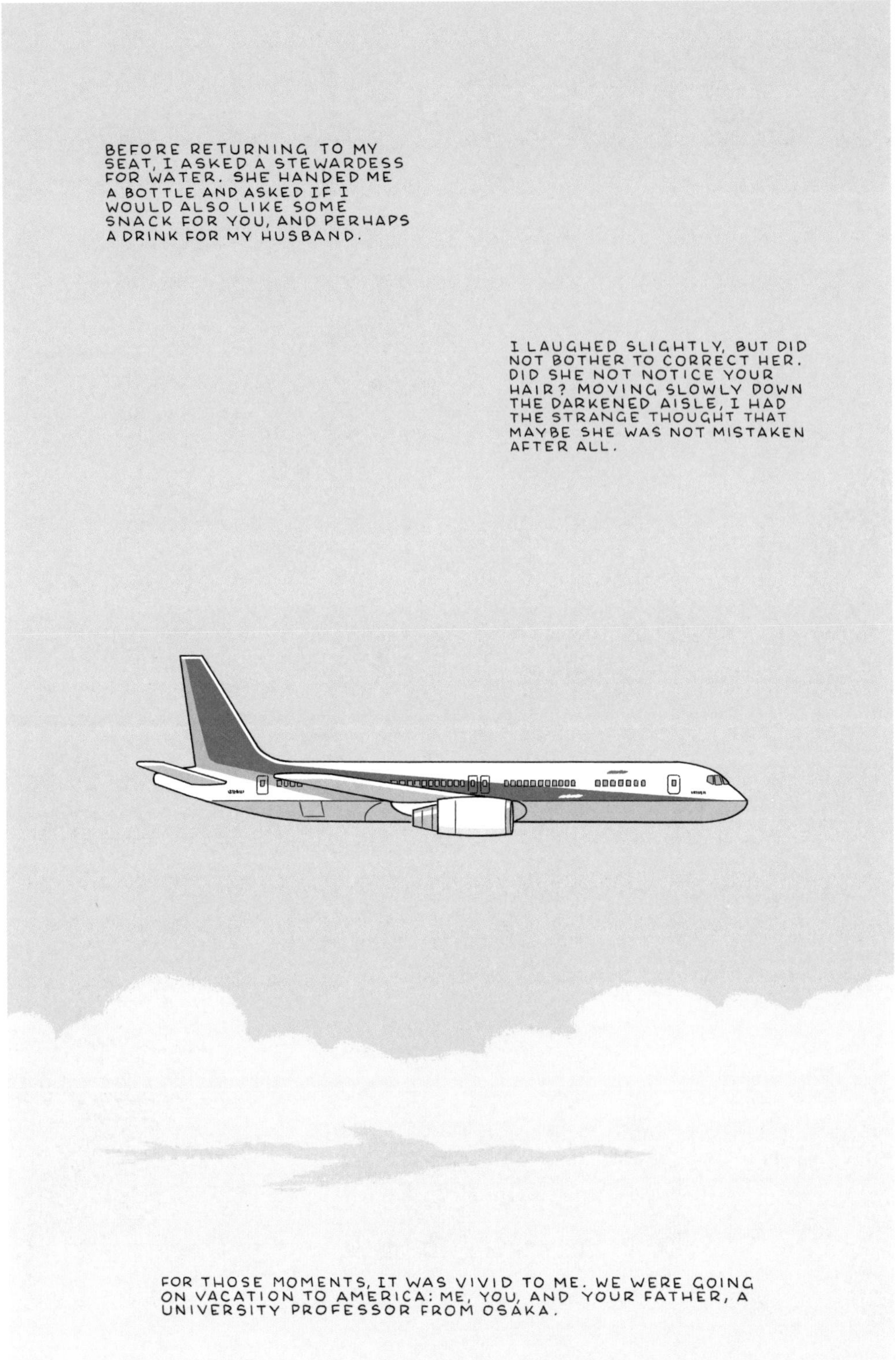

BEFORE RETURNING TO MY
SEAT, I ASKED A STEWARDESS
FOR WATER. SHE HANDED ME
A BOTTLE AND ASKED IF I
WOULD ALSO LIKE SOME
SNACK FOR YOU, AND PERHAPS
A DRINK FOR MY HUSBAND.

I LAUGHED SLIGHTLY, BUT DID
NOT BOTHER TO CORRECT HER.
DID SHE NOT NOTICE YOUR
HAIR? MOVING SLOWLY DOWN
THE DARKENED AISLE, I HAD
THE STRANGE THOUGHT THAT
MAYBE SHE WAS NOT MISTAKEN
AFTER ALL.

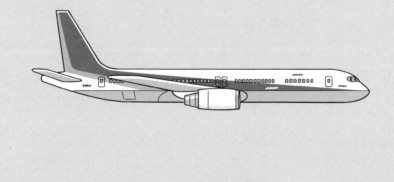

FOR THOSE MOMENTS, IT WAS VIVID TO ME. WE WERE GOING
ON VACATION TO AMERICA: ME, YOU, AND YOUR FATHER, A
UNIVERSITY PROFESSOR FROM OSAKA.

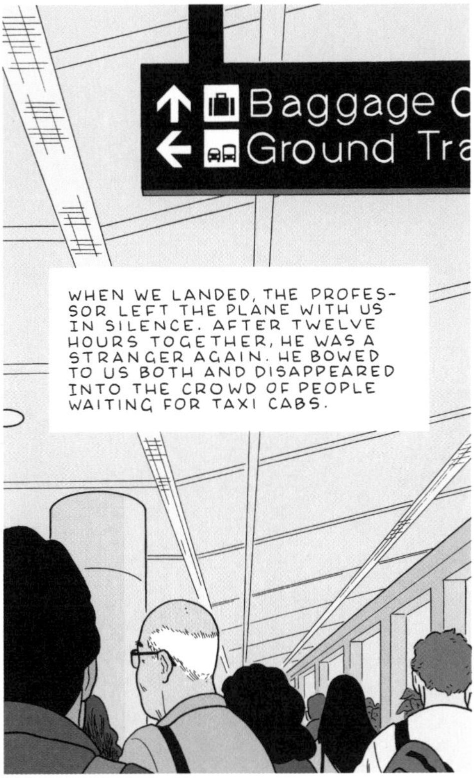
Baggage C
Ground Tra
WHEN WE LANDED, THE PROFESSOR LEFT THE PLANE WITH US IN SILENCE. AFTER TWELVE HOURS TOGETHER, HE WAS A STRANGER AGAIN. HE BOWED TO US BOTH AND DISAPPEARED INTO THE CROWD OF PEOPLE WAITING FOR TAXI CABS.

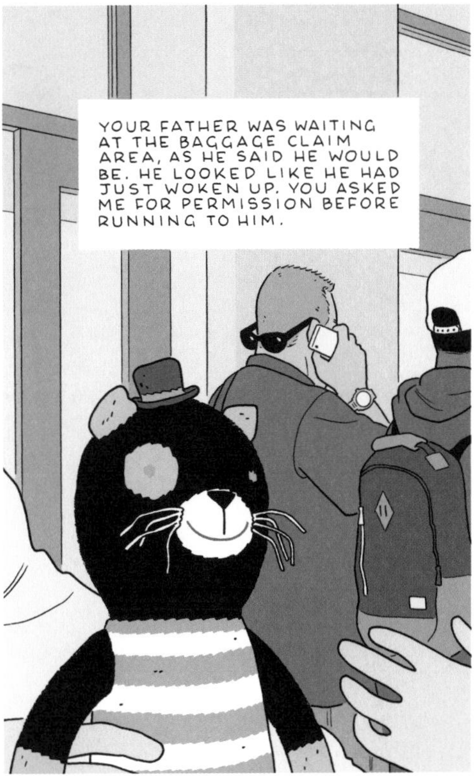
YOUR FATHER WAS WAITING AT THE BAGGAGE CLAIM AREA, AS HE SAID HE WOULD BE. HE LOOKED LIKE HE HAD JUST WOKEN UP. YOU ASKED ME FOR PERMISSION BEFORE RUNNING TO HIM.

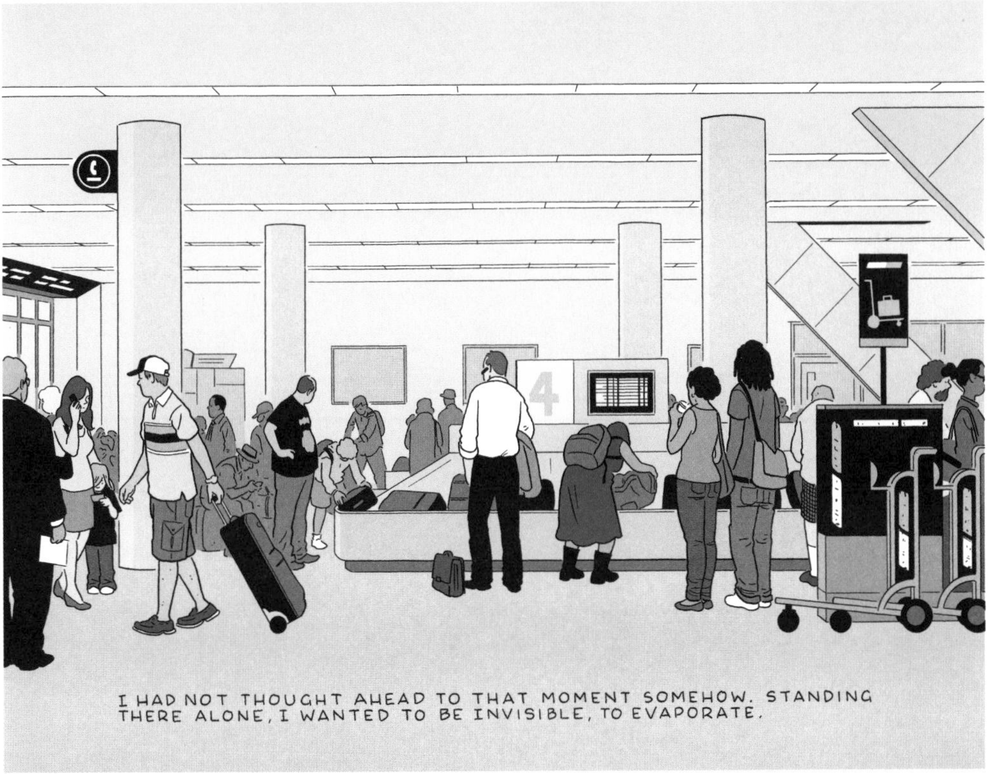
4
I HAD NOT THOUGHT AHEAD TO THAT MOMENT SOMEHOW. STANDING THERE ALONE, I WANTED TO BE INVISIBLE, TO EVAPORATE.

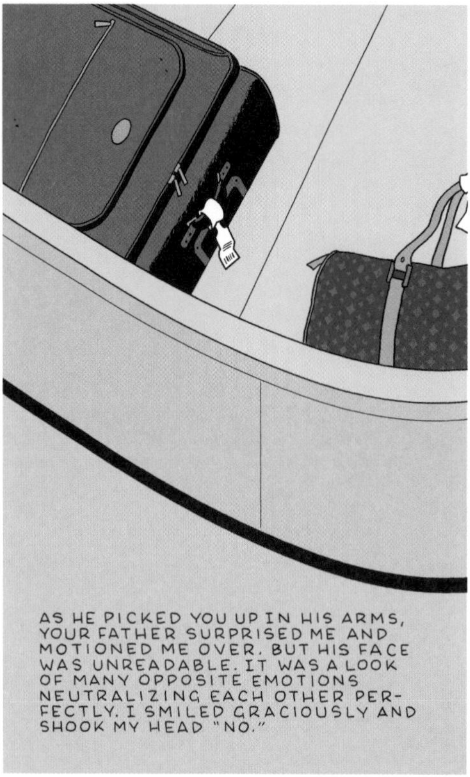
AS HE PICKED YOU UP IN HIS ARMS, YOUR FATHER SURPRISED ME AND MOTIONED ME OVER. BUT HIS FACE WAS UNREADABLE. IT WAS A LOOK OF MANY OPPOSITE EMOTIONS NEUTRALIZING EACH OTHER PERFECTLY. I SMILED GRACIOUSLY AND SHOOK MY HEAD "NO."

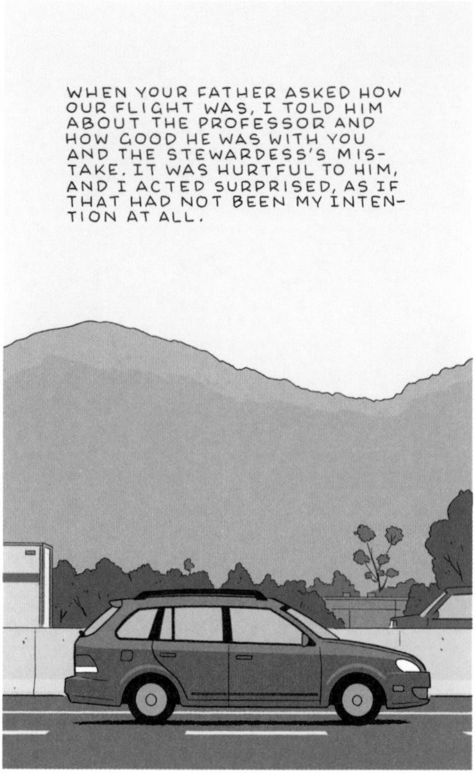
WHEN YOUR FATHER ASKED HOW OUR FLIGHT WAS, I TOLD HIM ABOUT THE PROFESSOR AND HOW GOOD HE WAS WITH YOU AND THE STEWARDESS'S MISTAKE. IT WAS HURTFUL TO HIM, AND I ACTED SURPRISED, AS IF THAT HAD NOT BEEN MY INTENTION AT ALL.

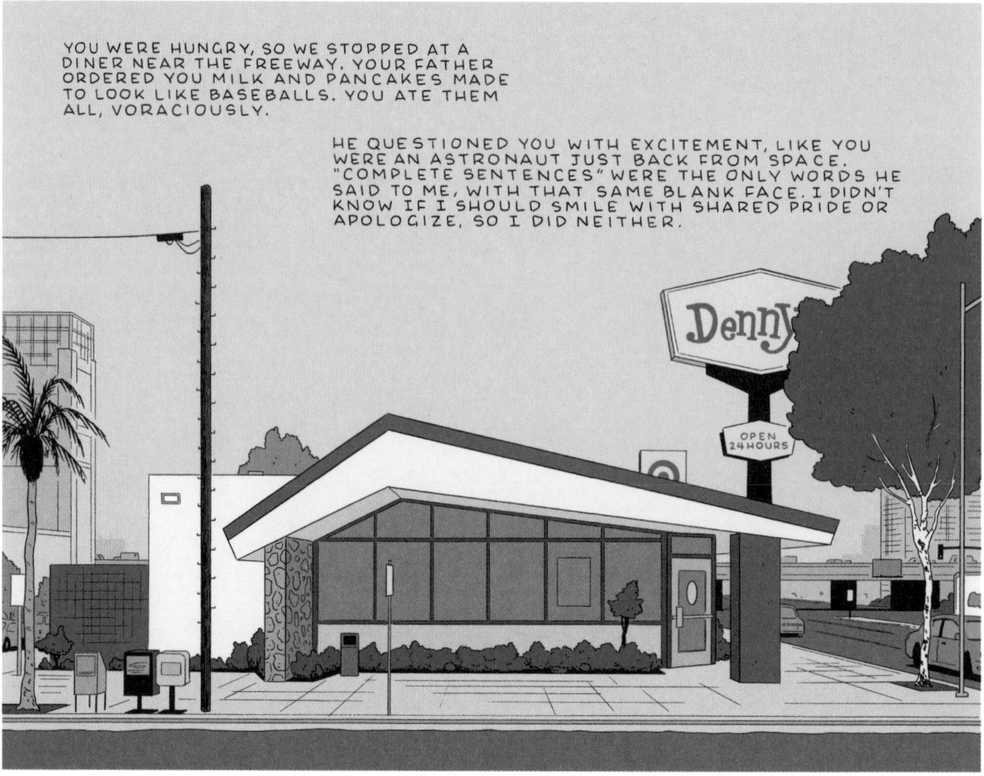
YOU WERE HUNGRY, SO WE STOPPED AT A DINER NEAR THE FREEWAY. YOUR FATHER ORDERED YOU MILK AND PANCAKES MADE TO LOOK LIKE BASEBALLS. YOU ATE THEM ALL, VORACIOUSLY.
HE QUESTIONED YOU WITH EXCITEMENT, LIKE YOU WERE AN ASTRONAUT JUST BACK FROM SPACE. "COMPLETE SENTENCES" WERE THE ONLY WORDS HE SAID TO ME, WITH THAT SAME BLANK FACE. I DIDN'T KNOW IF I SHOULD SMILE WITH SHARED PRIDE OR APOLOGIZE, SO I DID NEITHER.
OPEN 24 HOURS

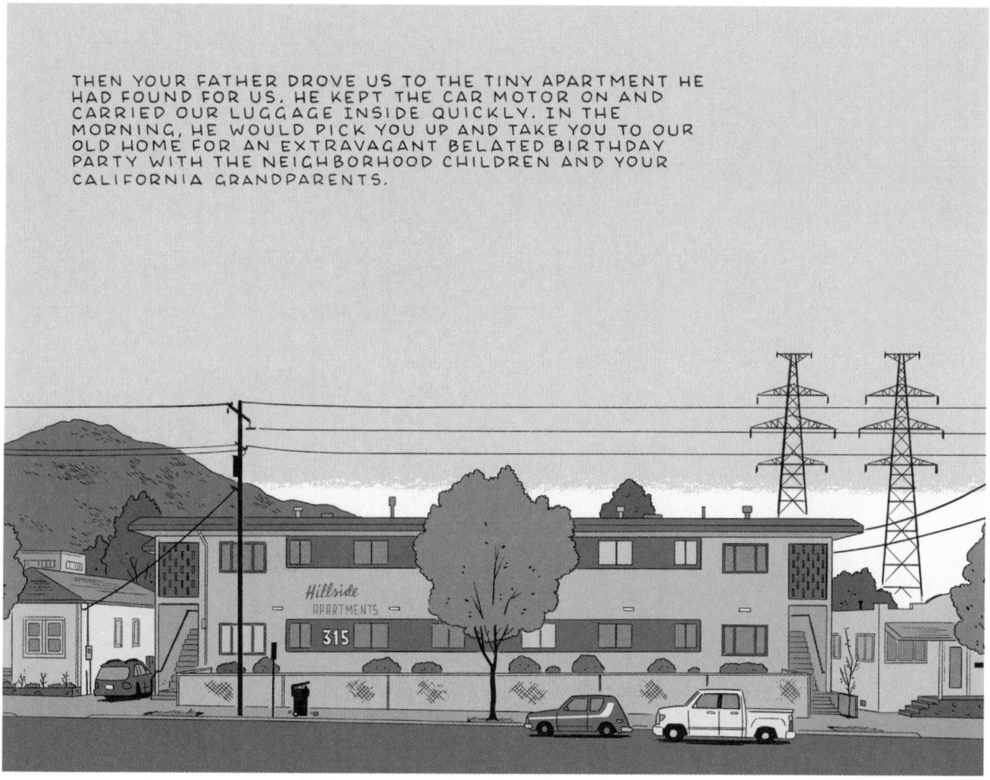
THEN YOUR FATHER DROVE US TO THE TINY APARTMENT HE HAD FOUND FOR US. HE KEPT THE CAR MOTOR ON AND CARRIED OUR LUGGAGE INSIDE QUICKLY. IN THE MORNING, HE WOULD PICK YOU UP AND TAKE YOU TO OUR OLD HOME FOR AN EXTRAVAGANT BELATED BIRTHDAY PARTY WITH THE NEIGHBORHOOD CHILDREN AND YOUR CALIFORNIA GRANDPARENTS.
Hillside
APARTMENTS
315

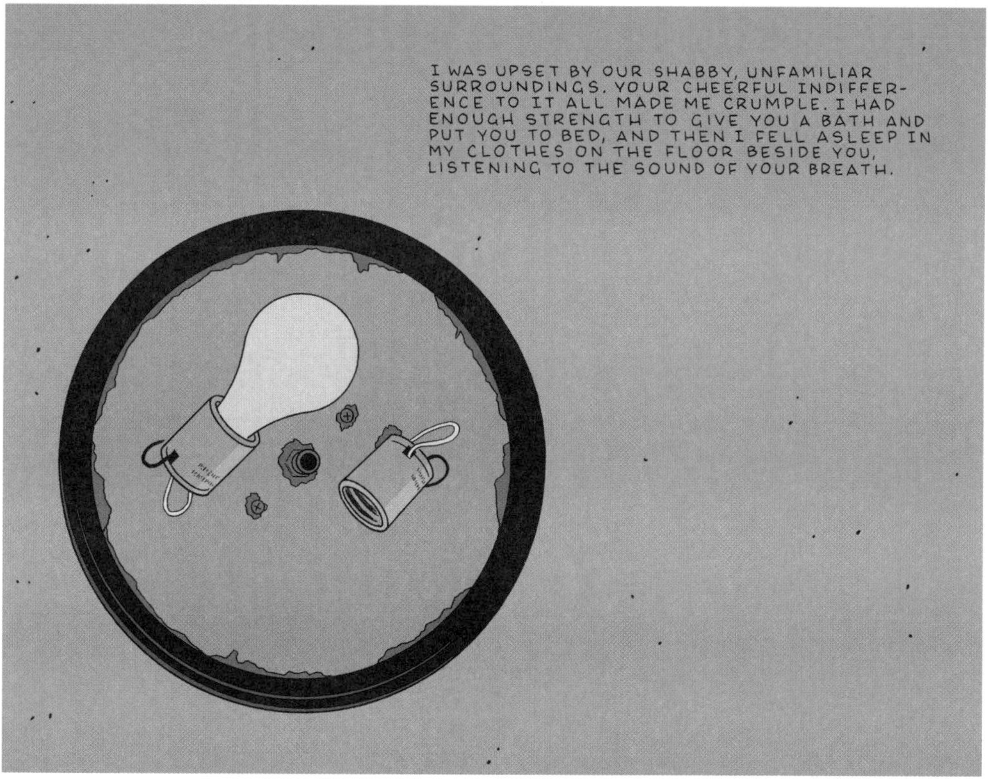
I WAS UPSET BY OUR SHABBY, UNFAMILIAR SURROUNDINGS. YOUR CHEERFUL INDIFFERENCE TO IT ALL MADE ME CRUMPLE. I HAD ENOUGH STRENGTH TO GIVE YOU A BATH AND PUT YOU TO BED, AND THEN I FELL ASLEEP IN MY CLOTHES ON THE FLOOR BESIDE YOU, LISTENING TO THE SOUND OF YOUR BREATH.

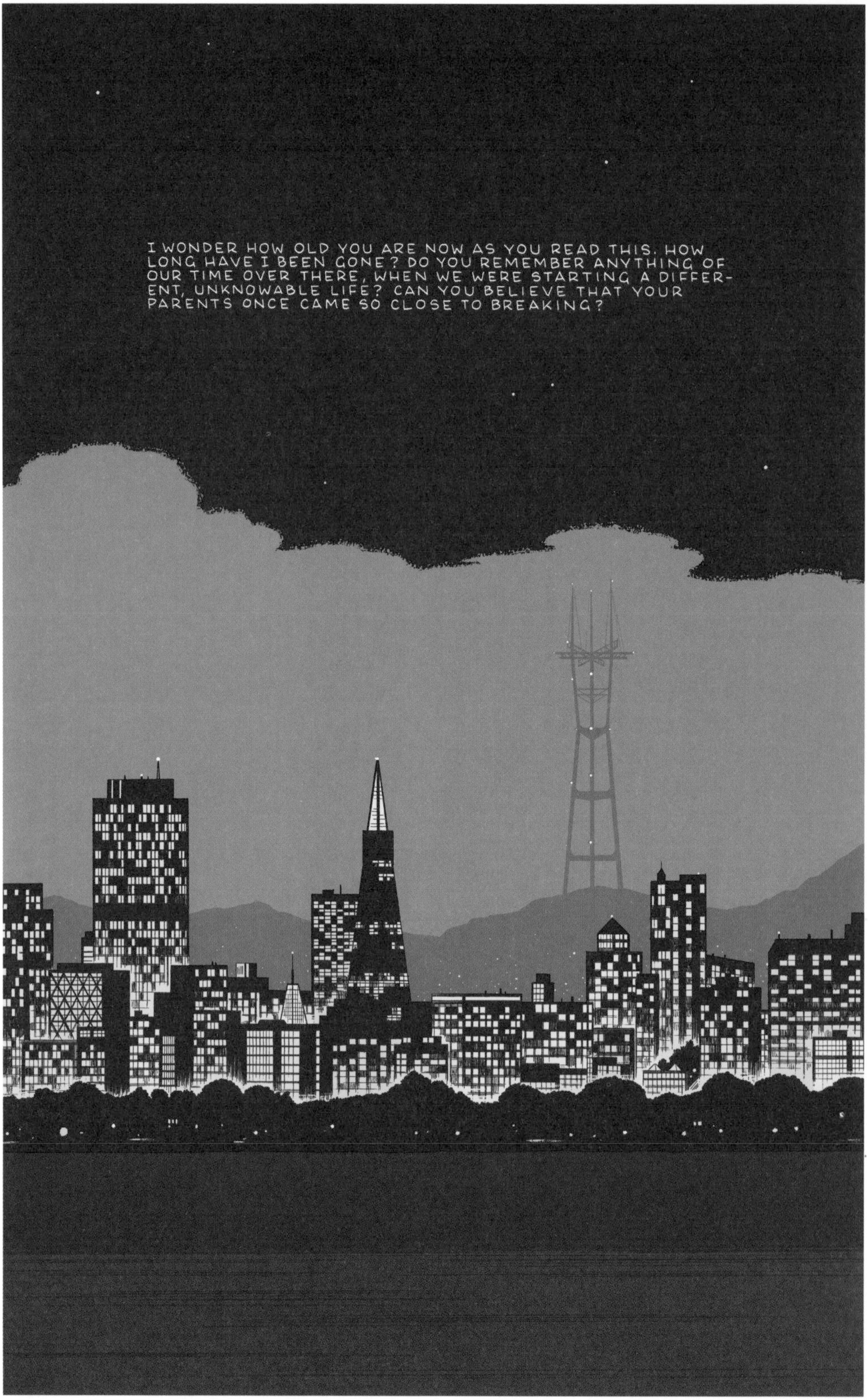
I WONDER HOW OLD YOU ARE NOW AS YOU READ THIS. HOW LONG HAVE I BEEN GONE? DO YOU REMEMBER ANYTHING OF OUR TIME OVER THERE, WHEN WE WERE STARTING A DIFFERENT, UNKNOWABLE LIFE? CAN YOU BELIEVE THAT YOUR PARENTS ONCE CAME SO CLOSE TO BREAKING?

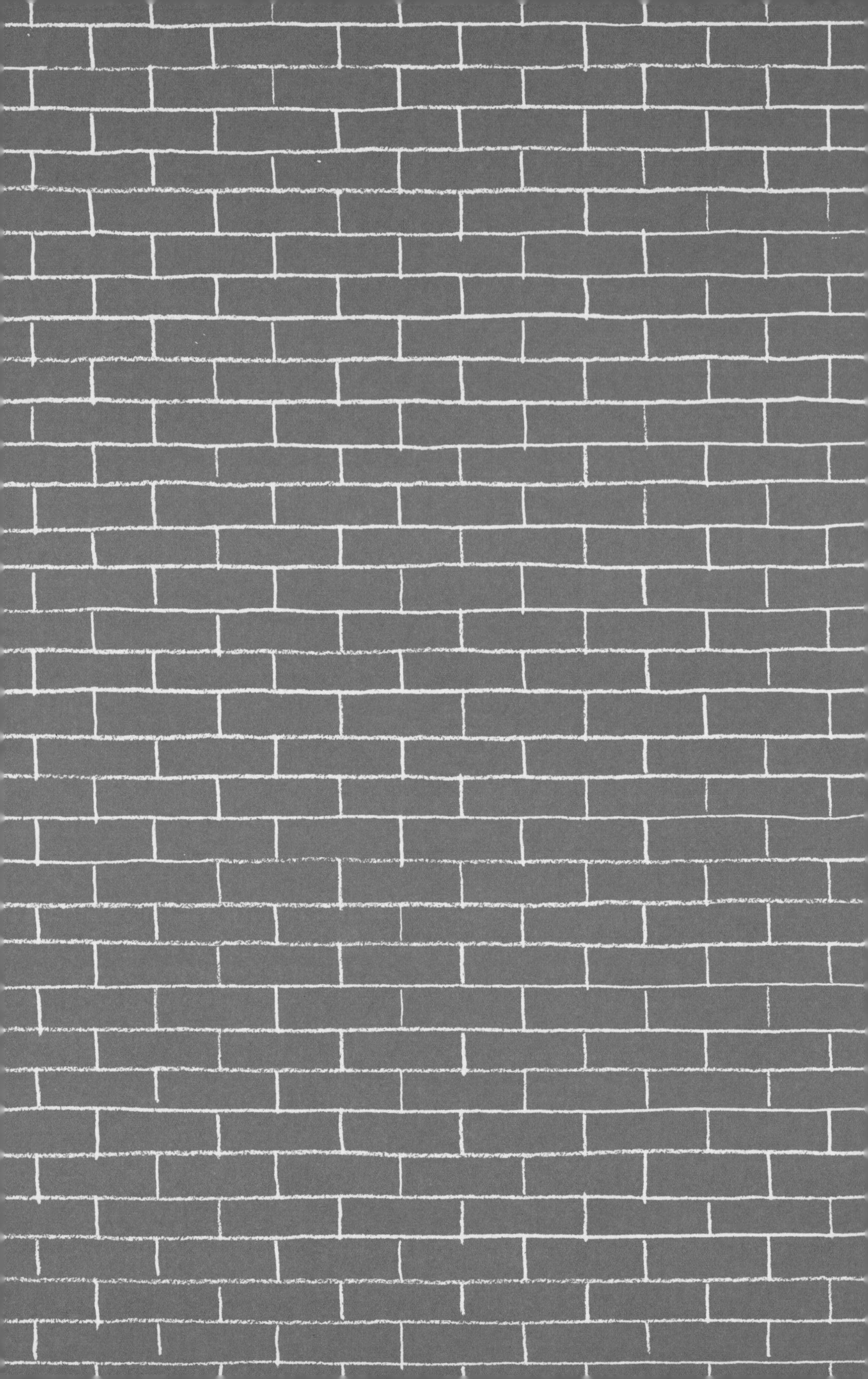

KILLING and DYING

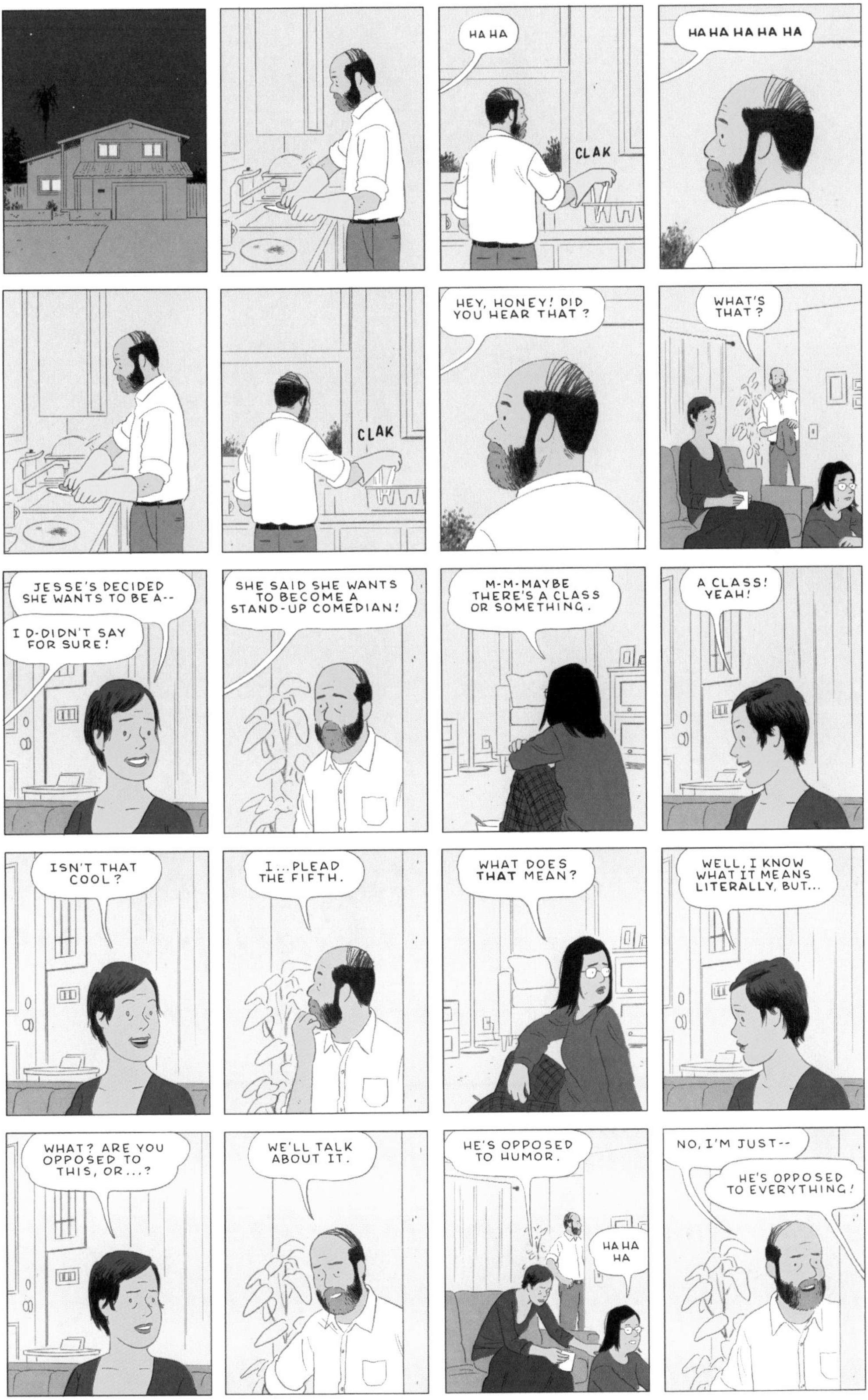
HA HA
CLAK
HA HA HA HA HA
CLAK
HEY, HONEY! DID YOU HEAR THAT?
WHAT'S THAT?
JESSE'S DECIDED SHE WANTS TO BE A--
I D-DIDN'T SAY FOR SURE!
SHE SAID SHE WANTS TO BECOME A STAND-UP COMEDIAN!
M-M-MAYBE THERE'S A CLASS OR SOMETHING.
A CLASS! YEAH!
ISN'T THAT COOL?
I...PLEAD THE FIFTH.
WHAT DOES THAT MEAN?
WELL, I KNOW WHAT IT MEANS LITERALLY, BUT...
WHAT? ARE YOU OPPOSED TO THIS, OR...?
WE'LL TALK ABOUT IT.
HE'S OPPOSED TO HUMOR.
HA HA HA
NO, I'M JUST--
HE'S OPPOSED TO EVERYTHING!

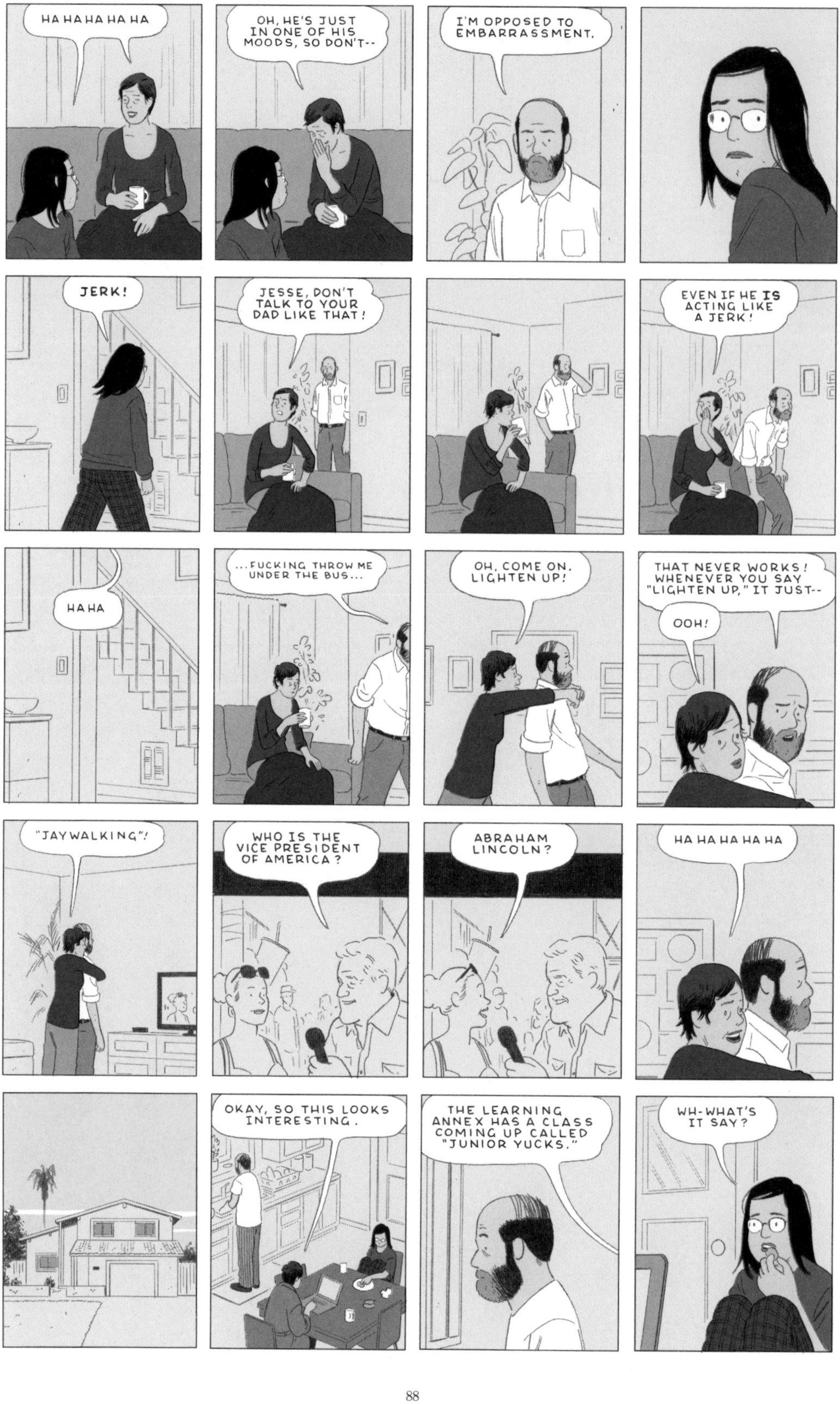
HA HA HA HA HA
OH, HE'S JUST IN ONE OF HIS MOODS, SO DON'T--
I'M OPPOSED TO EMBARRASSMENT.
JERK!
JESSE, DON'T TALK TO YOUR DAD LIKE THAT!
EVEN IF HE IS ACTING LIKE A JERK!
HA HA
...FUCKING THROW ME UNDER THE BUS...
OH, COME ON. LIGHTEN UP!
THAT NEVER WORKS! WHENEVER YOU SAY "LIGHTEN UP," IT JUST--
OOH!
"JAYWALKING"!
WHO IS THE VICE PRESIDENT OF AMERICA?
ABRAHAM LINCOLN?
HA HA HA HA HA
OKAY, SO THIS LOOKS INTERESTING.
THE LEARNING ANNEX HAS A CLASS COMING UP CALLED "JUNIOR YUCKS."
WH-WHAT'S IT SAY?

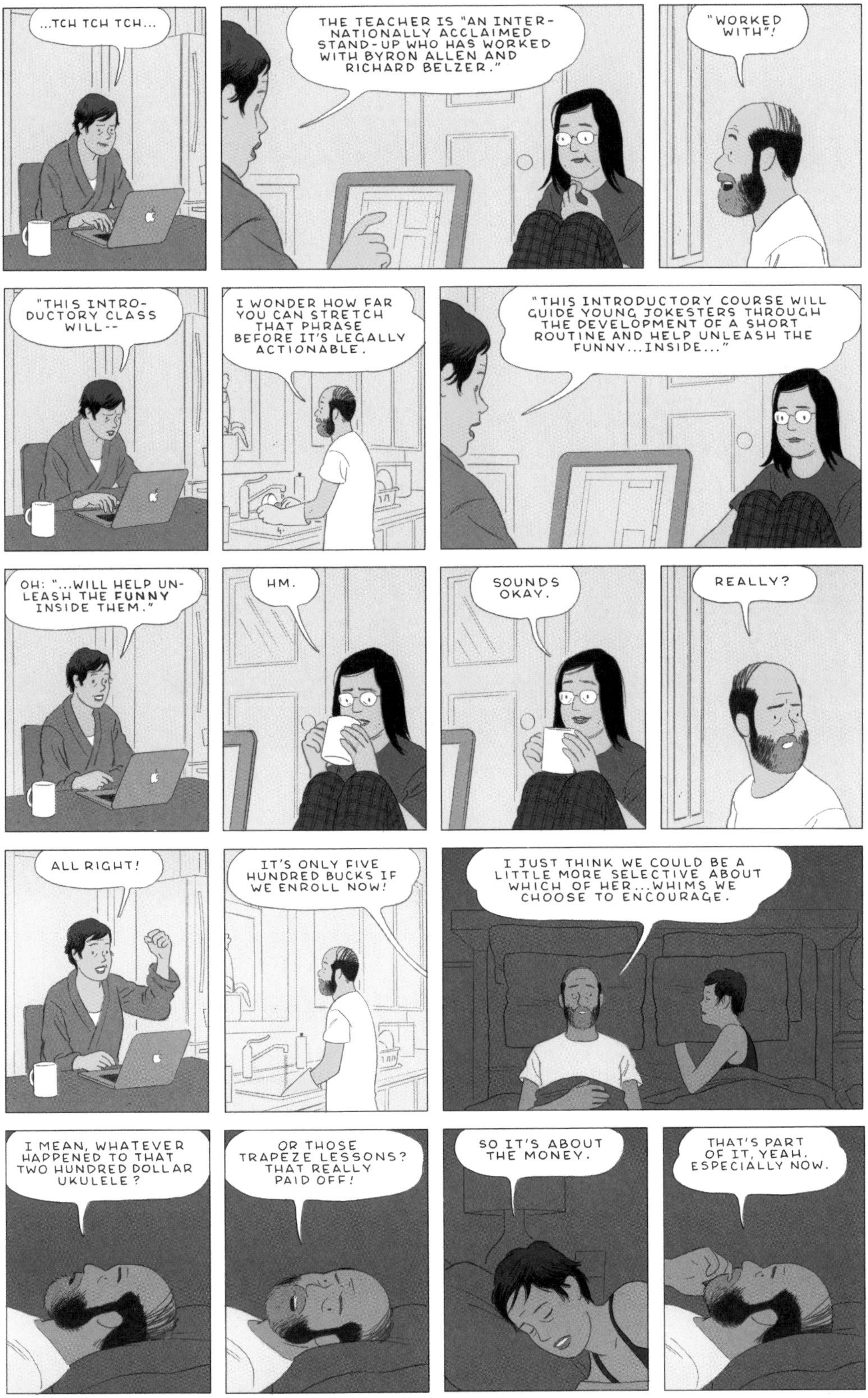
...TCH TCH TCH...
THE TEACHER IS "AN INTERNATIONALLY ACCLAIMED STAND-UP WHO HAS WORKED WITH BYRON ALLEN AND RICHARD BELZER."
"WORKED WITH"!
"THIS INTRODUCTORY CLASS WILL--
I WONDER HOW FAR YOU CAN STRETCH THAT PHRASE BEFORE IT'S LEGALLY ACTIONABLE.
"THIS INTRODUCTORY COURSE WILL GUIDE YOUNG JOKESTERS THROUGH THE DEVELOPMENT OF A SHORT ROUTINE AND HELP UNLEASH THE FUNNY...INSIDE..."
OH: "...WILL HELP UNLEASH THE **FUNNY** INSIDE THEM."
HM.
SOUNDS OKAY.
REALLY?
ALL RIGHT!
IT'S ONLY FIVE HUNDRED BUCKS IF WE ENROLL NOW!
I JUST THINK WE COULD BE A LITTLE MORE SELECTIVE ABOUT WHICH OF HER...WHIMS WE CHOOSE TO ENCOURAGE.
I MEAN, WHATEVER HAPPENED TO THAT TWO HUNDRED DOLLAR UKULELE?
OR THOSE TRAPEZE LESSONS? THAT REALLY PAID OFF!
SO IT'S ABOUT THE MONEY.
THAT'S PART OF IT, YEAH. ESPECIALLY NOW.

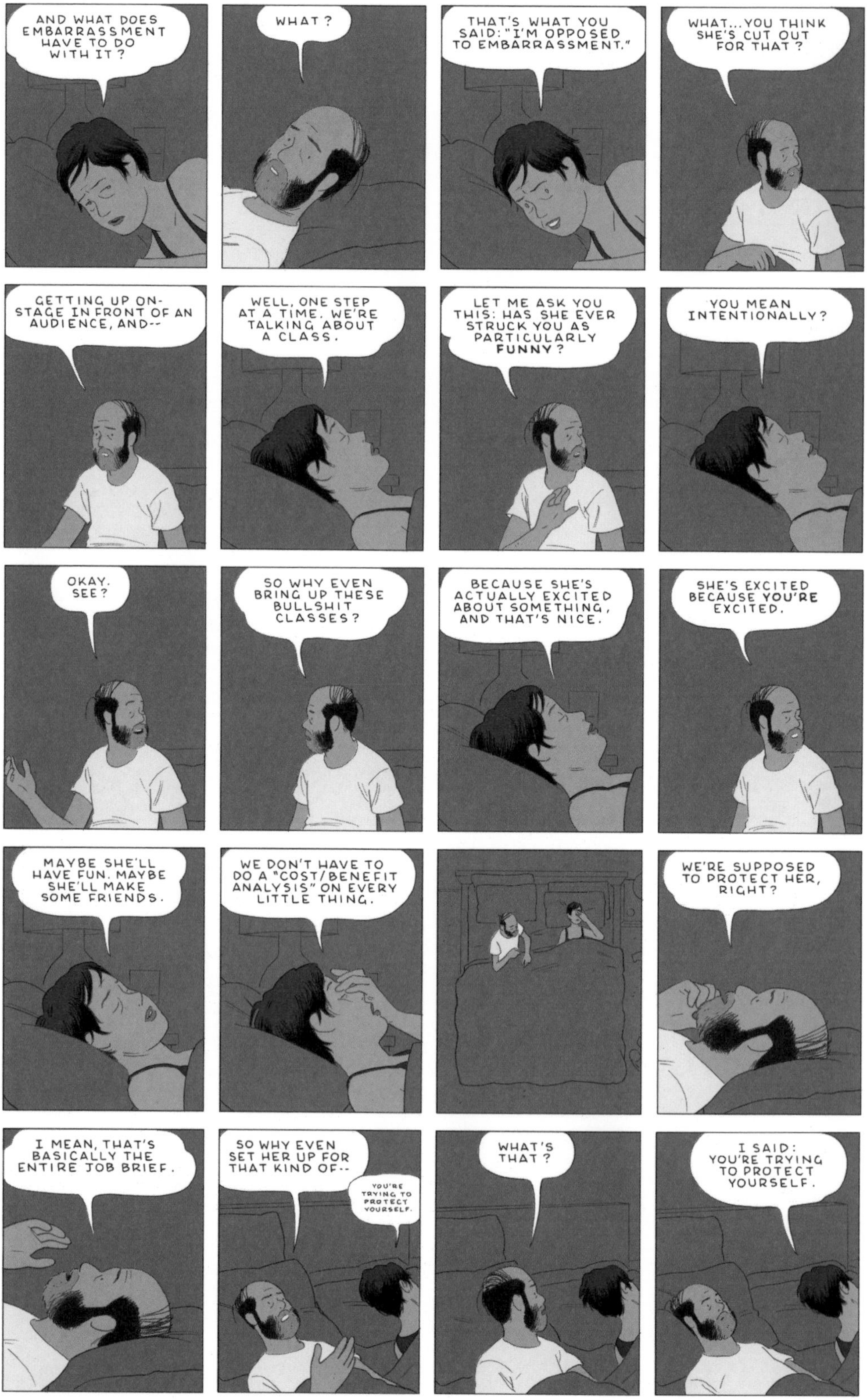
AND WHAT DOES EMBARRASSMENT HAVE TO DO WITH IT?
WHAT?
THAT'S WHAT YOU SAID: "I'M OPPOSED TO EMBARRASSMENT."
WHAT... YOU THINK SHE'S CUT OUT FOR THAT?
GETTING UP ON-STAGE IN FRONT OF AN AUDIENCE, AND--
WELL, ONE STEP AT A TIME. WE'RE TALKING ABOUT A CLASS.
LET ME ASK YOU THIS: HAS SHE EVER STRUCK YOU AS PARTICULARLY **FUNNY**?
YOU MEAN INTENTIONALLY?
OKAY. SEE?
SO WHY EVEN BRING UP THESE BULLSHIT CLASSES?
BECAUSE SHE'S ACTUALLY EXCITED ABOUT SOMETHING, AND THAT'S NICE.
SHE'S EXCITED BECAUSE **YOU'RE** EXCITED.
MAYBE SHE'LL HAVE FUN. MAYBE SHE'LL MAKE SOME FRIENDS.
WE DON'T HAVE TO DO A "COST/BENEFIT ANALYSIS" ON EVERY LITTLE THING.
WE'RE SUPPOSED TO PROTECT HER, RIGHT?
I MEAN, THAT'S BASICALLY THE ENTIRE JOB BRIEF.
SO WHY EVEN SET HER UP FOR THAT KIND OF--
YOU'RE TRYING TO PROTECT YOURSELF.
WHAT'S THAT?
I SAID: YOU'RE TRYING TO PROTECT YOURSELF.

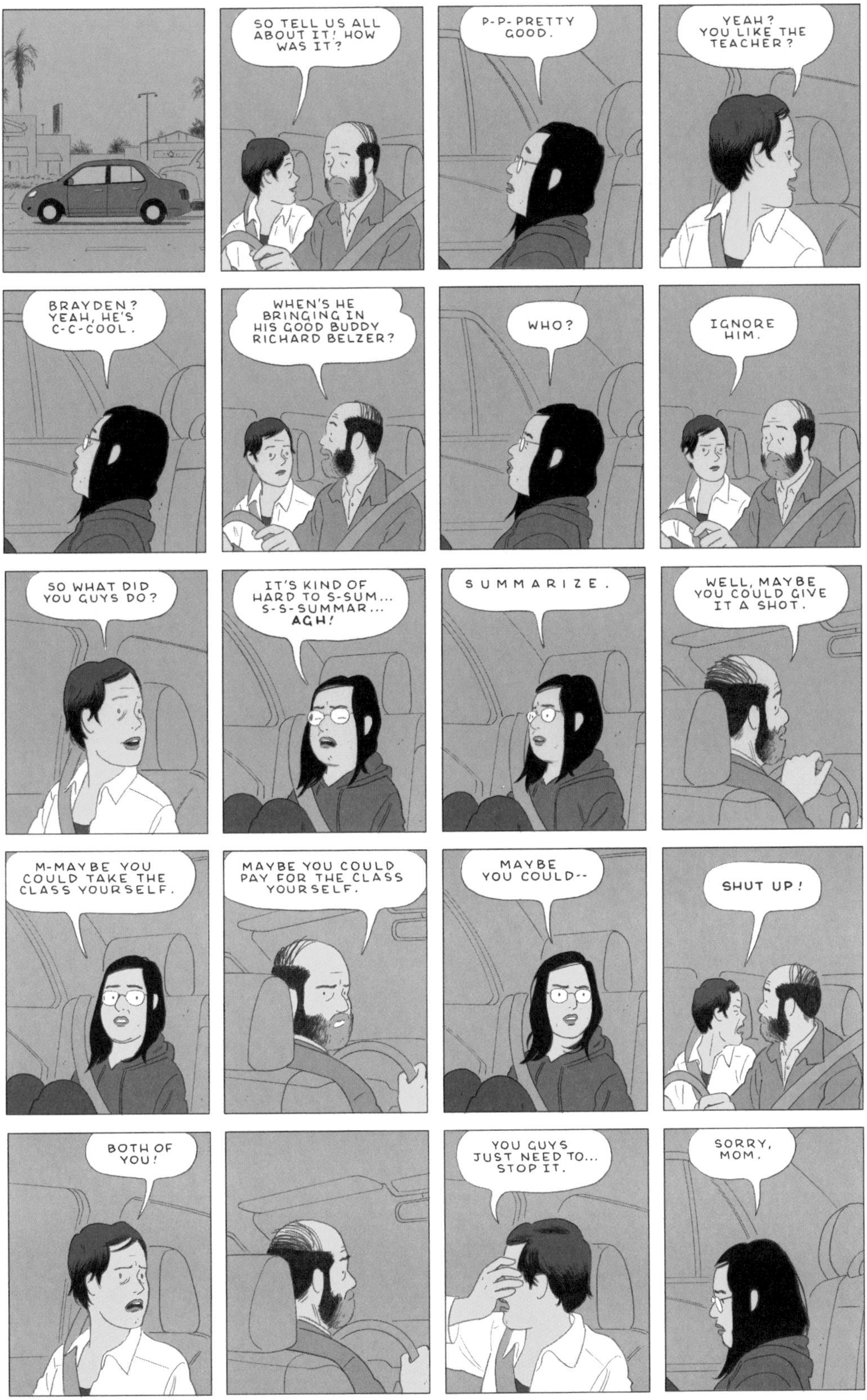
SO TELL US ALL ABOUT IT! HOW WAS IT?
P-P-PRETTY GOOD.
YEAH? YOU LIKE THE TEACHER?
BRAYDEN? YEAH, HE'S C-C-COOL.
WHEN'S HE BRINGING IN HIS GOOD BUDDY RICHARD BELZER?
WHO?
IGNORE HIM.
SO WHAT DID YOU GUYS DO?
IT'S KIND OF HARD TO S-SUM... S-S-SUMMAR... AGH!
SUMMARIZE.
WELL, MAYBE YOU COULD GIVE IT A SHOT.
M-MAYBE YOU COULD TAKE THE CLASS YOURSELF.
MAYBE YOU COULD PAY FOR THE CLASS YOURSELF.
MAYBE YOU COULD--
SHUT UP!
BOTH OF YOU!
YOU GUYS JUST NEED TO... STOP IT.
SORRY, MOM.

JUST A SEC!

OKAY.

THANK YOU!

CLAP CLAP CLAP CL

THANK YOU VERY M-M-MUCH!

CLAP CLAP AP CLAP

CLAP CLA CLAP C

UH... OKAY.

UM, SO I STARTED HIGH SCHOOL RE- CENTLY, AND I'M ALREADY LEARNING SO MUCH.

YEAH, I'VE READ SOME GREAT BOOKS, STARTED SPEAKING SPANISH, AND FIGURED OUT THAT MOST PEOPLE ARE DUMB ASSHOLES!

HEH HEH

HA HA HA

ACTUALLY, MY SCHOOL'S NOT SO BAD.

THEY'RE STARTING A "SPECIAL EDUCATION" PROGRAM NEXT YEAR, AND I THINK THAT'S WONDERFUL.

BECAUSE THAT MEANS THERE'LL BE TWENTY KIDS WHO GET THE SHIT BULLIED OUT OF THEM BEFORE ME!

AW, HONEY...

HA HA HA HA HA

CLAP CLA CLAP

CLAP CLA

S-S-SO THAT'S WHAT I HAVE SO FAR.

CLAP CLAP

CLAP CLAP CL CLAP

NICE JOB, HONEY.

YEAH!

HEH HEH HEH

GUESS I DON'T S-S-SUCK AT EVERYTHING.

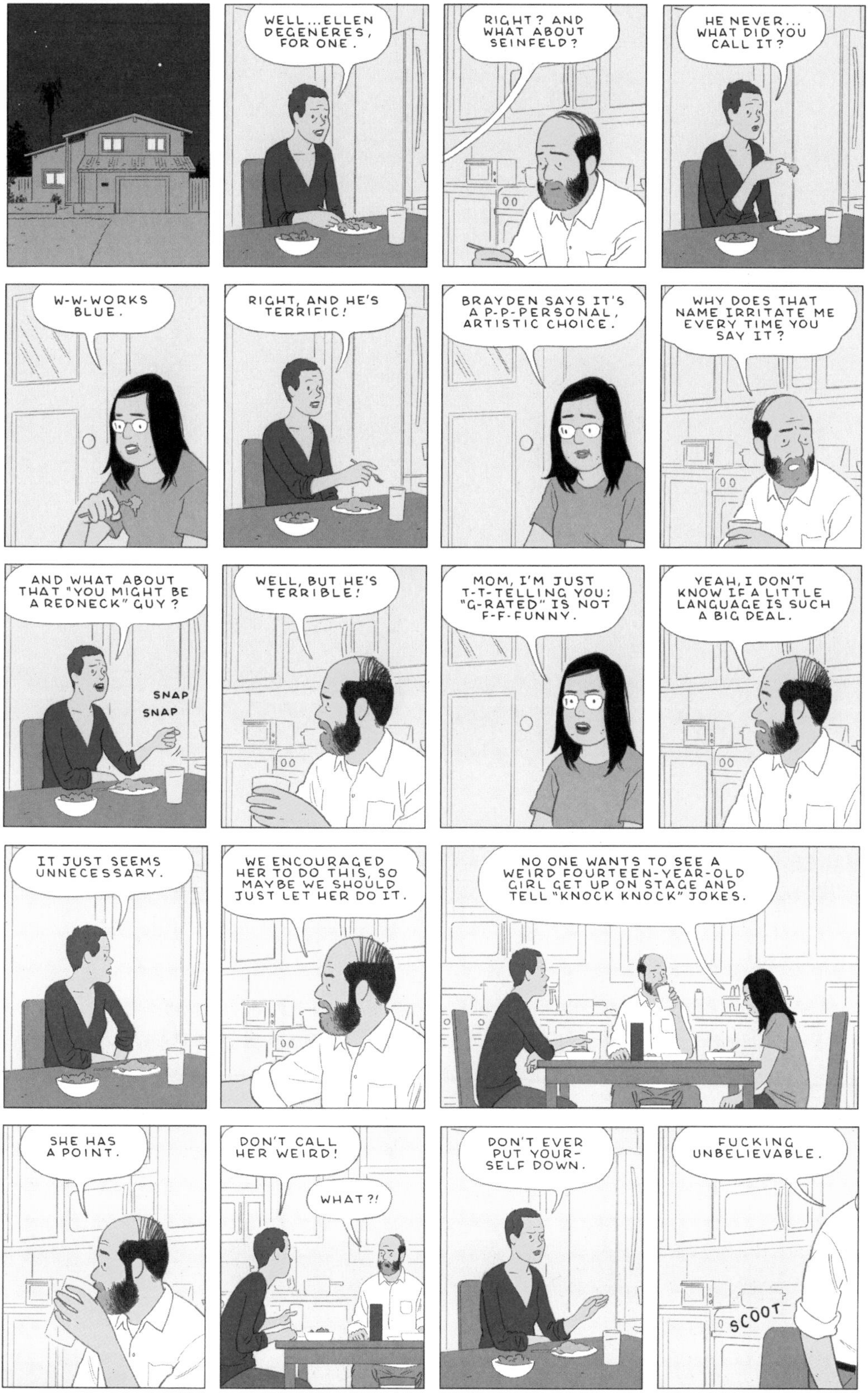
WELL...ELLEN DEGENERES, FOR ONE.
RIGHT? AND WHAT ABOUT SEINFELD?
HE NEVER... WHAT DID YOU CALL IT?
W-W-WORKS BLUE.
RIGHT, AND HE'S TERRIFIC!
BRAYDEN SAYS IT'S A P-P-PERSONAL, ARTISTIC CHOICE.
WHY DOES THAT NAME IRRITATE ME EVERY TIME YOU SAY IT?
AND WHAT ABOUT THAT "YOU MIGHT BE A REDNECK" GUY?
SNAP
SNAP
WELL, BUT HE'S TERRIBLE!
MOM, I'M JUST T-T-TELLING YOU: "G-RATED" IS NOT F-F-FUNNY.
YEAH, I DON'T KNOW IF A LITTLE LANGUAGE IS SUCH A BIG DEAL.
IT JUST SEEMS UNNECESSARY.
WE ENCOURAGED HER TO DO THIS, SO MAYBE WE SHOULD JUST LET HER DO IT.
NO ONE WANTS TO SEE A WEIRD FOURTEEN-YEAR-OLD GIRL GET UP ON STAGE AND TELL "KNOCK KNOCK" JOKES.
SHE HAS A POINT.
DON'T CALL HER WEIRD!
WHAT?!
DON'T EVER PUT YOURSELF DOWN.
FUCKING UNBELIEVABLE.
SCOOT

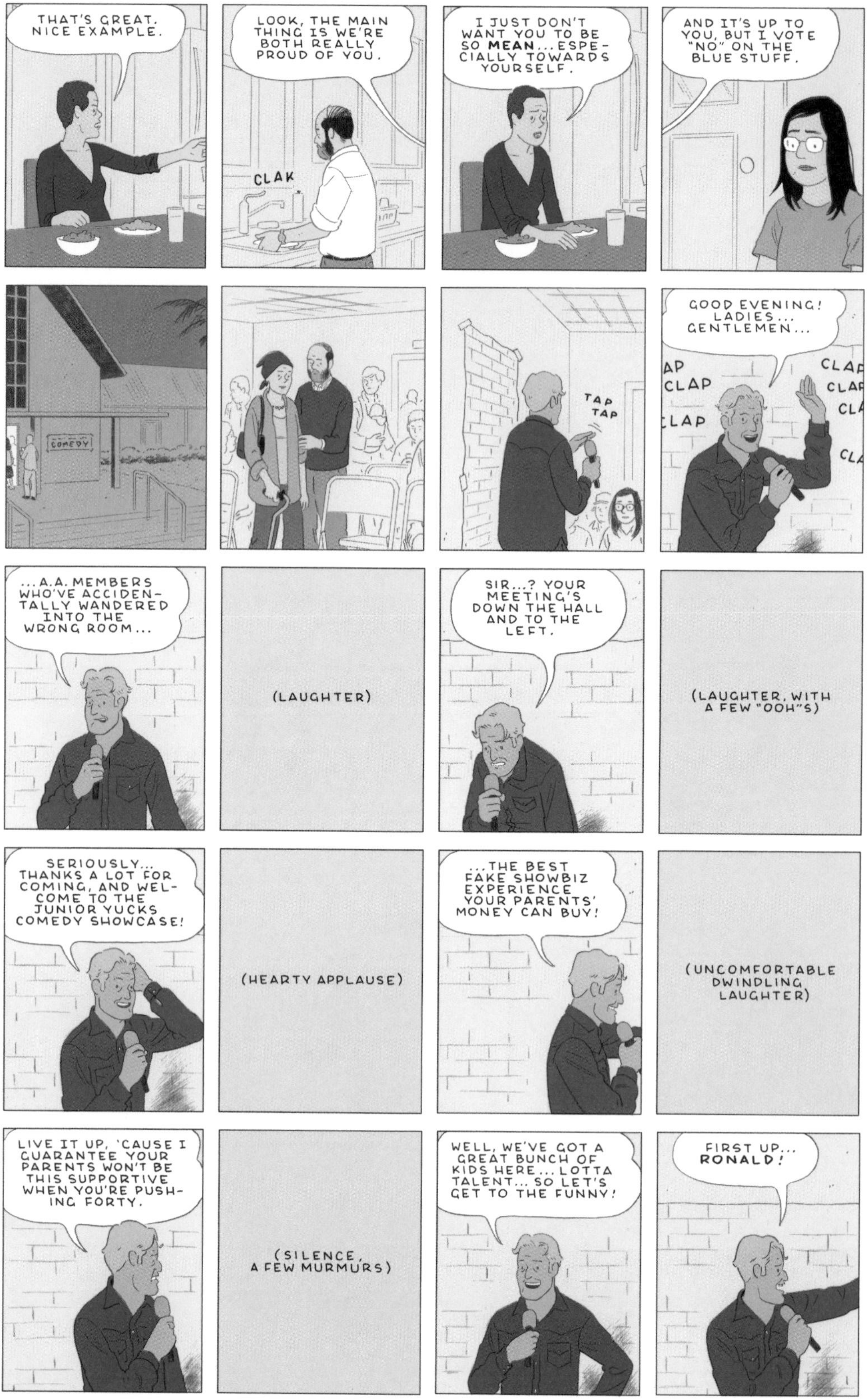
THAT'S GREAT. NICE EXAMPLE.
LOOK, THE MAIN THING IS WE'RE BOTH REALLY PROUD OF YOU.
CLAK
I JUST DON'T WANT YOU TO BE SO **MEAN**... ESPECIALLY TOWARDS YOURSELF.
AND IT'S UP TO YOU, BUT I VOTE "NO" ON THE BLUE STUFF.
COMEDY
TAP TAP
GOOD EVENING! LADIES... GENTLEMEN...
CLAP CLAP CLAP
...A.A. MEMBERS WHO'VE ACCIDENTALLY WANDERED INTO THE WRONG ROOM...
(LAUGHTER)
SIR...? YOUR MEETING'S DOWN THE HALL AND TO THE LEFT.
(LAUGHTER, WITH A FEW "OOH"S)
SERIOUSLY... THANKS A LOT FOR COMING, AND WELCOME TO THE JUNIOR YUCKS COMEDY SHOWCASE!
(HEARTY APPLAUSE)
...THE BEST FAKE SHOWBIZ EXPERIENCE YOUR PARENTS' MONEY CAN BUY!
(UNCOMFORTABLE DWINDLING LAUGHTER)
LIVE IT UP, 'CAUSE I GUARANTEE YOUR PARENTS WON'T BE THIS SUPPORTIVE WHEN YOU'RE PUSHING FORTY.
(SILENCE, A FEW MURMURS)
WELL, WE'VE GOT A GREAT BUNCH OF KIDS HERE... LOTTA TALENT... SO LET'S GET TO THE FUNNY!
FIRST UP... **RONALD**!

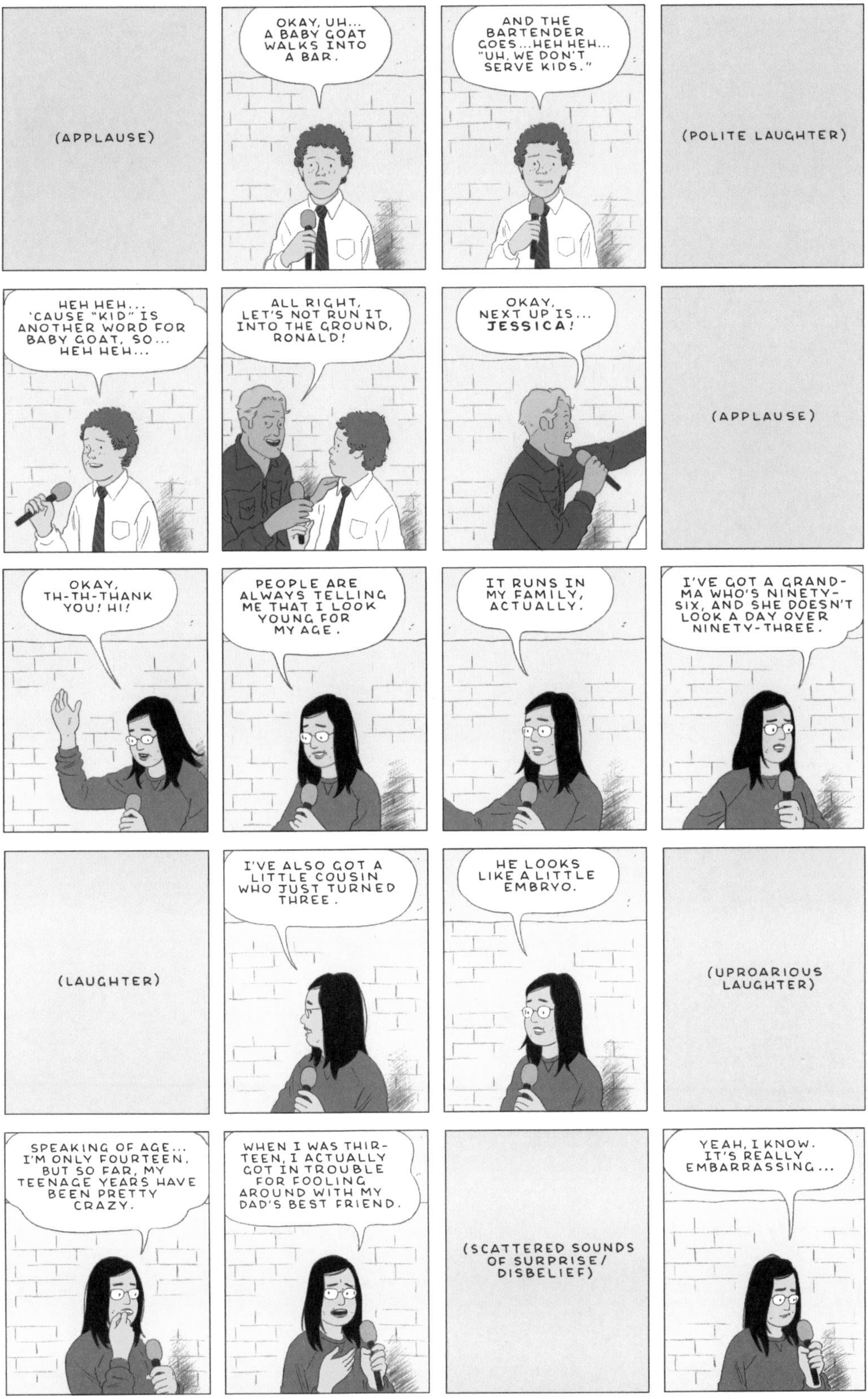
(APPLAUSE)
OKAY, UH... A BABY GOAT WALKS INTO A BAR.
AND THE BARTENDER GOES...HEH HEH... "UH, WE DON'T SERVE KIDS."
(POLITE LAUGHTER)
HEH HEH... 'CAUSE "KID" IS ANOTHER WORD FOR BABY GOAT, SO... HEH HEH...
ALL RIGHT, LET'S NOT RUN IT INTO THE GROUND, RONALD!
OKAY, NEXT UP IS... JESSICA!
(APPLAUSE)
OKAY, TH-TH-THANK YOU! HI!
PEOPLE ARE ALWAYS TELLING ME THAT I LOOK YOUNG FOR MY AGE.
IT RUNS IN MY FAMILY, ACTUALLY.
I'VE GOT A GRAND-MA WHO'S NINETY-SIX, AND SHE DOESN'T LOOK A DAY OVER NINETY-THREE.
(LAUGHTER)
I'VE ALSO GOT A LITTLE COUSIN WHO JUST TURNED THREE.
HE LOOKS LIKE A LITTLE EMBRYO.
(UPROARIOUS LAUGHTER)
SPEAKING OF AGE... I'M ONLY FOURTEEN, BUT SO FAR, MY TEENAGE YEARS HAVE BEEN PRETTY CRAZY.
WHEN I WAS THIR-TEEN, I ACTUALLY GOT IN TROUBLE FOR FOOLING AROUND WITH MY DAD'S BEST FRIEND.
(SCATTERED SOUNDS OF SURPRISE/ DISBELIEF)
YEAH, I KNOW. IT'S REALLY EMBARRASSING...

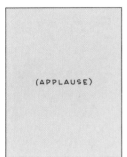

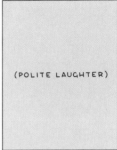

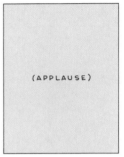

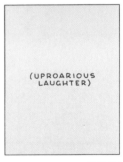

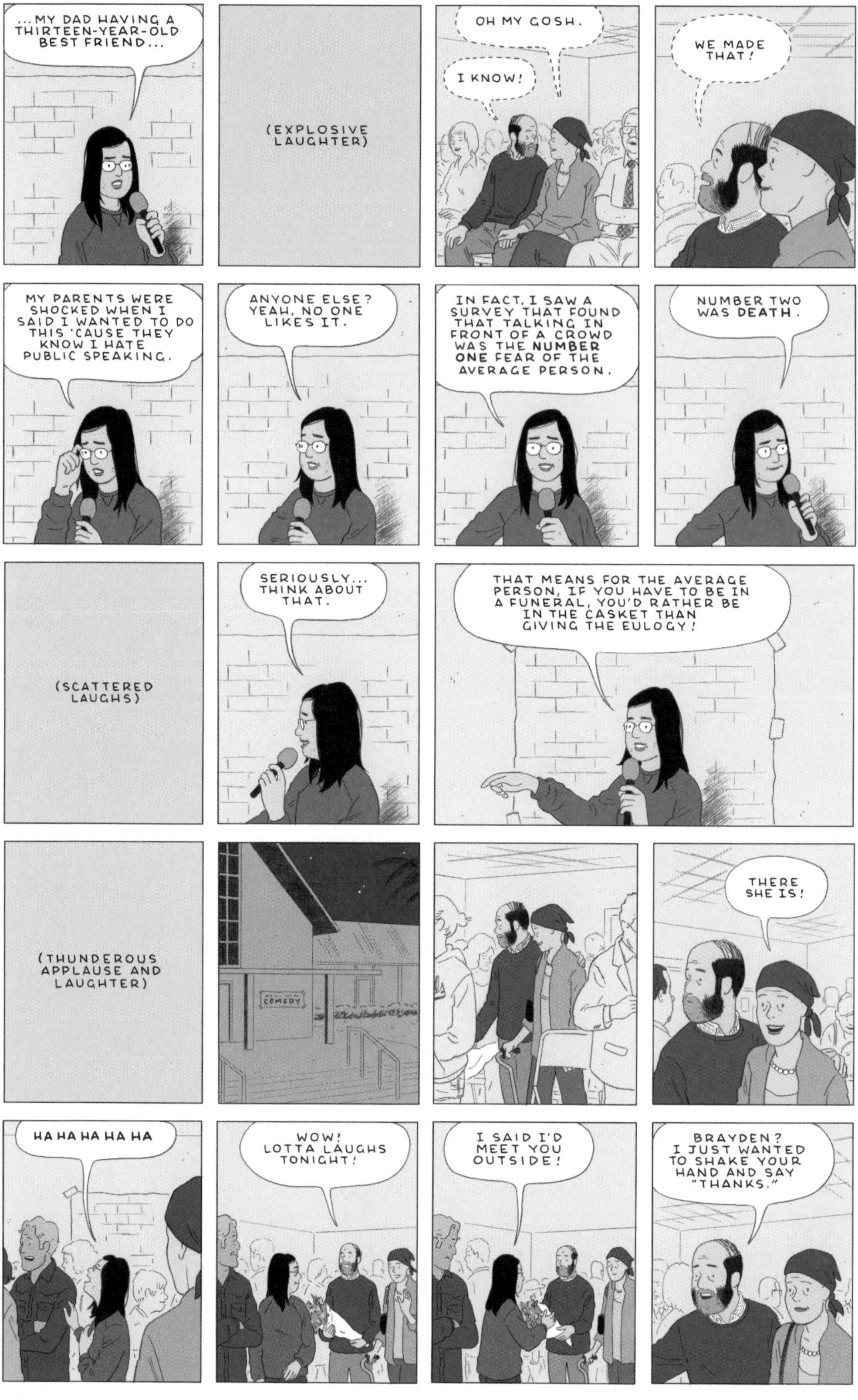
...MY DAD HAVING A THIRTEEN-YEAR-OLD BEST FRIEND...
(EXPLOSIVE LAUGHTER)
OH MY GOSH.
I KNOW!
WE MADE THAT!
MY PARENTS WERE SHOCKED WHEN I SAID I WANTED TO DO THIS 'CAUSE THEY KNOW I HATE PUBLIC SPEAKING.
ANYONE ELSE? YEAH, NO ONE LIKES IT.
IN FACT, I SAW A SURVEY THAT FOUND THAT TALKING IN FRONT OF A CROWD WAS THE **NUMBER ONE** FEAR OF THE AVERAGE PERSON.
NUMBER TWO WAS **DEATH**.
(SCATTERED LAUGHS)
SERIOUSLY... THINK ABOUT THAT.
THAT MEANS FOR THE AVERAGE PERSON, IF YOU HAVE TO BE IN A FUNERAL, YOU'D RATHER BE IN THE CASKET THAN GIVING THE EULOGY!
(THUNDEROUS APPLAUSE AND LAUGHTER)
COMEDY
THERE SHE IS!
HA HA HA HA HA
WOW! LOTTA LAUGHS TONIGHT!
I SAID I'D MEET YOU OUTSIDE!
BRAYDEN? I JUST WANTED TO SHAKE YOUR HAND AND SAY "THANKS."

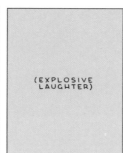

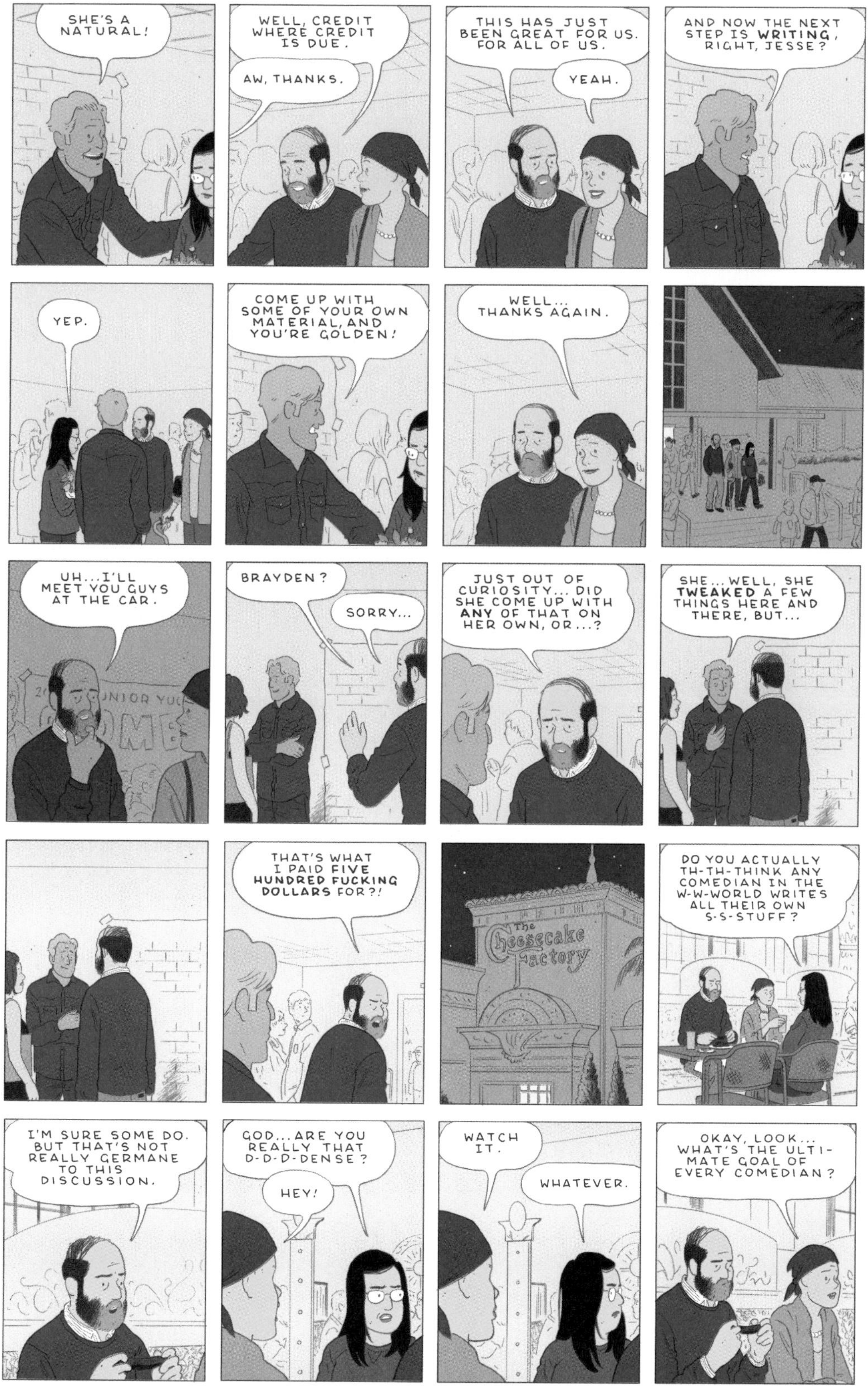
SHE'S A NATURAL!
WELL, CREDIT WHERE CREDIT IS DUE.
AW, THANKS.
THIS HAS JUST BEEN GREAT FOR US. FOR ALL OF US.
YEAH.
AND NOW THE NEXT STEP IS **WRITING**, RIGHT, JESSE?
YEP.
COME UP WITH SOME OF YOUR OWN MATERIAL, AND YOU'RE GOLDEN!
WELL... THANKS AGAIN.
UH... I'LL MEET YOU GUYS AT THE CAR.
BRAYDEN?
SORRY...
JUST OUT OF CURIOSITY... DID SHE COME UP WITH **ANY** OF THAT ON HER OWN, OR...?
SHE... WELL, SHE **TWEAKED** A FEW THINGS HERE AND THERE, BUT...
THAT'S WHAT I PAID **FIVE HUNDRED FUCKING DOLLARS** FOR?!
The Cheesecake Factory
DO YOU ACTUALLY TH-TH-THINK ANY COMEDIAN IN THE W-W-WORLD WRITES ALL THEIR OWN S-S-STUFF?
I'M SURE SOME DO. BUT THAT'S NOT REALLY GERMANE TO THIS DISCUSSION.
GOD... ARE YOU REALLY THAT D-D-D-DENSE?
HEY!
WATCH IT.
WHATEVER.
OKAY, LOOK... WHAT'S THE ULTI-MATE GOAL OF EVERY COMEDIAN?

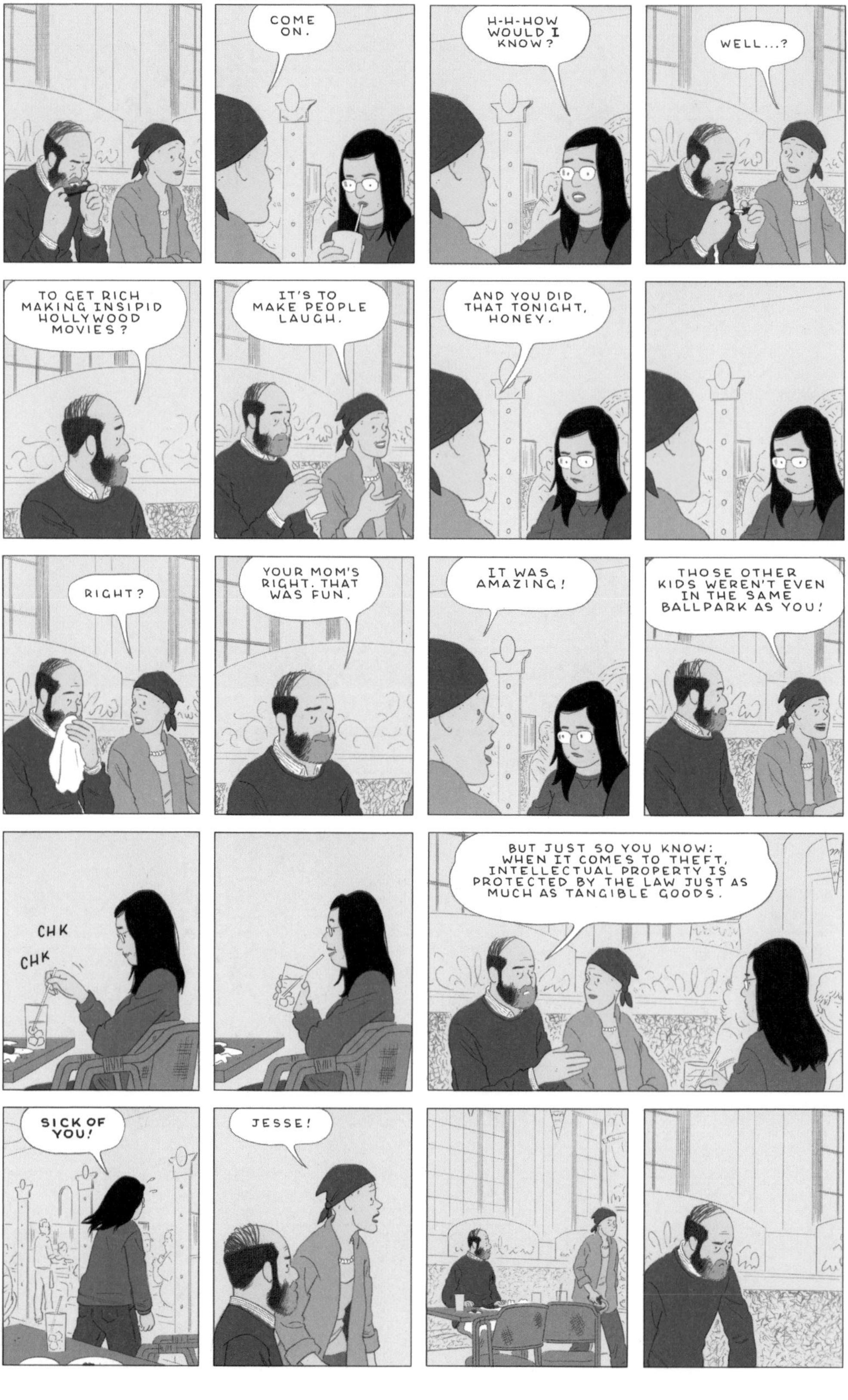
COME ON.
H-H-HOW WOULD I KNOW?
WELL...?
TO GET RICH MAKING INSIPID HOLLYWOOD MOVIES?
IT'S TO MAKE PEOPLE LAUGH.
AND YOU DID THAT TONIGHT, HONEY.
RIGHT?
YOUR MOM'S RIGHT. THAT WAS FUN.
IT WAS AMAZING!
THOSE OTHER KIDS WEREN'T EVEN IN THE SAME BALLPARK AS YOU!
CHK
CHK
BUT JUST SO YOU KNOW: WHEN IT COMES TO THEFT, INTELLECTUAL PROPERTY IS PROTECTED BY THE LAW JUST AS MUCH AS TANGIBLE GOODS.
SICK OF YOU!
JESSE!

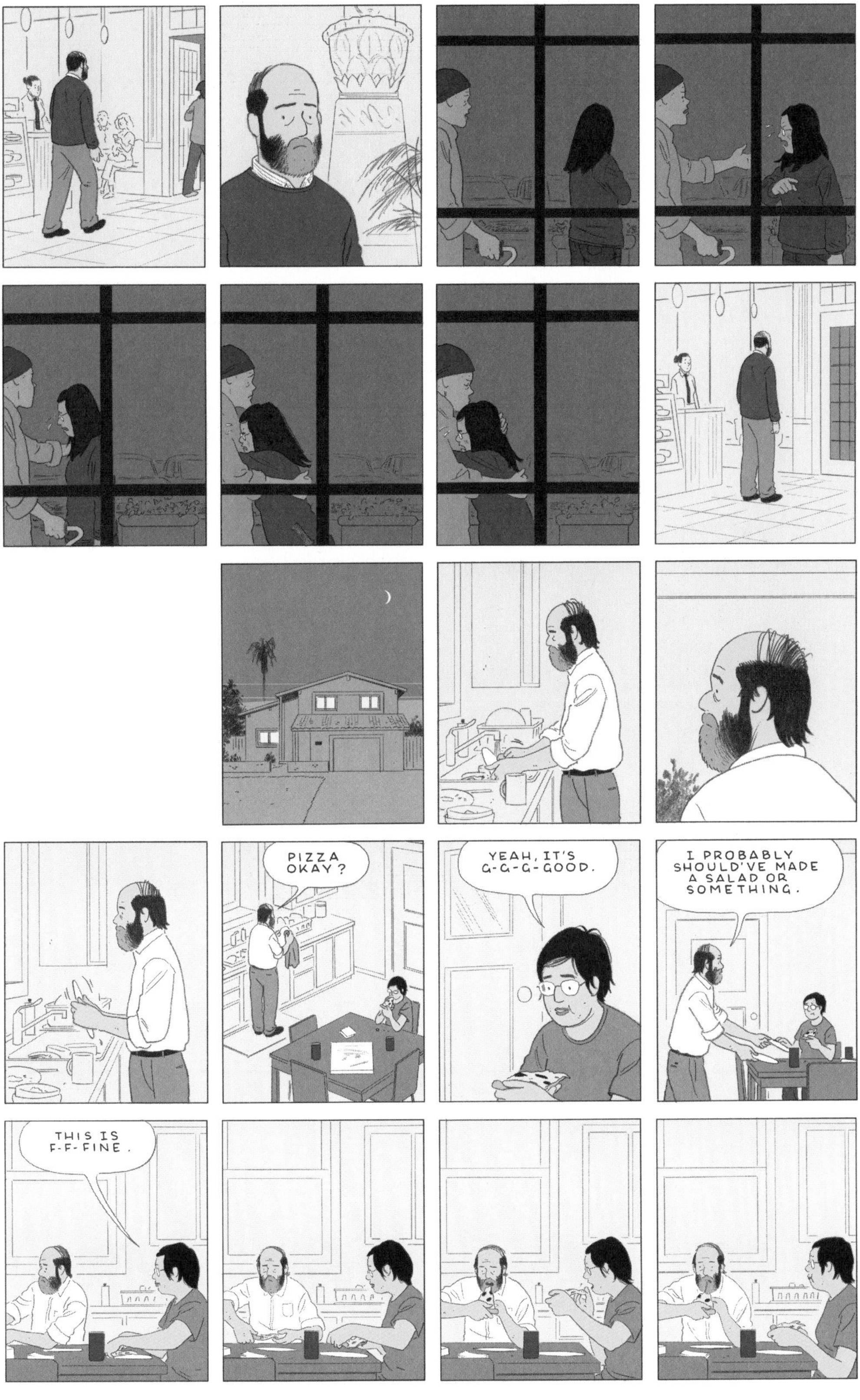
PIZZA OKAY?
YEAH, IT'S G-G-G-GOOD.
I PROBABLY SHOULD'VE MADE A SALAD OR SOMETHING.
THIS IS F-F-FINE.

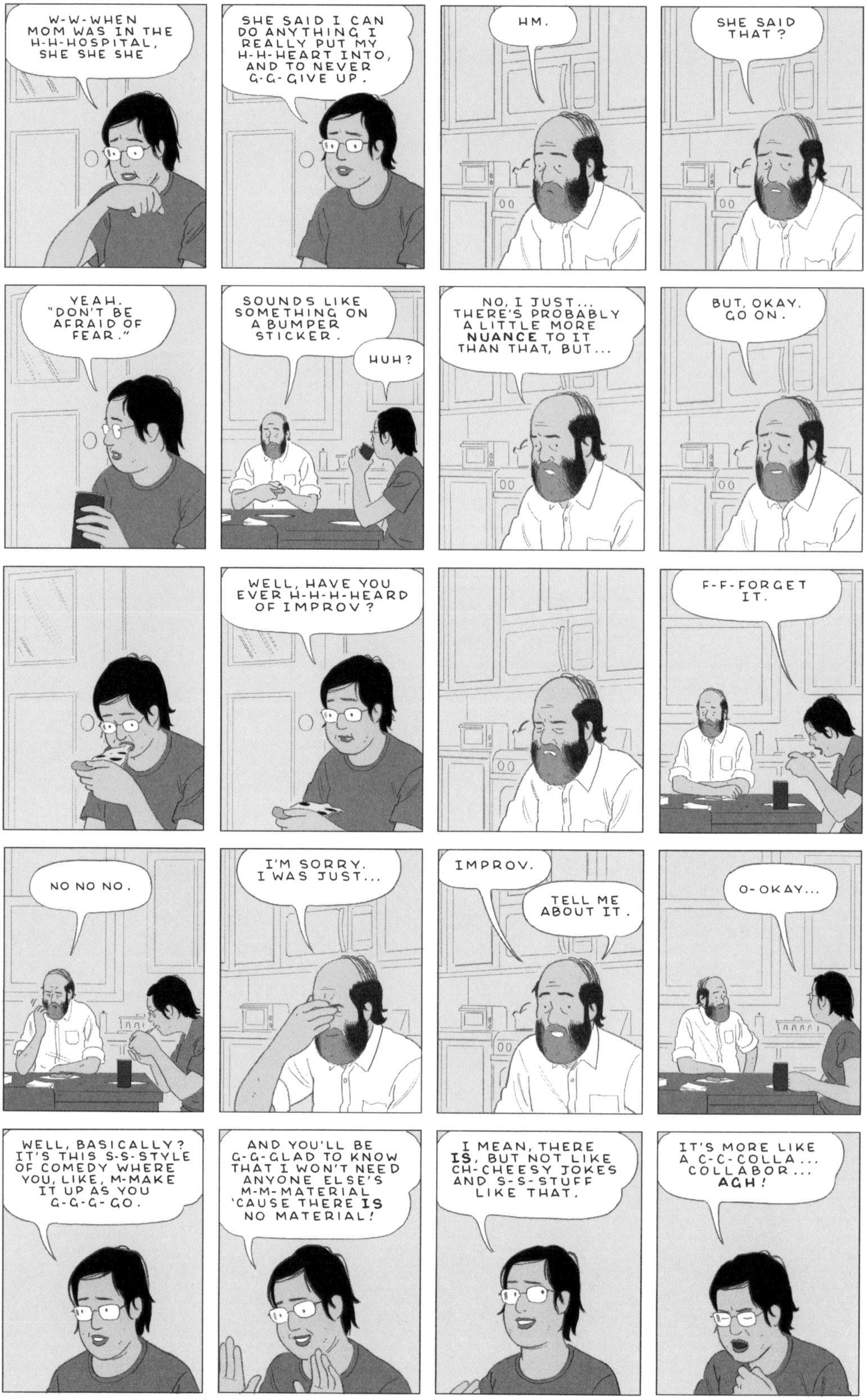
W-W-WHEN MOM WAS IN THE H-H-HOSPITAL, SHE SHE SHE
SHE SAID I CAN DO ANYTHING I REALLY PUT MY H-H-HEART INTO, AND TO NEVER G-G-GIVE UP.
HM.
SHE SAID THAT?
YEAH. "DON'T BE AFRAID OF FEAR."
SOUNDS LIKE SOMETHING ON A BUMPER STICKER.
HUH?
NO, I JUST... THERE'S PROBABLY A LITTLE MORE **NUANCE** TO IT THAN THAT, BUT...
BUT, OKAY. GO ON.
WELL, HAVE YOU EVER H-H-H-HEARD OF IMPROV?
F-F-FORGET IT.
NO NO NO.
I'M SORRY. I WAS JUST...
IMPROV.
TELL ME ABOUT IT.
O-OKAY...
WELL, BASICALLY? IT'S THIS S-S-STYLE OF COMEDY WHERE YOU, LIKE, M-MAKE IT UP AS YOU G-G-G-GO.
AND YOU'LL BE G-G-GLAD TO KNOW THAT I WON'T NEED ANYONE ELSE'S M-M-MATERIAL 'CAUSE THERE **IS** NO MATERIAL!
I MEAN, THERE **IS**, BUT NOT LIKE CH-CHEESY JOKES AND S-S-STUFF LIKE THAT.
IT'S MORE LIKE A C-C-COLLA... COLLABOR... **AGH!**

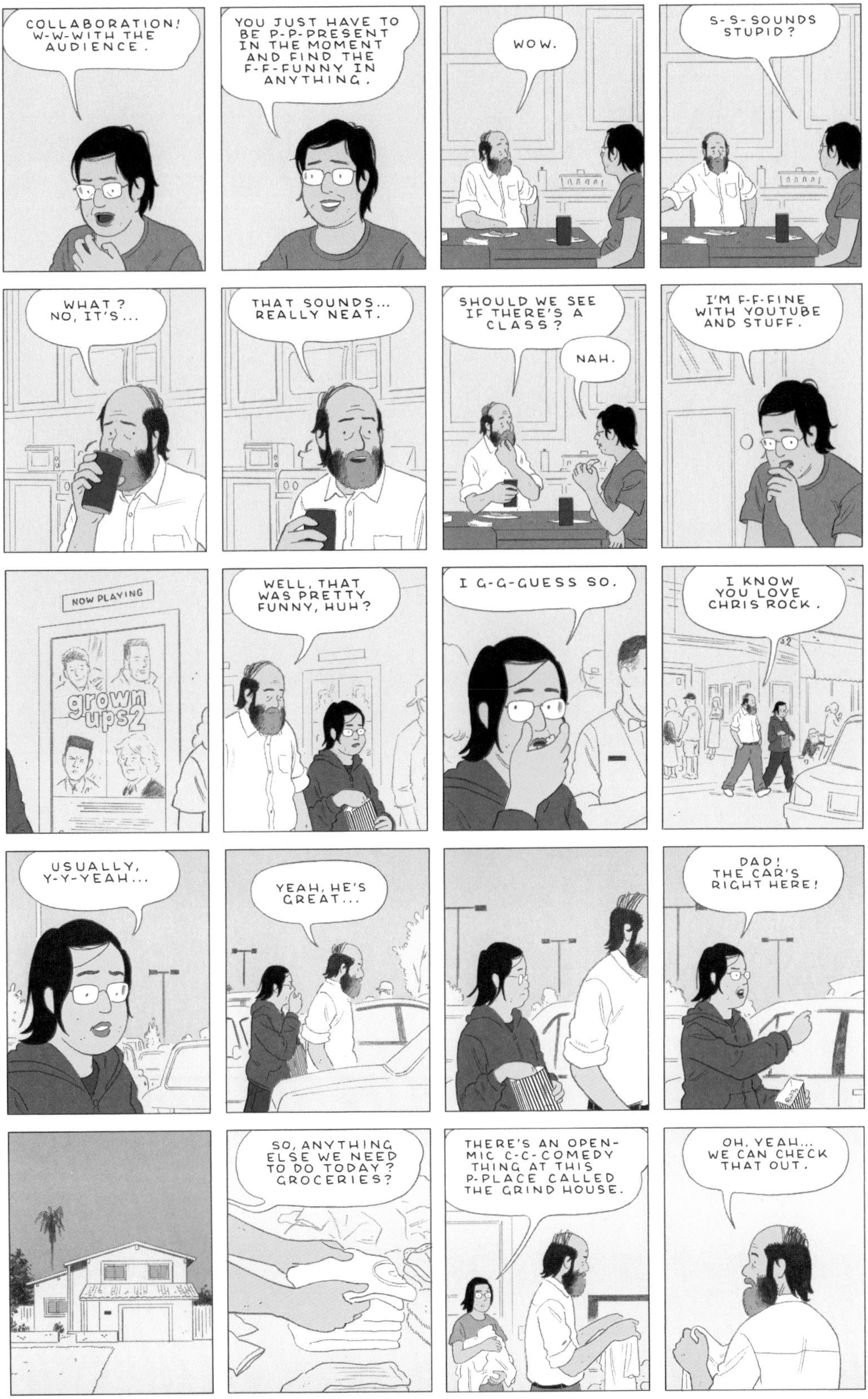
COLLABORATION! W-W-WITH THE AUDIENCE.
YOU JUST HAVE TO BE P-P-PRESENT IN THE MOMENT AND FIND THE F-F-FUNNY IN ANYTHING.
WOW.
S-S-SOUNDS STUPID?
WHAT? NO, IT'S...
THAT SOUNDS... REALLY NEAT.
SHOULD WE SEE IF THERE'S A CLASS?
NAH.
I'M F-F-FINE WITH YOUTUBE AND STUFF.
NOW PLAYING
grown ups2
WELL, THAT WAS PRETTY FUNNY, HUH?
I G-G-GUESS SO.
I KNOW YOU LOVE CHRIS ROCK.
USUALLY, Y-Y-YEAH...
YEAH, HE'S GREAT...
DAD! THE CAR'S RIGHT HERE!
SO, ANYTHING ELSE WE NEED TO DO TODAY? GROCERIES?
THERE'S AN OPEN-MIC C-C-COMEDY THING AT THIS P-PLACE CALLED THE GRIND HOUSE.
OH, YEAH... WE CAN CHECK THAT OUT.

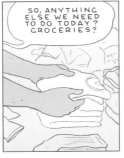

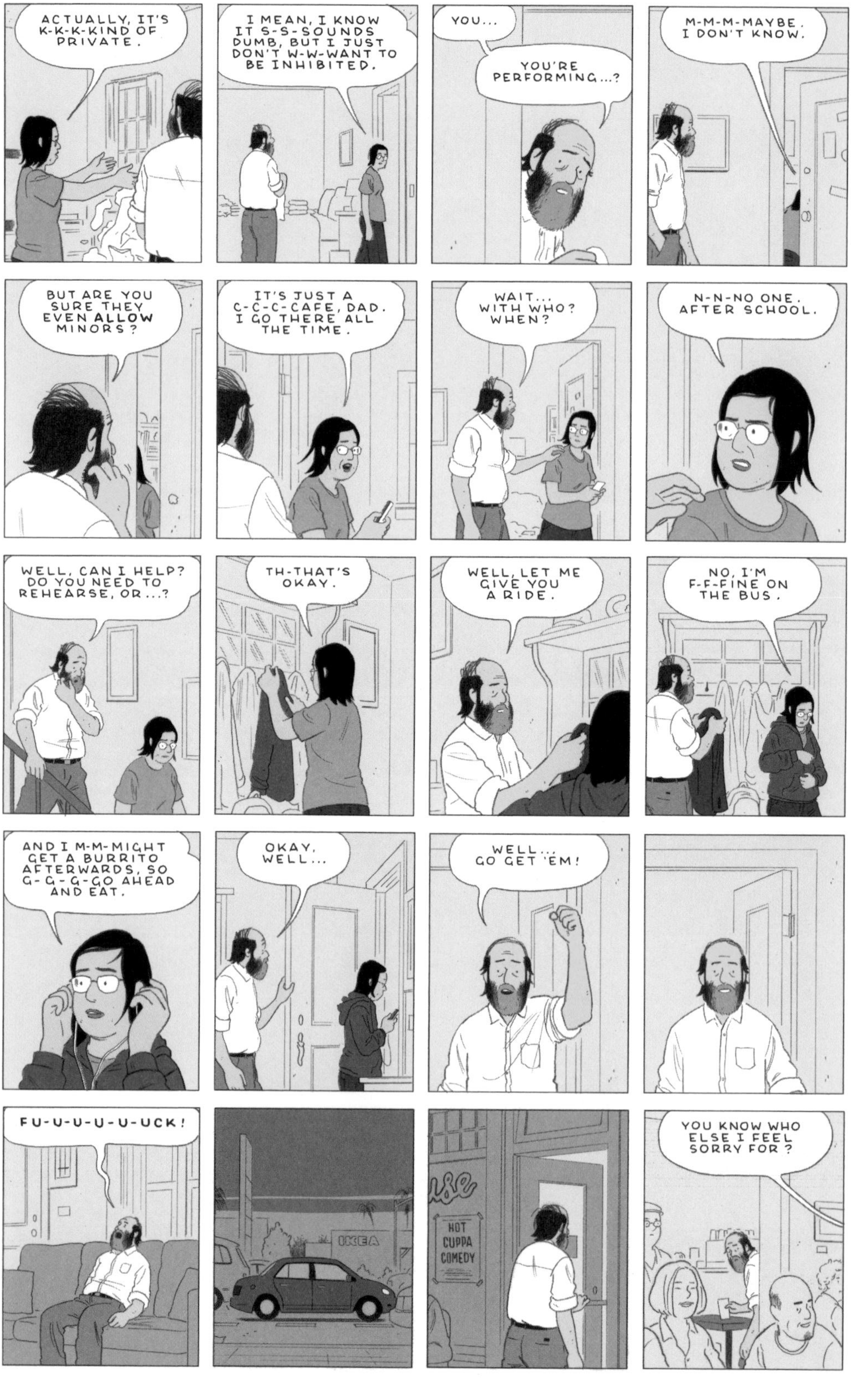
ACTUALLY, IT'S K-K-K-KIND OF PRIVATE.
I MEAN, I KNOW IT S-S-SOUNDS DUMB, BUT I JUST DON'T W-W-WANT TO BE INHIBITED.
YOU...
YOU'RE PERFORMING...?
M-M-M-MAYBE. I DON'T KNOW.
BUT ARE YOU SURE THEY EVEN ALLOW MINORS?
IT'S JUST A C-C-C-CAFE, DAD. I GO THERE ALL THE TIME.
WAIT... WITH WHO? WHEN?
N-N-NO ONE. AFTER SCHOOL.
WELL, CAN I HELP? DO YOU NEED TO REHEARSE, OR...?
TH-THAT'S OKAY.
WELL, LET ME GIVE YOU A RIDE.
NO, I'M F-F-FINE ON THE BUS.
AND I M-M-MIGHT GET A BURRITO AFTERWARDS, SO G-G-G-GO AHEAD AND EAT.
OKAY. WELL...
WELL... GO GET 'EM!
FU-U-U-U-U-UCK!
IKEA
HOT CUPPA COMEDY
YOU KNOW WHO ELSE I FEEL SORRY FOR?

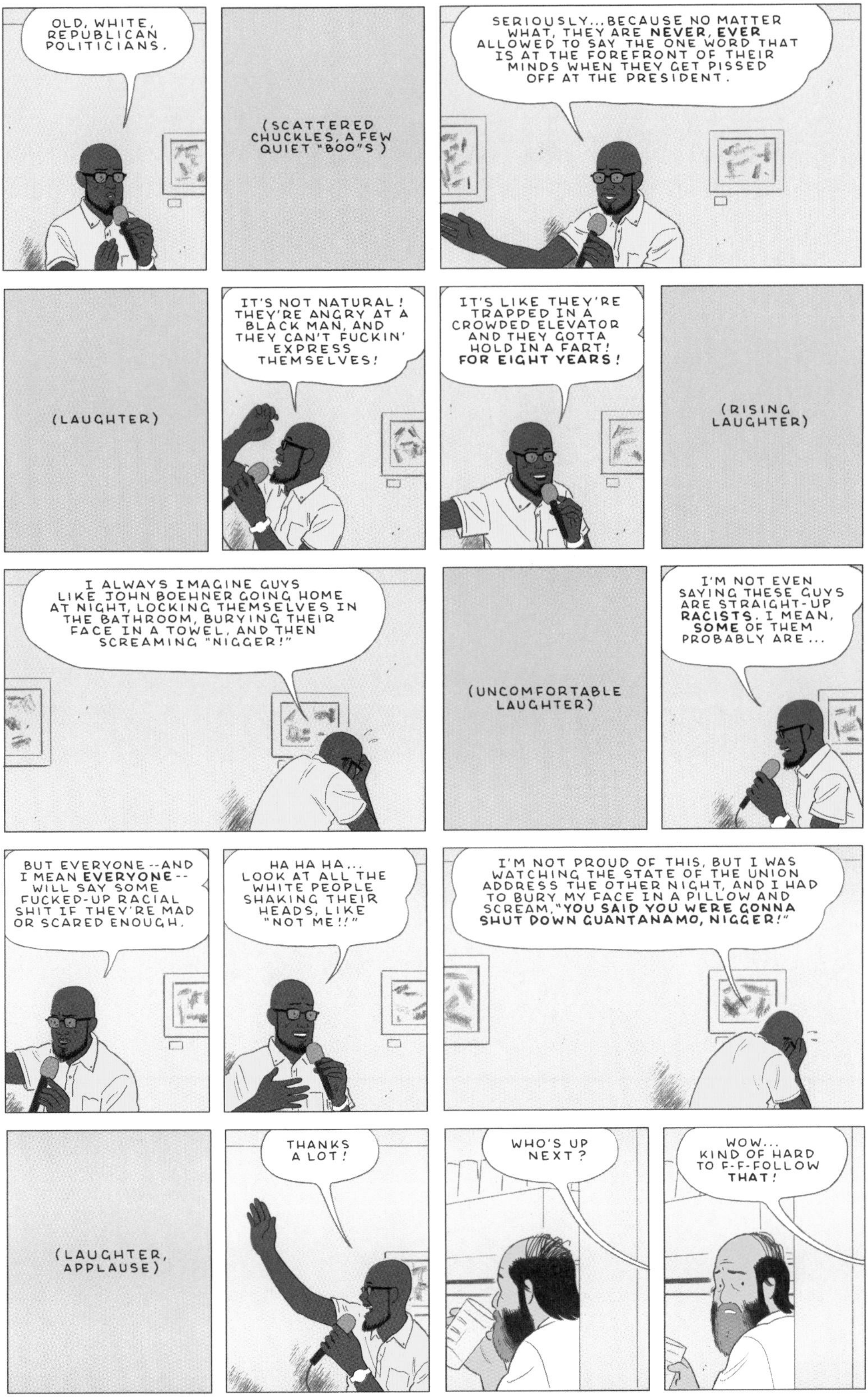
OLD, WHITE, REPUBLICAN POLITICIANS.
(SCATTERED CHUCKLES, A FEW QUIET "BOO"S)
SERIOUSLY...BECAUSE NO MATTER WHAT, THEY ARE NEVER, EVER ALLOWED TO SAY THE ONE WORD THAT IS AT THE FOREFRONT OF THEIR MINDS WHEN THEY GET PISSED OFF AT THE PRESIDENT.
(LAUGHTER)
IT'S NOT NATURAL! THEY'RE ANGRY AT A BLACK MAN, AND THEY CAN'T FUCKIN' EXPRESS THEMSELVES!
IT'S LIKE THEY'RE TRAPPED IN A CROWDED ELEVATOR AND THEY GOTTA HOLD IN A FART! FOR EIGHT YEARS!
(RISING LAUGHTER)
I ALWAYS IMAGINE GUYS LIKE JOHN BOEHNER GOING HOME AT NIGHT, LOCKING THEMSELVES IN THE BATHROOM, BURYING THEIR FACE IN A TOWEL, AND THEN SCREAMING "NIGGER!"
(UNCOMFORTABLE LAUGHTER)
I'M NOT EVEN SAYING THESE GUYS ARE STRAIGHT-UP RACISTS. I MEAN, SOME OF THEM PROBABLY ARE...
BUT EVERYONE--AND I MEAN EVERYONE--WILL SAY SOME FUCKED-UP RACIAL SHIT IF THEY'RE MAD OR SCARED ENOUGH.
HA HA HA... LOOK AT ALL THE WHITE PEOPLE SHAKING THEIR HEADS, LIKE "NOT ME!!"
I'M NOT PROUD OF THIS, BUT I WAS WATCHING THE STATE OF THE UNION ADDRESS THE OTHER NIGHT, AND I HAD TO BURY MY FACE IN A PILLOW AND SCREAM, "YOU SAID YOU WERE GONNA SHUT DOWN GUANTANAMO, NIGGER!"
(LAUGHTER, APPLAUSE)
THANKS A LOT!
WHO'S UP NEXT?
WOW... KIND OF HARD TO F-F-FOLLOW THAT!

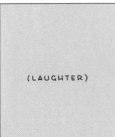

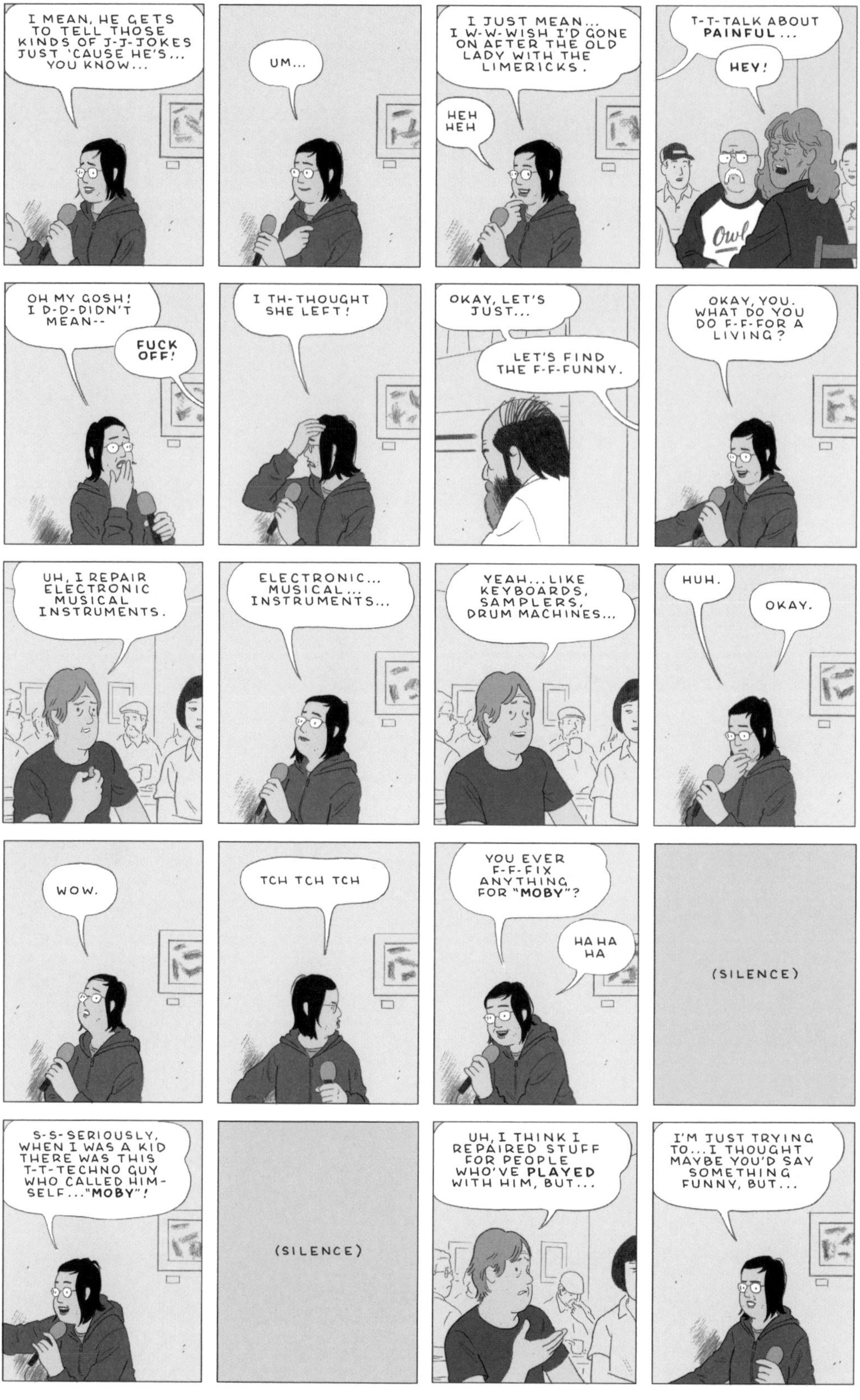
I MEAN, HE GETS TO TELL THOSE KINDS OF J-J-JOKES JUST 'CAUSE HE'S... YOU KNOW...
UM...
I JUST MEAN... I W-W-WISH I'D GONE ON AFTER THE OLD LADY WITH THE LIMERICKS.
HEH HEH
T-T-TALK ABOUT **PAINFUL**...
HEY!
OH MY GOSH! I D-D-DIDN'T MEAN--
FUCK OFF!
I TH-THOUGHT SHE LEFT!
OKAY, LET'S JUST...
LET'S FIND THE F-F-FUNNY.
OKAY, YOU. WHAT DO YOU DO F-F-FOR A LIVING?
UH, I REPAIR ELECTRONIC MUSICAL INSTRUMENTS.
ELECTRONIC... MUSICAL... INSTRUMENTS...
YEAH... LIKE KEYBOARDS, SAMPLERS, DRUM MACHINES...
HUH.
OKAY.
WOW.
TCH TCH TCH
YOU EVER F-F-FIX ANYTHING FOR "**MOBY**"?
HA HA HA
(SILENCE)
S-S-SERIOUSLY, WHEN I WAS A KID THERE WAS THIS T-T-TECHNO GUY WHO CALLED HIM-SELF..."**MOBY**"!
(SILENCE)
UH, I THINK I REPAIRED STUFF FOR PEOPLE WHO'VE **PLAYED** WITH HIM, BUT...
I'M JUST TRYING TO... I THOUGHT MAYBE YOU'D SAY SOMETHING FUNNY, BUT...

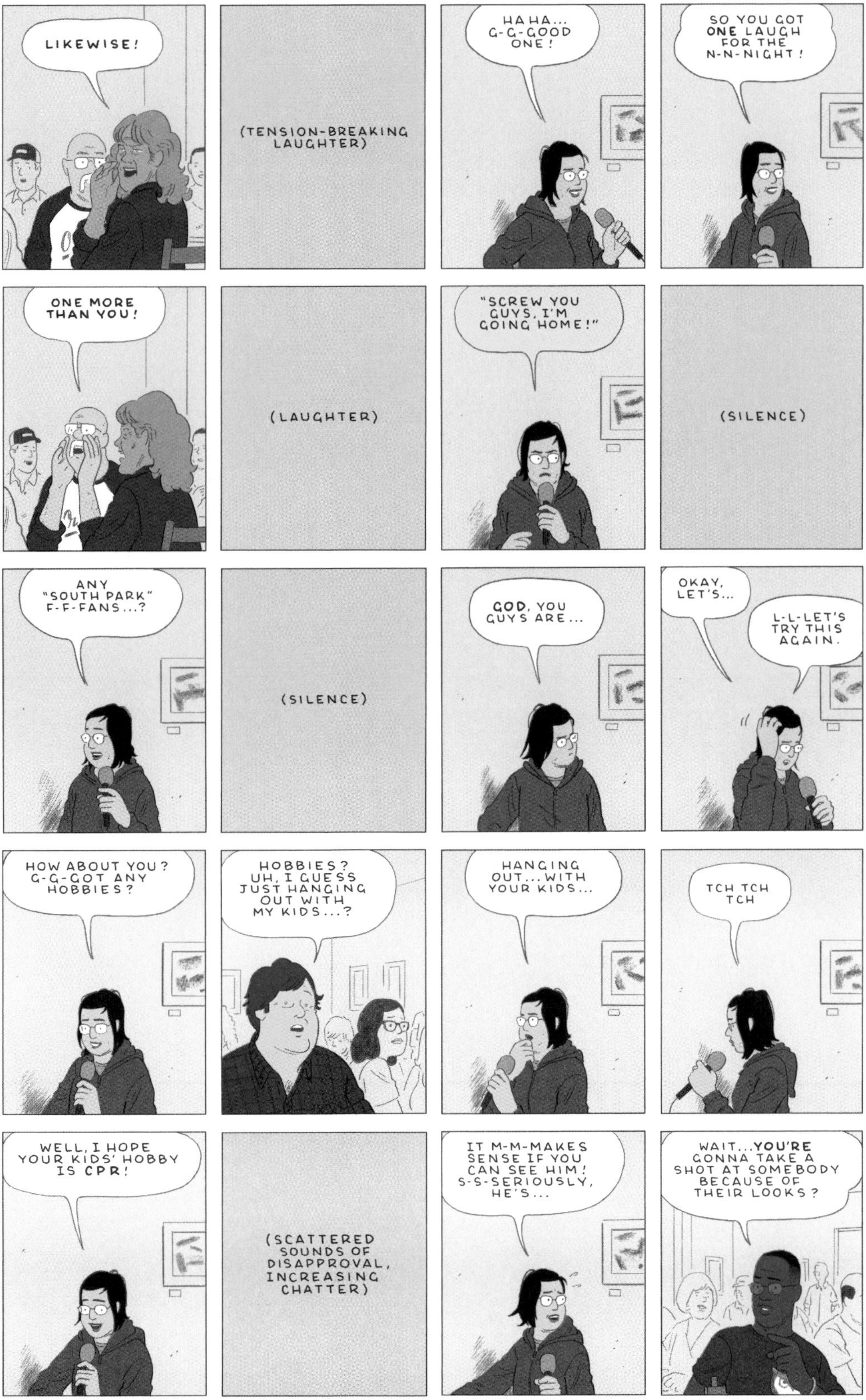
LIKEWISE!
(TENSION-BREAKING LAUGHTER)
HA HA... G-G-GOOD ONE!
SO YOU GOT ONE LAUGH FOR THE N-N-NIGHT!
ONE MORE THAN YOU!
(LAUGHTER)
"SCREW YOU GUYS, I'M GOING HOME!"
(SILENCE)
ANY "SOUTH PARK" F-F-FANS...?
(SILENCE)
GOD, YOU GUYS ARE...
OKAY, LET'S...
L-L-LET'S TRY THIS AGAIN.
HOW ABOUT YOU? G-G-GOT ANY HOBBIES?
HOBBIES? UH, I GUESS JUST HANGING OUT WITH MY KIDS...?
HANGING OUT... WITH YOUR KIDS...
TCH TCH TCH
WELL, I HOPE YOUR KIDS' HOBBY IS CPR!
(SCATTERED SOUNDS OF DISAPPROVAL, INCREASING CHATTER)
IT M-M-MAKES SENSE IF YOU CAN SEE HIM! S-S-SERIOUSLY, HE'S...
WAIT... YOU'RE GONNA TAKE A SHOT AT SOMEBODY BECAUSE OF THEIR LOOKS?

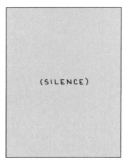

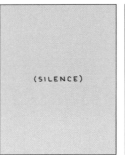

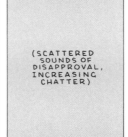

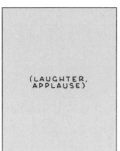

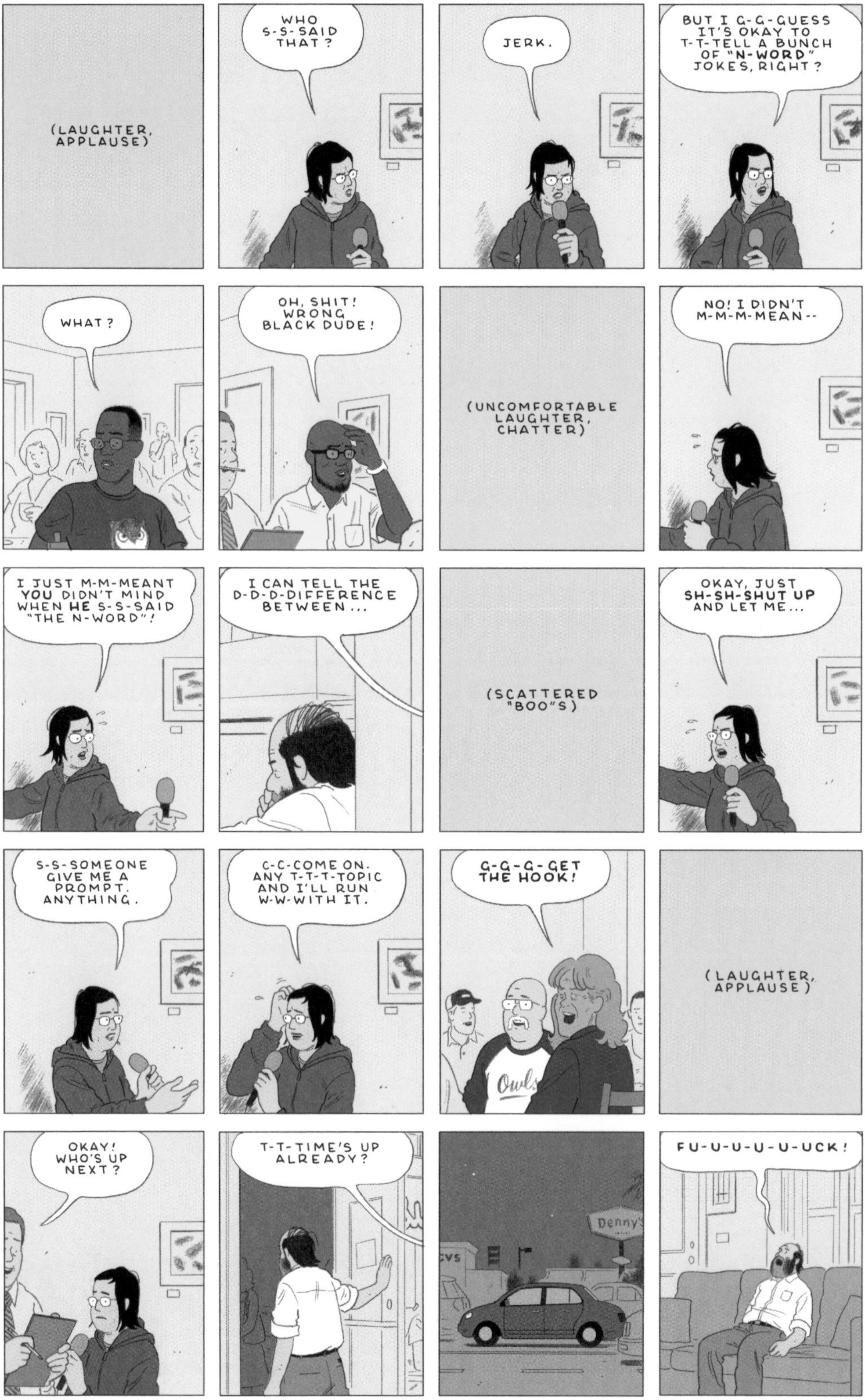
(LAUGHTER, APPLAUSE)
WHO S-S-SAID THAT?
JERK.
BUT I G-G-GUESS IT'S OKAY TO T-T-TELL A BUNCH OF "N-WORD" JOKES, RIGHT?
WHAT?
OH, SHIT! WRONG BLACK DUDE!
(UNCOMFORTABLE LAUGHTER, CHATTER)
NO! I DIDN'T M-M-M-MEAN--
I JUST M-M-MEANT YOU DIDN'T MIND WHEN HE S-S-SAID "THE N-WORD"!
I CAN TELL THE D-D-D-DIFFERENCE BETWEEN...
(SCATTERED "BOO"S)
OKAY, JUST SH-SH-SHUT UP AND LET ME...
S-S-SOMEONE GIVE ME A PROMPT. ANYTHING.
C-C-COME ON. ANY T-T-T-TOPIC AND I'LL RUN W-W-WITH IT.
G-G-G-GET THE HOOK!
Owls
(LAUGHTER, APPLAUSE)
OKAY! WHO'S UP NEXT?
T-T-TIME'S UP ALREADY?
Denny's
CVS
FU-U-U-U-U-UCK!

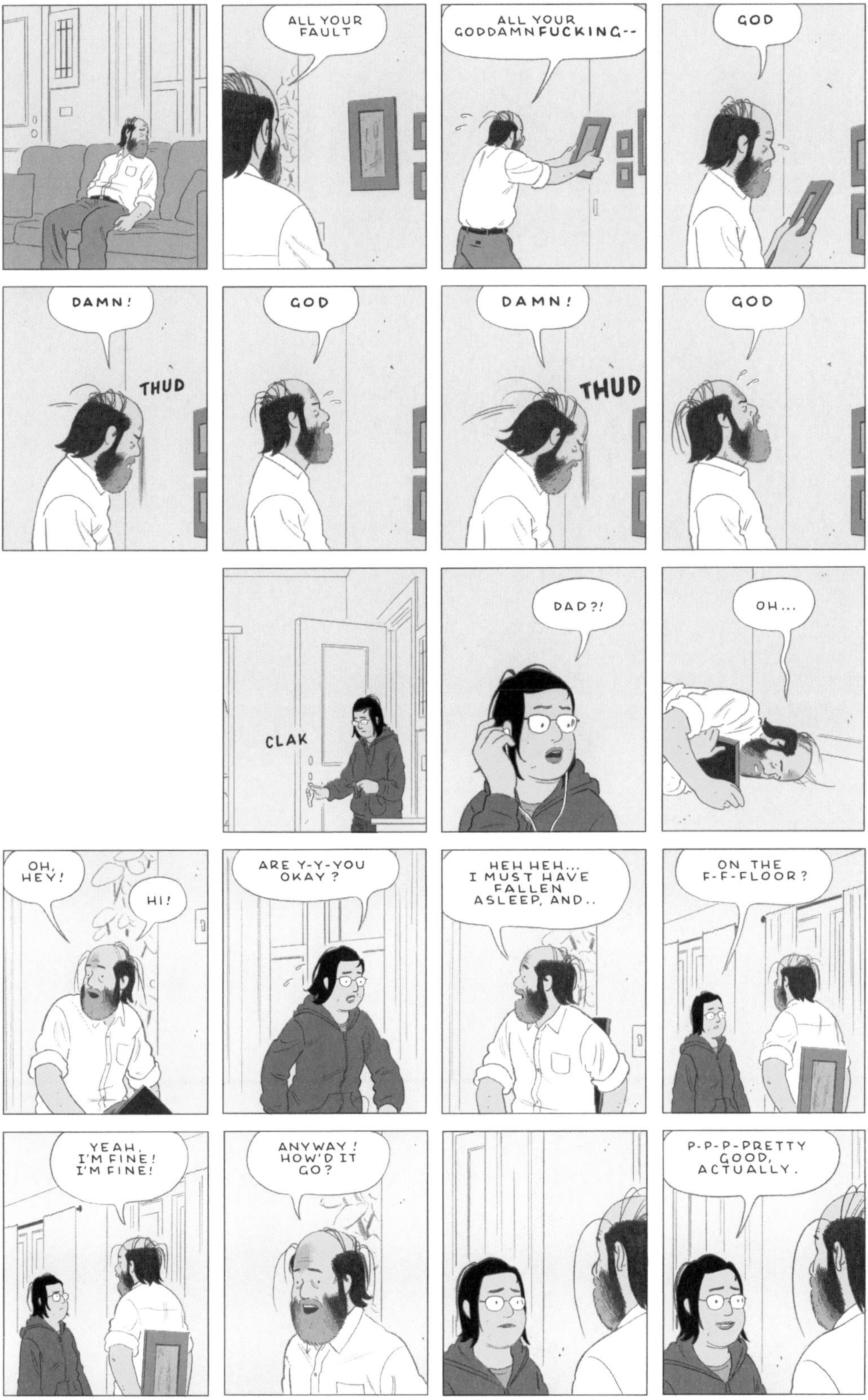
ALL YOUR FAULT
ALL YOUR GODDAMNFUCKING--
GOD
DAMN!
THUD
GOD
DAMN!
THUD
GOD
CLAK
DAD?!
OH...
OH, HEY!
HI!
ARE Y-Y-YOU OKAY?
HEH HEH... I MUST HAVE FALLEN ASLEEP, AND..
ON THE F-F-FLOOR?
YEAH, I'M FINE! I'M FINE!
ANYWAY! HOW'D IT GO?
P-P-P-PRETTY GOOD, ACTUALLY.

THAT'S... THAT'S GREAT, HONEY!
I'M SO PROUD OF YOU!
SO TELL ME ABOUT IT! GOOD CROWD?
DAD.
OH...
HEH HEH

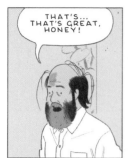

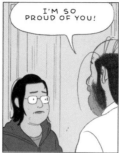

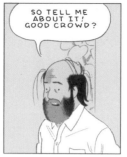

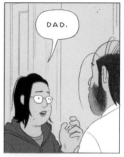

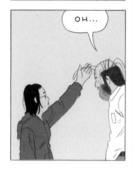

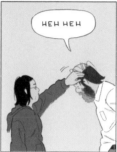

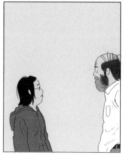

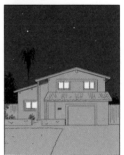

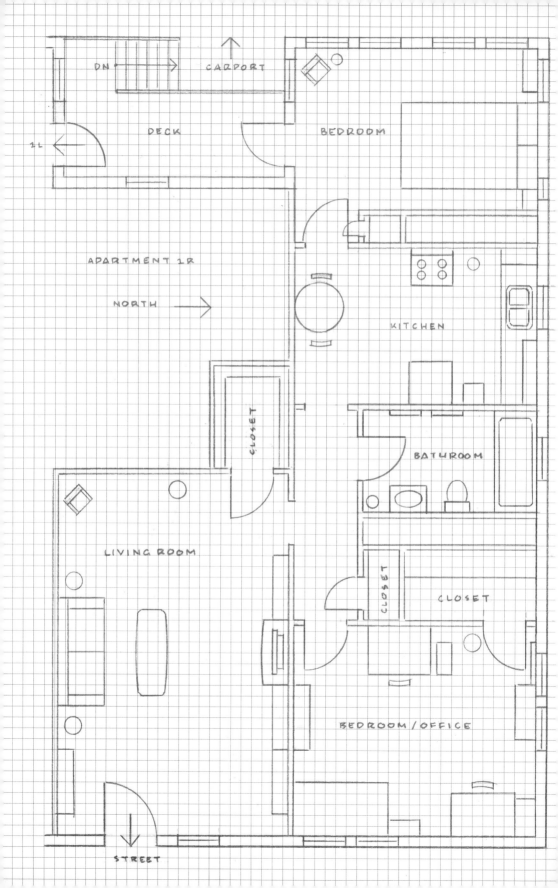

DN
CARPORT
1L
DECK
BEDROOM
APARTMENT 1R
NORTH
KITCHEN
CLOSET
BATHROOM
LIVING ROOM
CLOSET
CLOSET
BEDROOM/OFFICE
STREET

INTRUDERS

for Yoshihiro Tatsumi

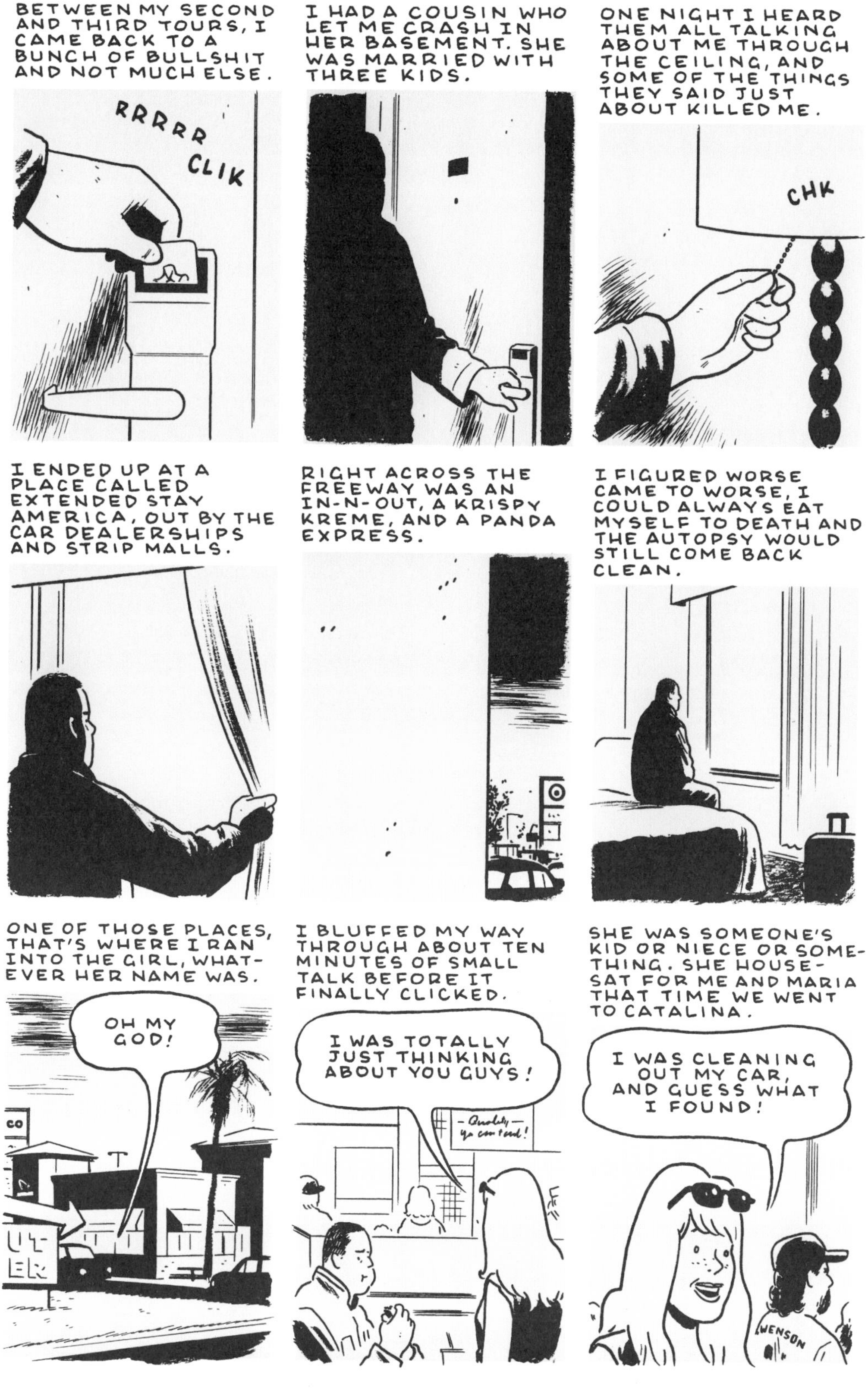
BETWEEN MY SECOND AND THIRD TOURS, I CAME BACK TO A BUNCH OF BULLSHIT AND NOT MUCH ELSE.
RRRRR
CLIK
I HAD A COUSIN WHO LET ME CRASH IN HER BASEMENT. SHE WAS MARRIED WITH THREE KIDS.
ONE NIGHT I HEARD THEM ALL TALKING ABOUT ME THROUGH THE CEILING, AND SOME OF THE THINGS THEY SAID JUST ABOUT KILLED ME.
CHK
I ENDED UP AT A PLACE CALLED EXTENDED STAY AMERICA, OUT BY THE CAR DEALERSHIPS AND STRIP MALLS.
RIGHT ACROSS THE FREEWAY WAS AN IN-N-OUT, A KRISPY KREME, AND A PANDA EXPRESS.
I FIGURED WORSE CAME TO WORSE, I COULD ALWAYS EAT MYSELF TO DEATH AND THE AUTOPSY WOULD STILL COME BACK CLEAN.
ONE OF THOSE PLACES, THAT'S WHERE I RAN INTO THE GIRL, WHATEVER HER NAME WAS.
OH MY GOD!
I BLUFFED MY WAY THROUGH ABOUT TEN MINUTES OF SMALL TALK BEFORE IT FINALLY CLICKED.
I WAS TOTALLY JUST THINKING ABOUT YOU GUYS!
SHE WAS SOMEONE'S KID OR NIECE OR SOMETHING. SHE HOUSESAT FOR ME AND MARIA THAT TIME WE WENT TO CATALINA.
I WAS CLEANING OUT MY CAR, AND GUESS WHAT I FOUND!

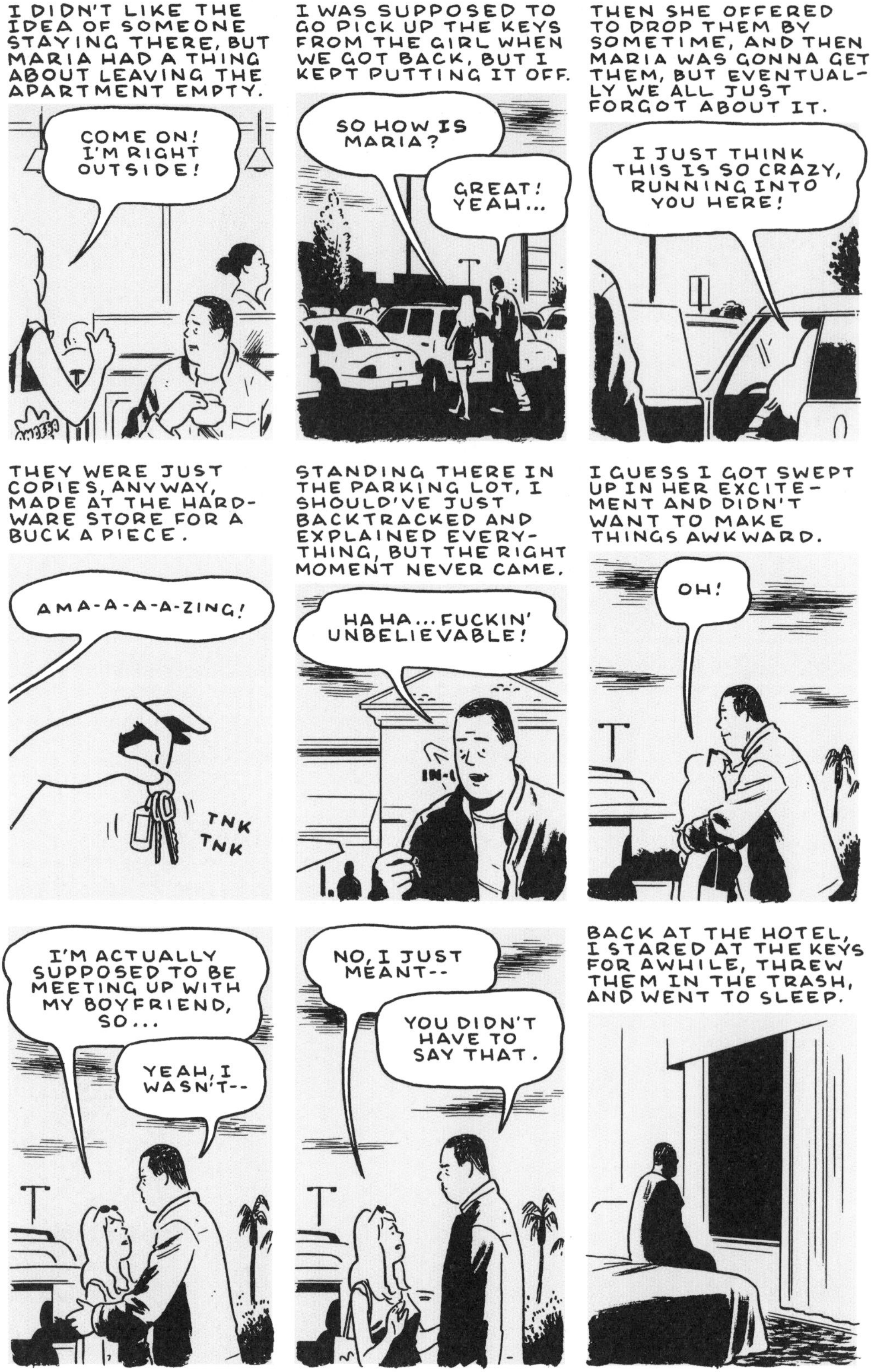
I DIDN'T LIKE THE IDEA OF SOMEONE STAYING THERE, BUT MARIA HAD A THING ABOUT LEAVING THE APARTMENT EMPTY.
COME ON! I'M RIGHT OUTSIDE!
I WAS SUPPOSED TO GO PICK UP THE KEYS FROM THE GIRL WHEN WE GOT BACK, BUT I KEPT PUTTING IT OFF.
SO HOW IS MARIA?
GREAT! YEAH...
THEN SHE OFFERED TO DROP THEM BY SOMETIME, AND THEN MARIA WAS GONNA GET THEM, BUT EVENTUALLY WE ALL JUST FORGOT ABOUT IT.
I JUST THINK THIS IS SO CRAZY, RUNNING INTO YOU HERE!
THEY WERE JUST COPIES, ANYWAY, MADE AT THE HARDWARE STORE FOR A BUCK A PIECE.
AMA-A-A-A-ZING!
TNK
TNK
STANDING THERE IN THE PARKING LOT, I SHOULD'VE JUST BACKTRACKED AND EXPLAINED EVERYTHING, BUT THE RIGHT MOMENT NEVER CAME.
HA HA... FUCKIN' UNBELIEVABLE!
I GUESS I GOT SWEPT UP IN HER EXCITEMENT AND DIDN'T WANT TO MAKE THINGS AWKWARD.
OH!
I'M ACTUALLY SUPPOSED TO BE MEETING UP WITH MY BOYFRIEND, SO...
YEAH, I WASN'T--
NO, I JUST MEANT--
YOU DIDN'T HAVE TO SAY THAT.
BACK AT THE HOTEL, I STARED AT THE KEYS FOR AWHILE, THREW THEM IN THE TRASH, AND WENT TO SLEEP.

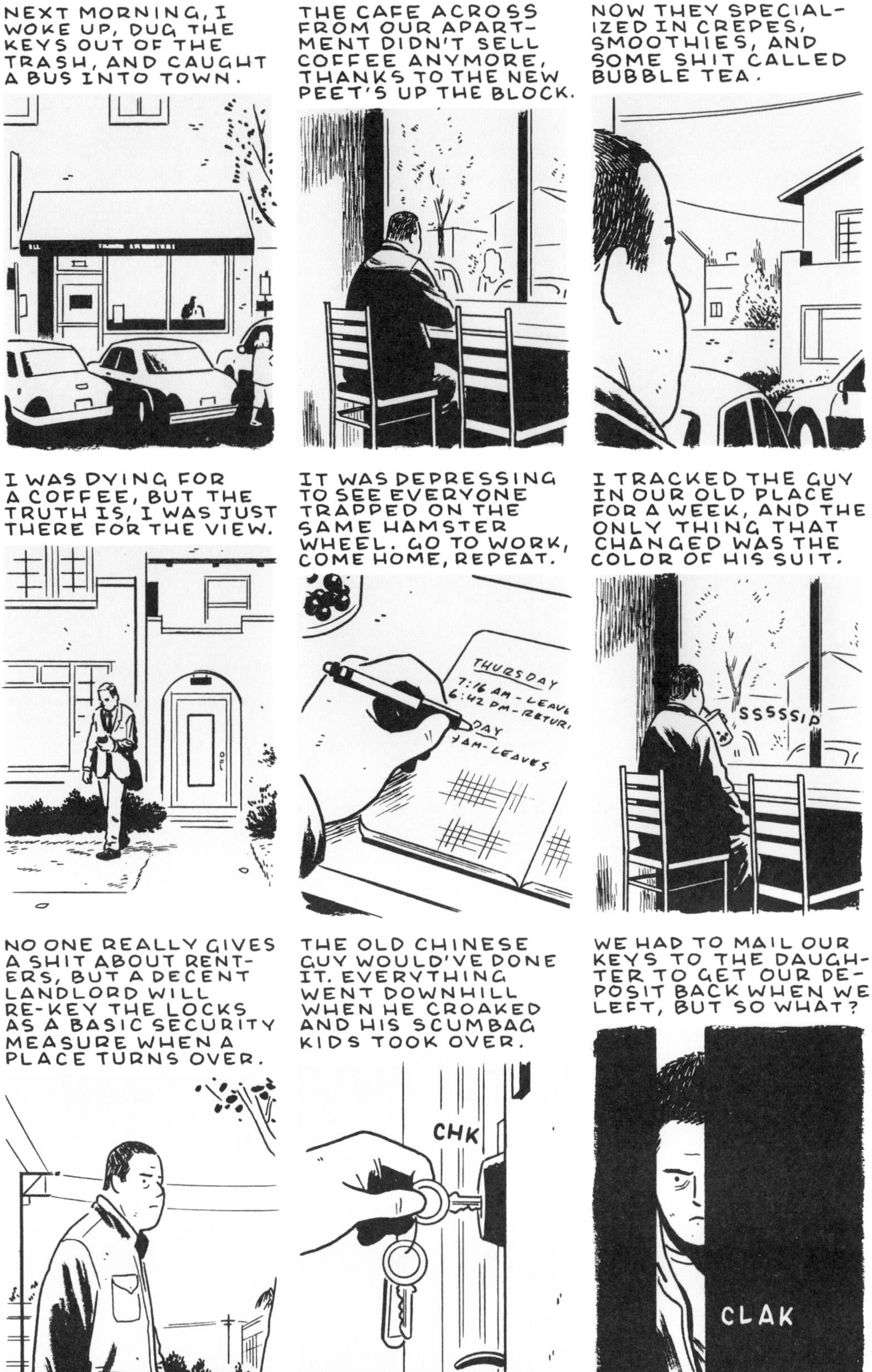
NEXT MORNING, I WOKE UP, DUG THE KEYS OUT OF THE TRASH, AND CAUGHT A BUS INTO TOWN.
THE CAFE ACROSS FROM OUR APARTMENT DIDN'T SELL COFFEE ANYMORE, THANKS TO THE NEW PEET'S UP THE BLOCK.
NOW THEY SPECIALIZED IN CREPES, SMOOTHIES, AND SOME SHIT CALLED BUBBLE TEA.
I WAS DYING FOR A COFFEE, BUT THE TRUTH IS, I WAS JUST THERE FOR THE VIEW.
IT WAS DEPRESSING TO SEE EVERYONE TRAPPED ON THE SAME HAMSTER WHEEL. GO TO WORK, COME HOME, REPEAT.
THURSDAY
I TRACKED THE GUY IN OUR OLD PLACE FOR A WEEK, AND THE ONLY THING THAT CHANGED WAS THE COLOR OF HIS SUIT.
SSSSSIP
NO ONE REALLY GIVES A SHIT ABOUT RENTERS, BUT A DECENT LANDLORD WILL RE-KEY THE LOCKS AS A BASIC SECURITY MEASURE WHEN A PLACE TURNS OVER.
THE OLD CHINESE GUY WOULD'VE DONE IT. EVERYTHING WENT DOWNHILL WHEN HE CROAKED AND HIS SCUMBAG KIDS TOOK OVER.
CHK
WE HAD TO MAIL OUR KEYS TO THE DAUGHTER TO GET OUR DEPOSIT BACK WHEN WE LEFT, BUT SO WHAT?
CLAK

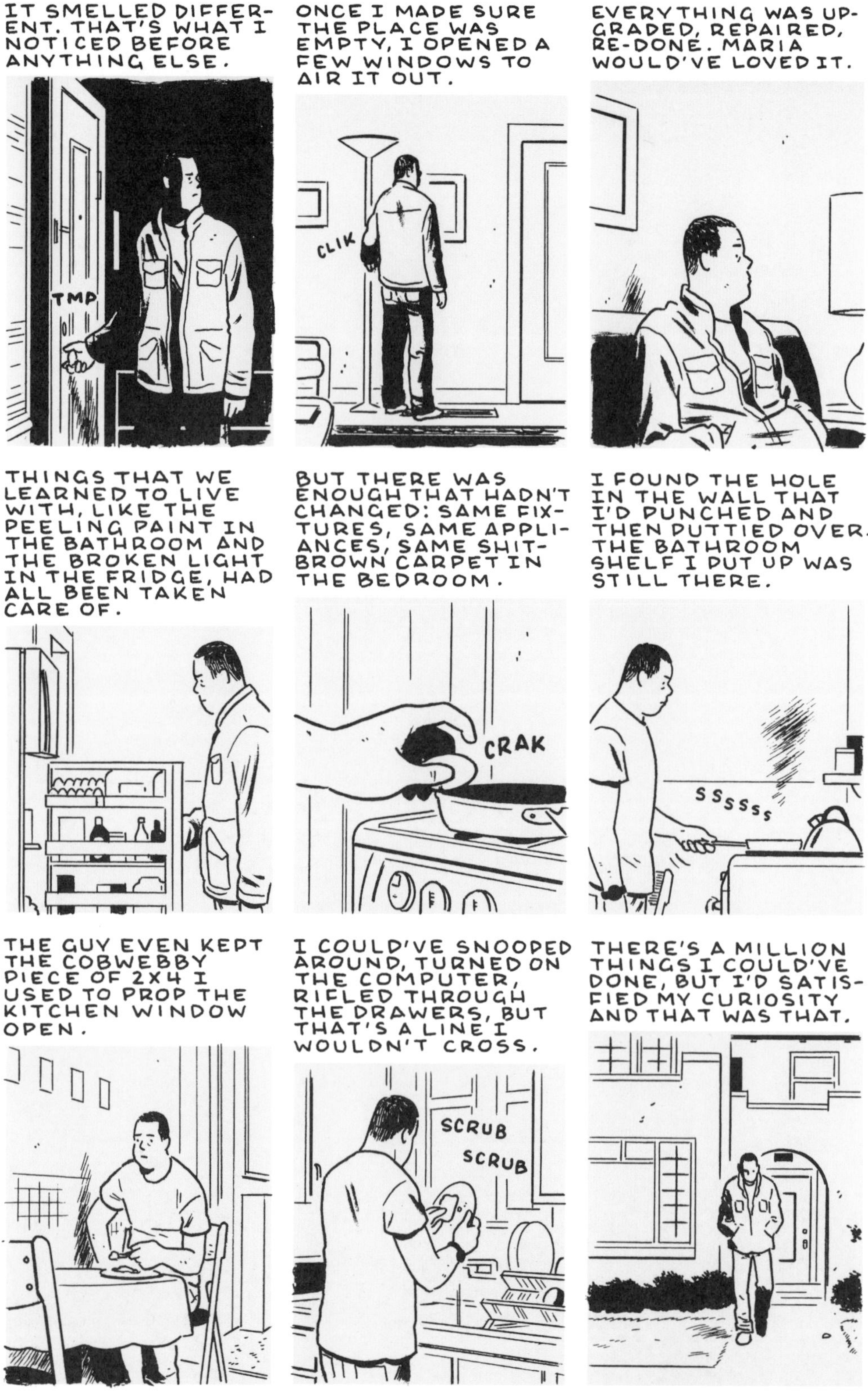
IT SMELLED DIFFERENT. THAT'S WHAT I NOTICED BEFORE ANYTHING ELSE.
TMP
ONCE I MADE SURE THE PLACE WAS EMPTY, I OPENED A FEW WINDOWS TO AIR IT OUT.
CLIK
EVERYTHING WAS UPGRADED, REPAIRED, RE-DONE. MARIA WOULD'VE LOVED IT.
THINGS THAT WE LEARNED TO LIVE WITH, LIKE THE PEELING PAINT IN THE BATHROOM AND THE BROKEN LIGHT IN THE FRIDGE, HAD ALL BEEN TAKEN CARE OF.
BUT THERE WAS ENOUGH THAT HADN'T CHANGED: SAME FIXTURES, SAME APPLIANCES, SAME SHIT-BROWN CARPET IN THE BEDROOM.
CRAK
I FOUND THE HOLE IN THE WALL THAT I'D PUNCHED AND THEN PUTTIED OVER. THE BATHROOM SHELF I PUT UP WAS STILL THERE.
SSSSSS
THE GUY EVEN KEPT THE COBWEBBY PIECE OF 2X4 I USED TO PROP THE KITCHEN WINDOW OPEN.
I COULD'VE SNOOPED AROUND, TURNED ON THE COMPUTER, RIFLED THROUGH THE DRAWERS, BUT THAT'S A LINE I WOULDN'T CROSS.
SCRUB
SCRUB
THERE'S A MILLION THINGS I COULD'VE DONE, BUT I'D SATISFIED MY CURIOSITY AND THAT WAS THAT.

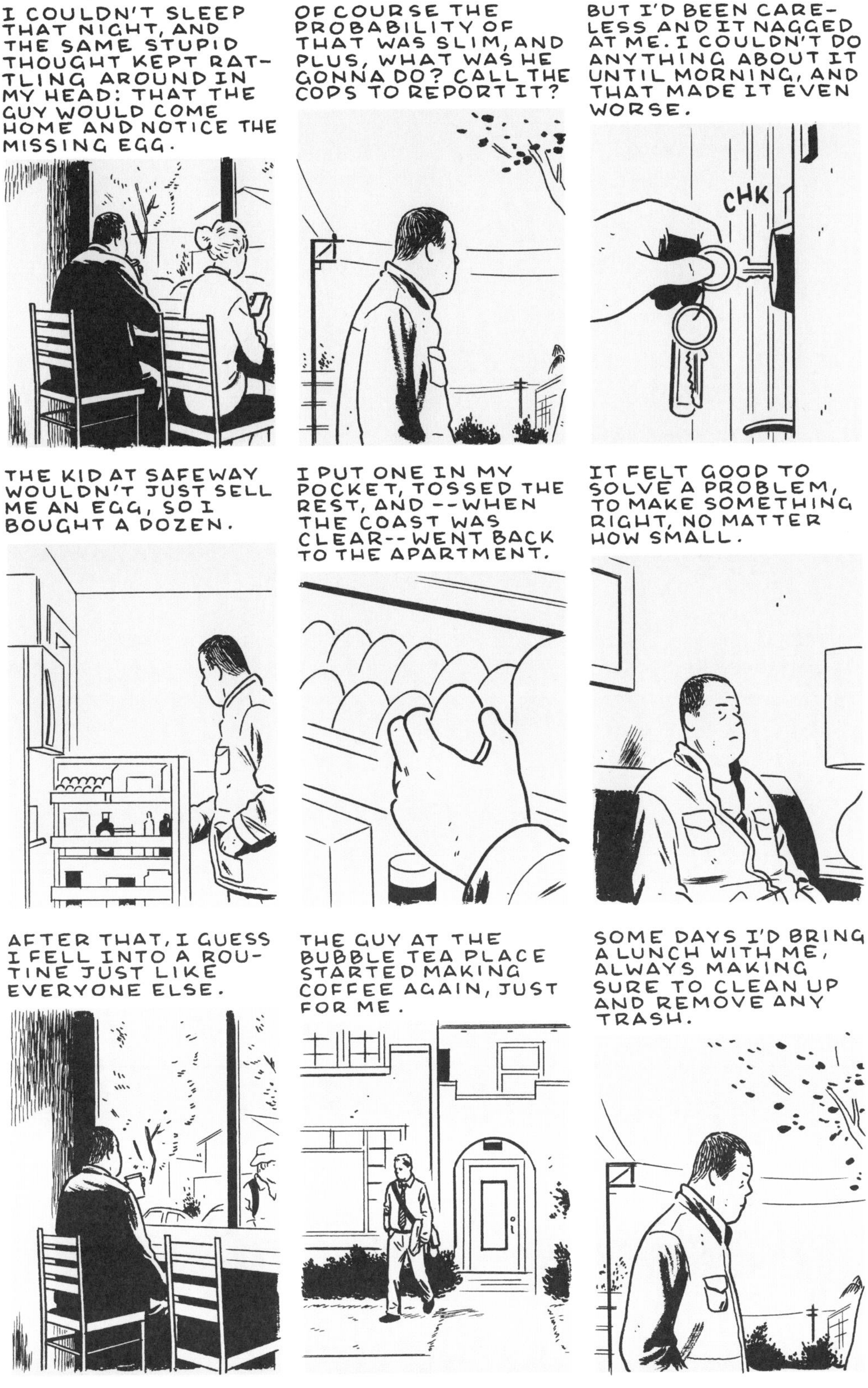
I COULDN'T SLEEP THAT NIGHT, AND THE SAME STUPID THOUGHT KEPT RATTLING AROUND IN MY HEAD: THAT THE GUY WOULD COME HOME AND NOTICE THE MISSING EGG.
OF COURSE THE PROBABILITY OF THAT WAS SLIM, AND PLUS, WHAT WAS HE GONNA DO? CALL THE COPS TO REPORT IT?
BUT I'D BEEN CARELESS AND IT NAGGED AT ME. I COULDN'T DO ANYTHING ABOUT IT UNTIL MORNING, AND THAT MADE IT EVEN WORSE.
CHK
THE KID AT SAFEWAY WOULDN'T JUST SELL ME AN EGG, SO I BOUGHT A DOZEN.
I PUT ONE IN MY POCKET, TOSSED THE REST, AND -- WHEN THE COAST WAS CLEAR -- WENT BACK TO THE APARTMENT.
IT FELT GOOD TO SOLVE A PROBLEM, TO MAKE SOMETHING RIGHT, NO MATTER HOW SMALL.
AFTER THAT, I GUESS I FELL INTO A ROUTINE JUST LIKE EVERYONE ELSE.
THE GUY AT THE BUBBLE TEA PLACE STARTED MAKING COFFEE AGAIN, JUST FOR ME.
SOME DAYS I'D BRING A LUNCH WITH ME, ALWAYS MAKING SURE TO CLEAN UP AND REMOVE ANY TRASH.

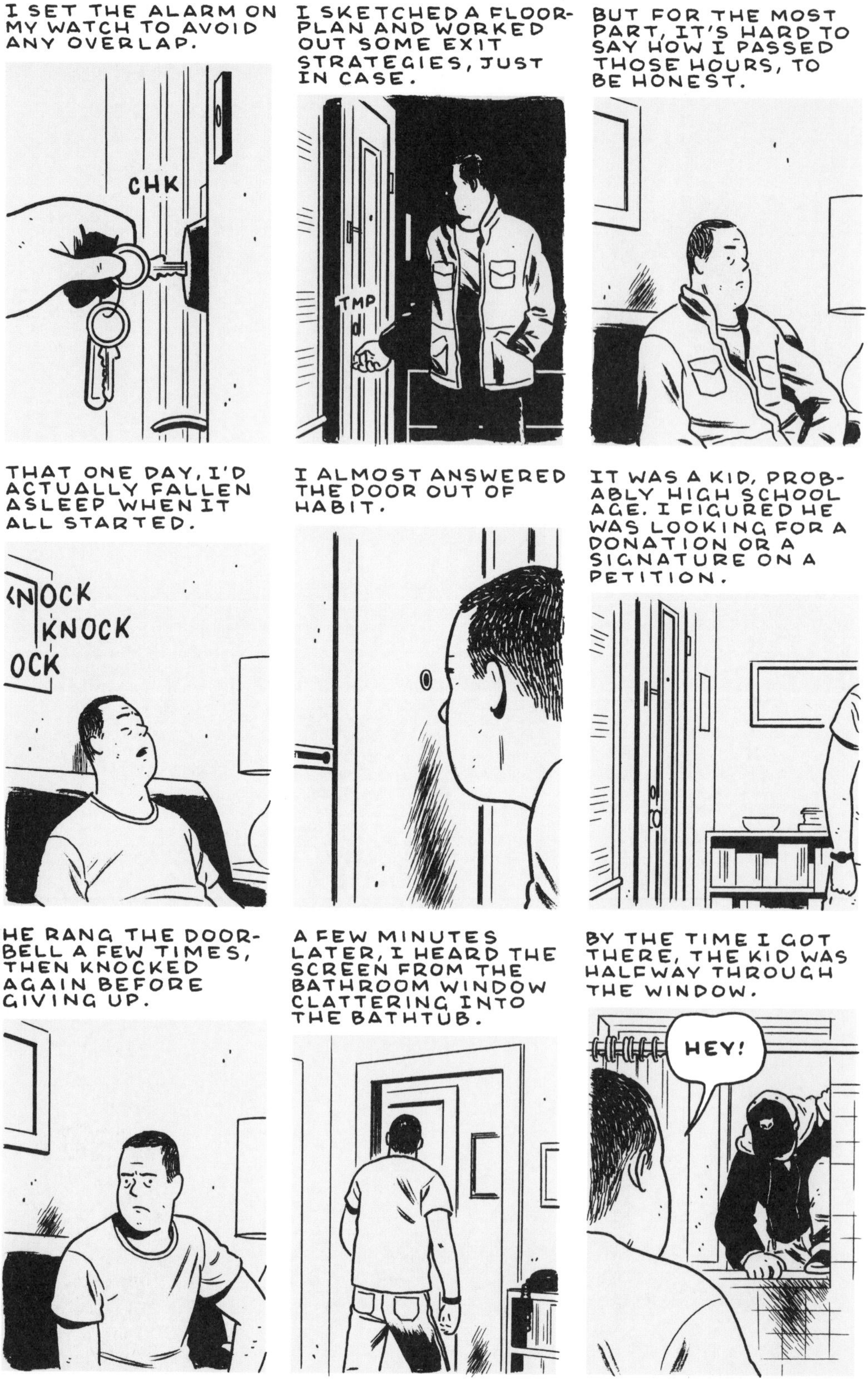
I SET THE ALARM ON MY WATCH TO AVOID ANY OVERLAP.
CHK
I SKETCHED A FLOOR-PLAN AND WORKED OUT SOME EXIT STRATEGIES, JUST IN CASE.
TMP
BUT FOR THE MOST PART, IT'S HARD TO SAY HOW I PASSED THOSE HOURS, TO BE HONEST.
THAT ONE DAY, I'D ACTUALLY FALLEN ASLEEP WHEN IT ALL STARTED.
KNOCK
KNOCK
OCK
I ALMOST ANSWERED THE DOOR OUT OF HABIT.
IT WAS A KID, PROBABLY HIGH SCHOOL AGE. I FIGURED HE WAS LOOKING FOR A DONATION OR A SIGNATURE ON A PETITION.
HE RANG THE DOORBELL A FEW TIMES, THEN KNOCKED AGAIN BEFORE GIVING UP.
A FEW MINUTES LATER, I HEARD THE SCREEN FROM THE BATHROOM WINDOW CLATTERING INTO THE BATHTUB.
BY THE TIME I GOT THERE, THE KID WAS HALFWAY THROUGH THE WINDOW.
HEY!

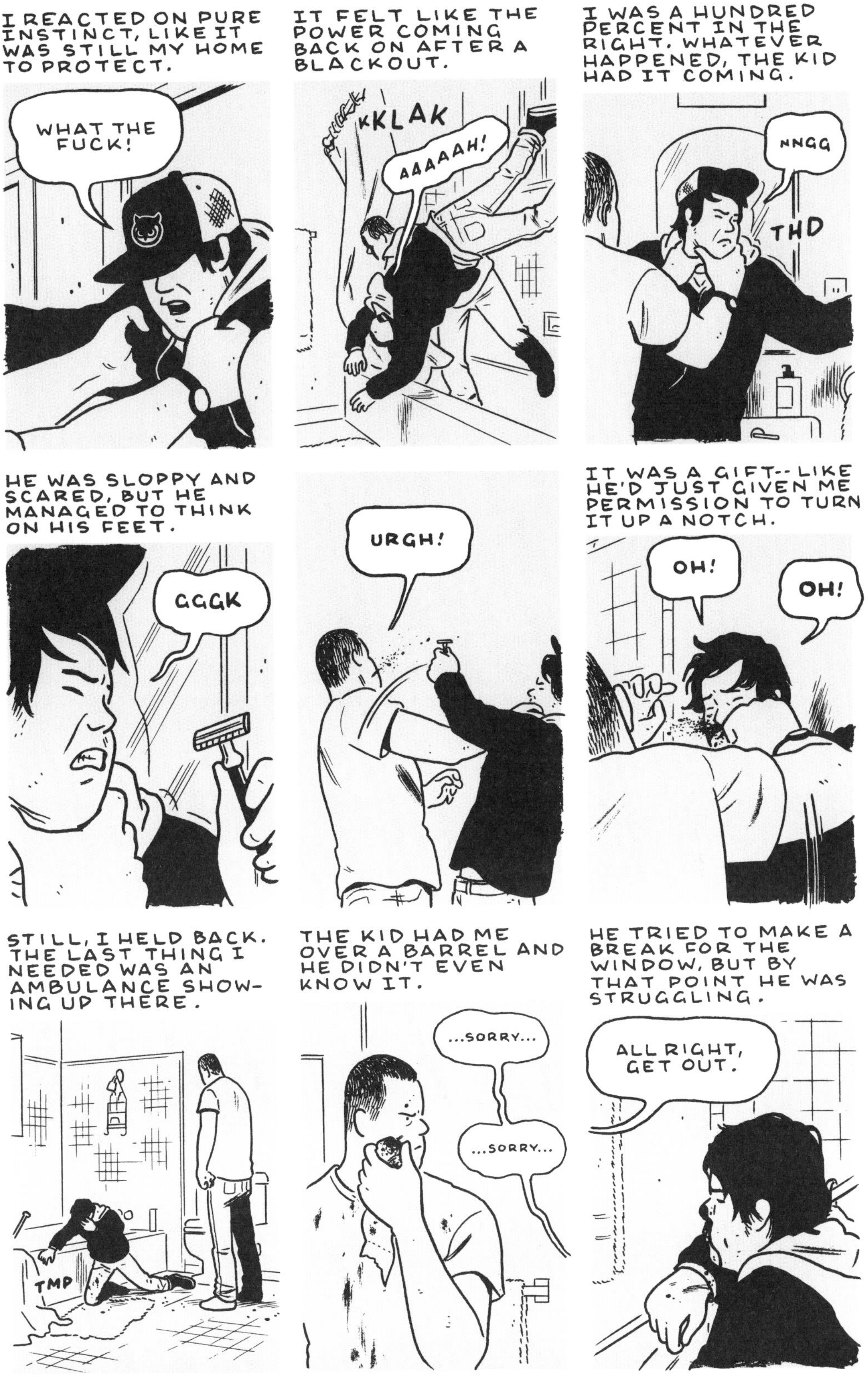
I REACTED ON PURE INSTINCT, LIKE IT WAS STILL MY HOME TO PROTECT.
WHAT THE FUCK!
IT FELT LIKE THE POWER COMING BACK ON AFTER A BLACKOUT.
KKLAK
AAAAAH!
I WAS A HUNDRED PERCENT IN THE RIGHT. WHATEVER HAPPENED, THE KID HAD IT COMING.
NNGG
THD
HE WAS SLOPPY AND SCARED, BUT HE MANAGED TO THINK ON HIS FEET.
GGGK
URGH!
IT WAS A GIFT-- LIKE HE'D JUST GIVEN ME PERMISSION TO TURN IT UP A NOTCH.
OH!
OH!
STILL, I HELD BACK. THE LAST THING I NEEDED WAS AN AMBULANCE SHOWING UP THERE.
TMP
THE KID HAD ME OVER A BARREL AND HE DIDN'T EVEN KNOW IT.
...SORRY...
...SORRY...
HE TRIED TO MAKE A BREAK FOR THE WINDOW, BUT BY THAT POINT HE WAS STRUGGLING.
ALL RIGHT, GET OUT.

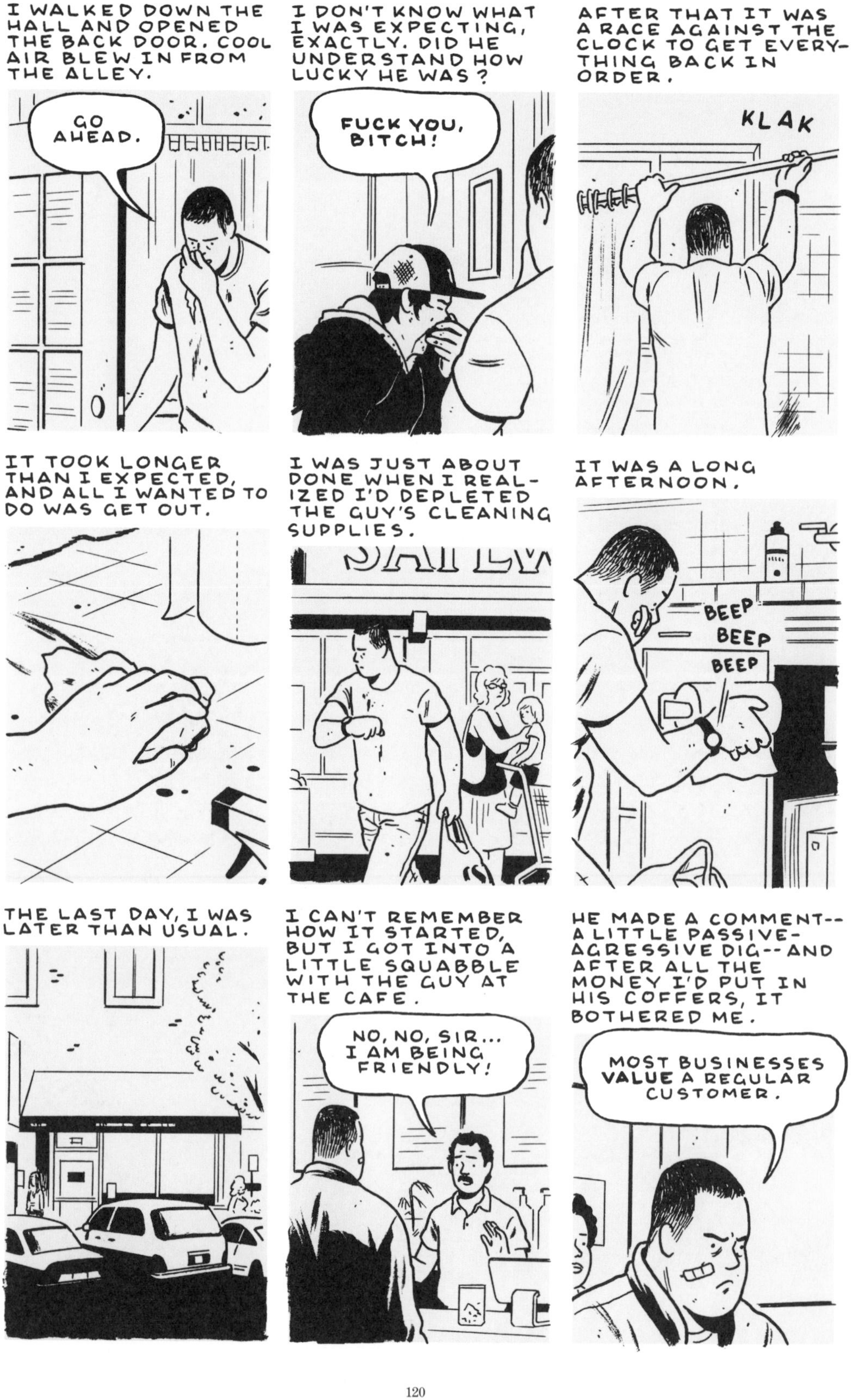
I WALKED DOWN THE HALL AND OPENED THE BACK DOOR. COOL AIR BLEW IN FROM THE ALLEY.
GO AHEAD.
I DON'T KNOW WHAT I WAS EXPECTING, EXACTLY. DID HE UNDERSTAND HOW LUCKY HE WAS?
FUCK YOU, BITCH!
AFTER THAT IT WAS A RACE AGAINST THE CLOCK TO GET EVERY-THING BACK IN ORDER.
KLAK
IT TOOK LONGER THAN I EXPECTED, AND ALL I WANTED TO DO WAS GET OUT.
I WAS JUST ABOUT DONE WHEN I REAL-IZED I'D DEPLETED THE GUY'S CLEANING SUPPLIES.
IT WAS A LONG AFTERNOON.
BEEP
BEEP
BEEP
THE LAST DAY, I WAS LATER THAN USUAL.
I CAN'T REMEMBER HOW IT STARTED, BUT I GOT INTO A LITTLE SQUABBLE WITH THE GUY AT THE CAFE.
NO, NO, SIR... I AM BEING FRIENDLY!
HE MADE A COMMENT-- A LITTLE PASSIVE-AGRESSIVE DIG--AND AFTER ALL THE MONEY I'D PUT IN HIS COFFERS, IT BOTHERED ME.
MOST BUSINESSES **VALUE** A REGULAR CUSTOMER.

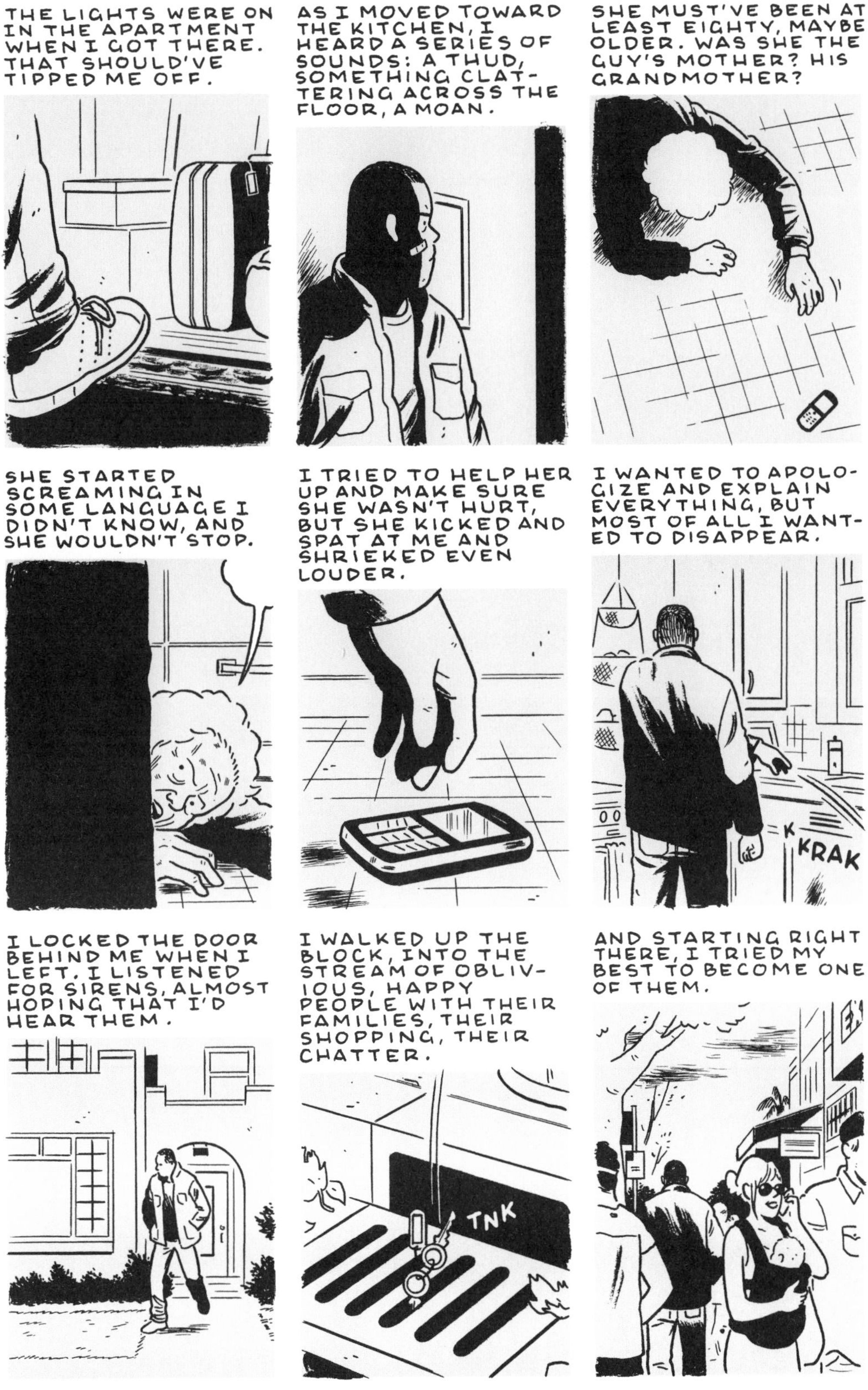
THE LIGHTS WERE ON IN THE APARTMENT WHEN I GOT THERE. THAT SHOULD'VE TIPPED ME OFF.
AS I MOVED TOWARD THE KITCHEN, I HEARD A SERIES OF SOUNDS: A THUD, SOMETHING CLATTERING ACROSS THE FLOOR, A MOAN.
SHE MUST'VE BEEN AT LEAST EIGHTY, MAYBE OLDER. WAS SHE THE GUY'S MOTHER? HIS GRANDMOTHER?
SHE STARTED SCREAMING IN SOME LANGUAGE I DIDN'T KNOW, AND SHE WOULDN'T STOP.
I TRIED TO HELP HER UP AND MAKE SURE SHE WASN'T HURT, BUT SHE KICKED AND SPAT AT ME AND SHRIEKED EVEN LOUDER.
I WANTED TO APOLOGIZE AND EXPLAIN EVERYTHING, BUT MOST OF ALL I WANTED TO DISAPPEAR.
K
KRAK
I LOCKED THE DOOR BEHIND ME WHEN I LEFT. I LISTENED FOR SIRENS, ALMOST HOPING THAT I'D HEAR THEM.
I WALKED UP THE BLOCK, INTO THE STREAM OF OBLIVIOUS, HAPPY PEOPLE WITH THEIR FAMILIES, THEIR SHOPPING, THEIR CHATTER.
TNK
AND STARTING RIGHT THERE, I TRIED MY BEST TO BECOME ONE OF THEM.

ACKNOWLEDGMENTS

The quote on page 11 is from *The Isamu Noguchi Museum*, published by Harry N. Abrams, 1999. The lyrics on page 51 are a brief excerpt from the song "Starting a New Life," written by Van Morrison, copyright © 1971 Caledonia Soul Music Co., WB Music Corp. The jokes on pages 95 and 96 were originally performed by Ellen DeGeneres, Sarah Silverman, and Jerry Seinfeld.

The author would like to thank: Kathleen Alcott, Alexandra Auger, Jonathan Bennett, Peggy Burns, Daniel Clowes, Ann Cunningham, Tom Devlin, Mark Everett, Charles Ferraro, Denise Goldberg, Samantha J. Haywood, Mayumi Horiguchi, Tracy Hurren, Mina Kaneko, Daisuke Kawasaki, Keya Khayatian, Chip Kidd, John Kuramoto, Marie-Jade Menni, Françoise Mouly, Chris Oliveros, Mark Parker, Julia Pohl-Miranda, Jon Resnik, Richard Sala, Seth, Alyson Sinclair, Zadie Smith, Dylan Tomine, Chris Ware, John Wray, and most of all, Sarah, Nora, and May.

Killing and Dying

 The material in this book was serialized in issues twelve through fourteen of *Optic Nerve* (published by Drawn & Quarterly). The story "Amber Sweet" originally appeared, under a different title and in substantially different form, in *Kramers Ergot* #7 (published by Buenaventura Press). The characters and events depicted in this book are fictitious. Any similarities to real persons, living or dead, is coincidental and not intended by the author.

www.faber.co.uk
www.adrian–tomine.com

First hardcover edition: October 2015.
Second hardcover printing: March 2016.
Printed in China.

10 9 8 7 6 5 4 3 2

Published in the United Kingdom by Faber and Faber Limited,
Bloombury House, 74-77 Great Russell St, London, WC1B 3DA

Published in the USA by Drawn & Quarterly, a client publisher of Farrar, Straus and Giroux.

A CIP record for this book is available from the British Library.

ISBN 978-0-571-32514-6